THE WINE OF LIFE

A Testimony to Vital Encounter

by

John McLachlan

"Friendship, the wine of life"
James Boswell

I count myself in nothing else so happy
As in a soul remembering my good friends
Richard II, Act ii, Scene 3

Distributed by
Dr John McLachlan
112 Brincliffe Edge Road
Sheffield S11 9BX
UK

First published 1991

ISBN: 0 9516911 0 4

Laserprinter typeset by Martin Lister Publishing Services, Bolton-le-Sands, Carnforth, Lancs.

Printed in Great Britain by Antony Rowe Ltd, Bumper's Farm, Chippenham, Wiltshire

Contents

List of Illustrations

Preface

When living in Oxford I used to cycle up to Shotover to visit the veteran philosopher, Dr L.P. Jacks. One day, over a cup of tea, he mentioned that he had just received a letter from an old friend, the Dean of St Paul's, W.R. Inge. "We have both come to the conclusion (he said) that we have had the best of it". His meaning was clear. Two old experienced, widely-travelled scholars and philosophers had reached the same verdict. Their generation had lived through some of the most eventful years of human history, but Western man, and probably humanity as a whole, had reached a zenith point, beyond which it was unlikely that our kind of civilisation would proceed. The 'Decline of the West' foreshadowed by Oswald Spengler, unlikely as it seemed when first propounded, was probably a correct diagnosis of the state of the world. To put it crudely, we were 'on our way out'! Like many another civilisation in the past, the best was over and behind us: the future held little hope of better things to come....

Was this, perhaps, too pessimistic a conclusion?

Recollection of this conversation has long haunted me. Being an optimist, and having been, in large measure, a privileged person by reason of birth, upbringing, health and occupation, I have rarely dwelt upon the thought of the eventual destruction of my familiar, everyday world. It has not troubled my sleep or spoilt my appetite. Yet, ever and again, I, too, have had the uneasy feeling that I belong to a generation which has "had the best of it", that, in fact, we may be the last of a particular kind of folk. Our aftercomers may not be so fortunate, physically, mentally, and spiritually, as we have been. Occasionally, the realisation of the possibility, or even the probability, of an almost universal collapse has forced itself upon me. This has happened twice, with exceptional vividness.

The first time was shortly after the end of the Second World War. I was in the Sheldonian Theatre in Oxford, listening to a lecture on "The Economic and Social Consequences of the Atomic Bomb". The lecturer was E.L. Woodward, Fellow of Balliol and Professor of International Relations. He said that the nature of the nation-state was such, that the possession of 'the bomb' would prove an irresistible temptation to most, if not all, governments, and that the race to possess it and indeed to replicate it as a military weapon in one hideous form or another, would undoubtedly dominate the years ahead. As we came away from that lecture, I remarked to Dr Ernest Payne of Regent's Park College, afterwards a Companion of Honour, "Well, that is a gloomy prospect for mankind"! To which he sadly assented.

The second time I felt oppressed by 'the shape of things to come' was in 1986, when Sir John Rowlands, assistant-principal of Sheffield Polytechnic and a leading authority on training for the Royal Air Force and Civil Aviation, addressed our Probus Club in Sheffield on "Technology and the Future". He discussed the effect of micro-electronics in general and the application of the micro-chip in particular. He indicated the speed, novelty, and vast implications of the electronic revolution of our time. The prospect was terrifying, since technology threatens to overwhelm society and create social, political, and spiritual problems at present seemingly insoluble.

As I write, it appears that Karel Čapek's vision of robots ruling the world, which the Czech author illustrated in his play R.U.R., will be realised. He protested against the mechanisation of the age and prophesied the capture of the human spirit by material forces. People would construct their own prison and eventually die in it. The irony of such an outcome must weigh heavily upon the mind and spirit.

But of course another scenario now seems possible. Some of us have always believed in the innate dynamism of the human spirit. We have pinned our faith to the possibility of the revival of civilised values, though we may not have expected it to take place in our lifetime. Nevertheless, we are now open to less pessimistic conclusions. Granted 'to err is human' yet the perception is making headway that 'to make an absolute mess of things it takes a computer' (as a notice in a local library reminded me the other day). The important point to grasp is that humanity must not become dehumanised. We must not submit to robots. Violence, atheistic determinism and computerised controls cannot be the last word in human history.

Perhaps, when our generation has become merely a memory and a new Renaissance is about to emerge, it may be of some slight interest to posterity to learn something of the feelings and experiences of one living through the closing years of what has been termed the 'post-Christian age'.

It could be more than a matter of idle curiosity that, through years of increasing violence, instability, and breakdown of civilised behaviour, there were those who maintained their loyalty to the values of truth, beauty, liberty and sheer goodwill, were members of a society which still held family-life in high regard, and were unwilling to sacrifice humane and social values to the rat-race of materialist and 'market-forces' determinism.

1

BEGINNINGS

Family Background and Childhood

"Home is where one starts from"
T.S. Eliot, *East Coker*

My father was born on 22nd August, 1876 at Dulesgate between Todmorden and Bacup, which makes him, I reckon, half a Yorkshireman and half Lancastrian. The latter half was to preponderate. He was the second son and third child of John and Sarah (née Gladwell). His grandfather, John, was six years dead when my father was born. This John appears to have been something of what is known in these northern counties as 'a character'. By trade a journeyman-tailor, he was self-taught and could read and write, accomplishments which in his early days distinguished him from many of his contemporaries. He has been described as a 'Peterloo man', that is to say he had been present on the 16th August, 1819 at the Chartist meeting in St Peter's Fields, Manchester. Like many Chartists, he had become a 'freethinker', and political sympathy combined with interest in education led him to send his children (two sons and a daughter) to the Methodist Unitarian Sunday School at Newchurch-in-Rossendale. I imagine that I owe more than a little of my leaning towards a radical appraisal of society and a general feeling of sympathy for the underprivileged to this paternal great-grandparent who was a well known figure in The Valley, smoking his churchwarden and ever-ready to engage in conversation on political or religious topics of the day.

His wife, Mary, my father's grandmother, hailed from Chester. Twenty-two years younger than her husband, she was for a time caretaker of the Newchurch Mechanics' Institute, of which, from 1867 to 1874, my grandfather was honorary secretary. She died aged 73. My father used to visit her every fortnight, carrying an allowance in cash from my grandfather so that she might be free from anxiety about her housekeeping and able to 'keep the wolf from the door'. This continued for the twenty years of her widowhood. My father recalled that she was seldom without company on these occasions. Apparently, several Irish dames, her neighbours, would be present when the regular alms arrived; this could scarcely be a mere coincidence, for they were not averse from drinking my great grandmother's health....

I have often wondered whether, in fact, Mary was of Irish extraction herself. She may well have been, for many Irish folk did make their way to Chester and Liverpool during the hard times of the nineteenth century and Mary is, of course, a popular Christian name in Ireland.

My grandfather (1840–99), another John, must have been a child when his parents migrated to Newchurch. At the age of seven, he went to work in a cotton mill, and throughout his life remained, in various capacities, connected with the cotton trade. He began his education at the age of five in the Unitarian Sunday School and at the Mechanic's Institute after work in the factory was over. He was, in fact, a half-timer. My grandmother, Sarah, was born on the 12th April, 1849 and came of Suffolk stock. I can just remember her, a short, stout little lady, always dressed in black, to me quite uncongenial and, clearly, not fond of children, as I have good reason to know. A pity, is it not, that the only grandparent whom I was destined to meet was one who did not like me and whom I, for my part, detested? 'Herbert', she cried, when she was staying with us in Manchester about 1911–12, "your little boy is spitting at me!" Animals and little children infallibly detect when 'grown-ups' dislike them.

The Gladwells were farmers and saddlers. Her father, Elijah, moved into Rossendale from Stowmarket during the time when the cotton trade was flourishing in what was then called 'The Golden Valley'. He was originally a Primitive Methodist local-preacher but became a Baptist and first minister of Mount Zion Baptist Church, Newchurch. Later, he transferred back to Methodism and became a preacher in the Bacup circuit. On this side, at least, my forbears came of convinced evangelical persuasion.

John and Sarah were married on 11th July, 1872 at Waterburn Baptist Chapel, Stacksteads, a hamlet 1½ miles south-west of Bacup, grandfather being 31 and grandmother 23. There were seven children of this union, four girls and three boys. Of the boys, Jack, Herbert and William, my uncle Jack, whom I hardly knew, died in Rio de Janeiro in 1917. He and my father were good friends and I have several letters of his, written in intimate and supportive terms to my father as the latter established himself in the ministry and academic world. William, whom I never knew, died in Auckland in 1940. Jack had one daughter, my cousin Jean, now living in Formby, near Liverpool; and William had two sons, one of whom met an early death on a motor-cycle, and Bruce Herbert (called after my father) and five daughters, all (at one time) settled and married in New Zealand.

At Dulesgate, my father's birthplace, the family lived in the manager's house, close to the mill, of which grandfather was manager. Like a number of mills in Lancashire, it suffered destruction from a huge fire which threatened the house in which the McLachlans were living. My father was carried to safety in his cradle, like John Wesley, "a brand plucked from the burning". The family then removed to Stacksteads where my grandfather was in charge of Banks Mill. Aged three and a half, my father was sent to an elementary school, where he learnt to read. As a youngster, he put this achievement to continuous use and progressed through the board school at Cloughfold to the Higher Grade School at Bacup, where a schools-inspector picked him out as a promising candidate for further education. However, at the age of ten he was sent as a half-timer to the mill which my grandfather managed, earning five shillings a week for two years as an errand and office boy. Here he became familiar with looms and engines and the general workings of a cotton mill, though he regarded this period in his life as "a sad waste of time". The autobiography which he composed for the family and which, alas, is incomplete, contains valuable descriptions of social and industrial life in Rossendale and Manchester during the last decade of the nineteenth century. It also depicts the progress of the child who was 'father of the man' – from business to night-school; from university student to teacher and lecturer; and from assistant-minister to warden, principal of a college, author, and bibliophile.

The year 1889 was a crucial one for my paternal grandparents. By this time the task of managing a mill must have palled, for grandfather decided to purchase an oil and dry-salter's business in Ardwick, Manchester, with the result that the family moved to Longsight to be near at hand. One consequence of this was that my father finished his regular schooling at the age of 13 and went into business with his father.

From 1891 to 1897, however, the family returned to Boothfold in the Rossendale valley, where my father lived at Bridge House for six and a half years, travelling up to Manchester every day to the Ardwick business and back every night, reading hard all the time: the daily press, in particular the *Manchester Guardian*, novels and poets, books in his father's collection and borrowed from a local book-club, and learning Pitman's Shorthand at an evening class in Newchurch Grammar School. He attended the Unitarian Church in Newchurch, taught a class in the Sunday School, and began to turn his thoughts to theology. At Christmas, 1896 he decided to enter the Unitarian ministry, and in order to do this he started to attend evening classes at Lower Mosley Street Schools with a view to matriculation at the Victoria University of Manchester. Here his classical tutor was Mr C.S. Lodge, brother of the famous scientist, Sir Oliver Lodge.

The account of my father's student days, from 1987 to 1906, reads almost like fiction, so strange and utterly different from my own. He and his fellow-students existed (just) on 15s. per week! Plain living and high thinking was the order of the day. Father proved a 'natural' when it came to exams and lecture-courses: he simply revelled in Academe, making remarkable progress in every subject he tackled. He won all the class-prizes and finished his college and university career with a first in the Honours School of History, an M.A., and B.D. with distinction. His professors (Tout and Tait in history and Peake in theology) regarded him as an outstanding scholar and provided him with glowing testimonials when he applied for, and was awarded, a Hibbert scholarship. He was, in fact, the first man from the Unitarian College, Manchester ever to have gained that distinction.

On leaving college, he was invited to a ministry in Swansea, but accepted an urgent request to become assistant to Dr Charles Hargrove, a distinguished ex-Dominican, at Mill Hill Chapel, Leeds, to which city he moved in October, 1906. Already in 1905 he had become engaged to my mother, then a member of the choir of the Longsight Free Christian Church, Manchester. They were married on Guy Fawkes' Day, November, 1906 and set up house at 152, Tempest Road, Beeston Hill, Leeds. Here I was born on the 7th or 8th July, 1908. There is some confusion about the exact date. We always celebrated my birthday on the 8th, but the birth certificate carries date, the 7th. Dr Hargrove baptised me a few weeks afterwards, a fact which I like to remember, since it is a modest link with a departed generation of Unitarian thinkers and statesmen the like of which are not likely to be encountered again. Hargrove's remarkable religious pilgrimage has been chronicled by Dr L.P. Jacks in a volume entitled *From Authority to Freedom*.

A short but busy ministry in Leeds, during which he was in sole charge of the daughter-church in Hunslet, terminated in 1909, when my father moved to become minister at Chapel Lane Chapel, Bradford. His stipend remained at £200 per annum, as in Leeds, and there was no manse. Actually, he was slightly worse off financially, for the rent was more than in Leeds and removal-expenses at this time were not defrayed by the churches. Later, he paid a well-earned tribute to my mother, who, as long as she lived, was his loyal self-sacrificing aid: "That I never got into debt at any time, despite a weakness for buying books, was due entirely to my wife, whose skill in all that pertained to a home was beyond praise".

My mother was a woman who united a sweet nature with natural courage, resolution, and self-control. To her I was entirely devoted, as she to me. My father's duties took him, as we shall see, into the wider world of academic, college, university, and denominational life, and a great deal of his time was spent in his study. In fact, when he became principal of the Unitarian College, he acted as administrator, librarian, and general curator, saving that institution untold expense. Needless to say, this may be said to have deprived him and his wife of much domestic delight that otherwise they would have enjoyed together. Indeed, as one contemplates the lot of many men of the cloth, it is not difficult to see that their vocation often imposes a loss of private and family weal. Moreover, within the churches there are, unfortunately, those who are quite ready to exploit their clergy, preferring always to spend money on bricks and mortar rather than pay their minister a decent stipend....

More happily, one can say that behind almost every successful man stands a woman, whose love and support is an overriding factor, often overlooked, but nonetheless, indispensable. My mother's personality and spirit were influential not only in the conduct of family affairs, but also in the fine example which she set both my father and myself of quiet, devoted attachment to the religious values and moral standards which she treasured and for which she was always ready to make considerable personal sacrifice. I set down here what a friend of over thirty years, the Quaker president of the Manchester branch of the Women's International League, wrote on her death from cancer in 1940: "She was a beautiful woman with a corresponding beauty of character". Two

Mary Jane McLachlan and the author, aged 7.

women, quite unknown to each other, both said, "She was the sweetest woman I ever knew".

Mary Jane Taylor (1872–1940) belonged to an old Dissenting family, tracing its descent back to John Taylor (1719–1796), a Yorkshire yeoman who lived at Snape Hill, a small farm near Whitefield, six miles north of Manchester. He was a farmer and handloom-weaver, a combination of crafts not unusual in the outskirts of 'Cottonopolis'. On his death he left six sons who, like their father, were connected with Stand Unitarian Chapel, near the lych-gate of which he lies buried. One of his sons was the father of the founder of the *Manchester Guardian*, John Edward Taylor (1791–1844). John Edward's father was a Quaker and his mother, Mary, a Unitarian, and daughter of the Rev. Russell Scott, for forty-five years minister of the High Street Chapel in Portsmouth, friend of Joseph Priestley and of radical reform. From a relative of John

Taylor came a water-colour of Snape Hill farm, a corner cupboard, a large bureau, and some articles of porcelain and silver that originally belonged to the Taylor family and are now in my possession. At the turn of the century my mother's branch of the family came to live in the Longsight district of Manchester, which explains my mother's membership of the choir at the Free Christian church. I never knew my maternal grandparents since they were both dead before I reached boyhood. But I well remember three uncles, John Edward (the eldest) who had been at Manchester Grammer School and was a member of the Minnehaha Minstrels, a pierrot troupe who used to entertain in aid of charities; Frank, and Charles, who, I believe, had a good singing voice, which, however, hardly earned him a living. My two aunts, Florence and Kitty, who, with my mother, belonged to the unprivileged class of females whom their parents did not consider needed to continue their schooling beyond the age of twelve or thirteen, eventually went into business together. They ran a dress-making shop until Kitty and my mother both got married and Flo', whom my father christened "the wicked Aunty" because she always petted me, moved 'up-market' and became the well-loved and very able manager of a Manchester clothing factory. Occasionally, my mother would visit the factory, taking me with her. She did not leave empty-handed, but benefited from an allowance of dress-materials which my generous aunt would bestow upon her. For my part, I would wander through the serried ranks of girls at sewing-machines, marvelling at their skill and enjoying their smiles and banter. Mother herself was no mean proficient with her treadle sewing-machine, on which she made most of her own dresses. Later, when I was sent away to boarding-school, it was she who made the bulk of my trousseau, including an Eton jacket and waistcoat, dressing-gown, breeches, pyjamas, and even shirts. One of my earliest (and latest) memories of her is the pulsating noise and vibration of her sewing-machine from an adjacent room.

My father met his future wife at Longsight Free Christian Church whilst he was a student teaching in the Sunday School. I still possess the illuminated address presented to her as a "Memento of her long and valued association with the Choir... by her fellow-members on her retirement" to get married. It speaks of her "faithfulness and devotion" and expresses gratitude "for all (her) helpfulness". She had a good contralto voice which, as a boy, I used to admire, as she sat at the piano and sang such ditties as "The little silver ring" and "Three fishers went sailing..."

Alas, as she grew older, deafness supervened and she was compelled to give up the solo-singing which delighted friends at the Mill Hill Musical Society's concerts in the Priestley Hall and elsewhere. Years later, a former Hungarian student at 'Summerville', the Unitarian College in Victoria Park, Manchester, described her in a letter to me as "petite, charming, but alas – deaf". It was a sad handicap, which she fought all her life with brave determination, and which the Manchester specialist whom she attended for years was unable to relieve. It made her all the more sympathetic, if that were possible, towards others who suffered from physical handicaps of one kind or another. Perhaps there were compensations? She could often hear people speaking in the noisy Manchester tramcars when we, sound-of-hearing people, could not. It seemed that the vibrations of the tram, running on its steel track, acted as a kind of 'deaf-aid'; remarkable, but I never came across anyone else who made this observation.

At Bradford we lived at 5, Ashfield, a semi-detached house not far from the centre of the city. It boasted a lawn and garden in which I used to play, when not making expeditions into town, which seemed to have a strange attraction for a three-year old who learnt to walk long before he could talk! In the Spring, daffodils and other bulbs grew in the border, and being of an inquisitive turn of mind I decided to investigate these new arrivals, pulling them up to see what they *really* looked like. Fortunately, I was interrupted in the process of disinterment, and when warned of the mischievous nature of my occupation, I was compelled to investigate the local geography. Early I suffered from *Wanderlust*. I managed to open the garden gate and proceed citywards at leisure. This happened on several occasions, and newsboys, postmen, policemen all joined in the hue and cry: the quarry? a small boy who could not tell where he lived and was manifestly lost and loitering. Once, I was discovered sheltering in the Town hall caretaker's lodging, contentedly sucking a lump of sugar.

One early memory still haunts me. Shortly after his appointment as minister in Bradford, my father decided that the memorial tablets on the walls of the chapel needed to be spruced up. They had probably not been cleaned for a lifetime. At all events, I distinctly recall accompanying my parents to Chapel Lane, my mother always willing to share, if possible, in any scheme my father entertained for improving the looks of the house of worship. There, with soap and water, buckets and a ladder, they were busy washing the Bradford grime away, whilst I, times watched, times wandered, as was my wont. Eventually, my absence was noted and a search instituted. I was found in the pulpit, access to which was by a small door with a spring-lock. This had closed behind me as I entered, and I had become a prisoner. Looking back upon this incident, one realises the truth of the poet's line, "Coming events cast their shadows before". For, many years later, in 1941, a fully-fledged minister, I conducted morning and evening Services from that same pulpit.

In 1911, Alexander Gordon, my father's old teacher and college principal, resigned and retired, and his pupil was appointed tutor and resident warden. There was no increase in stipend, but the family was given board and lodging, and my mother – I am sure reluctantly – agreed to act as matron at a salary of £50 per annum. Dr Hargrove and other friends sent their congratulations. Wrote the former, "I have long regretted that your talents and acquirements should have so little encouragement and your learning be of use neither to yourself nor the world.... I heartily hope that the connection on which you enter will last as long as you live – to the great benefit of the College and your own happiness and usefulness". That hope was fulfilled. My father had at last found his true vocation – that of a scholar and teacher. In due course he succeeded to the principalship. At Manchester University he became lecturer in Hellenistic Greek and for many years hon. secretary of the New Testament Greek seminar. He had already published work on St Luke. During his term in Manchester, he was very active in University circles, Dean of the Faculty of Theology, and a frequent examiner. The degree of D.D. was conferred upon him in 1920 (for work done) and D.Litt. later (a foregone conclusion) on the submission of some of his many published works. He it was who built up and catalogued the library at the college, for years his hobby, which, in view of all the work he had done for it, was later christened 'The McLachlan Library'. Few men could have researched and produced a great card-catalogue of this notable nonconformist library and written its interesting history, as he did. It was a labour of love, and the tragedy of its decline and eventual dispersal was, luckily, hidden from his eyes. (He died in December, 1958). Travelling from Oxford to London during the second World War, Professor E.F. Jacob, Regius Professor of Medieval History and formerly professor at Manchester, remarked to me, "Your father is a great bibliographer, and we all owe him a tremendous debt".

I was three years old when we arrived in Victoria Park, Manchester, and found myself living in a spacious Victorian mansion, 'Summerville', which was then the residential training college for the Unitarian ministry. A new world opened up before me. One of my earliest memories is that of being taken down to Albert Square where, hoisted on my father's shoulders, I watched the procession on the occasion of the Coronation of King George V. At that date, royalty did not have to submit to the indignity of being 'made up' for the TV cameras, which, in the late 'forties, was the fate of the King's second son, George VI, when he visited Oxford to open the Bodleian extension and passed immediately beneath our windows.

Victoria Park was at this time a quiet, private precinct, originally enclosed by a number of nineteenth century magnates and merchants, and later occupied by nursing homes, university halls of residence, hotels, and homes of the élite. The roads were not well-maintained, and the Park was entered through toll-gates where rather elderly gatekeepers kept watch in their tiny toll-houses. The Victoria Park Trust levied a voluntary rate, but this became difficult to collect as the number of small villas increased. At night, the streets were gloomy, gas-lit, almost deserted, and, to my youthful imagination, pregnant with mystery. I found the evening round of the lamp-lighter highly significant and entertaining. He carried a long pole crowned by a flickering light. This he inserted through a hinged pane of glass in the side of the lantern on each lamp post so as to ignite the gas-mantle. To me this was a never-ending source of wonder and delight. Lying in bed in my nursery, I would watch the moving panorama of light and shadow filtering through the branches of near-by trees and reflected upon the walls of the room with intense interest, trying to interpret the secret world of make-belief that was unfolding before my eyes.

'Summerville' had been purchased in 1905 for a mere £5,500, in celebration of the Jubilee of the college, to house students and staff. Eighty years later, riddled with dry-rot, it was sold to the Moslem community for £100,000 and became an 'Arabic Institute for Islamic Studies'. It had been the home of the Kesslers, a Unitarian family of German extraction, and, before that, of Major-General (later Sir) Harry Smith (1787–1860) "Soldier, Statesman, and Governor of the Cape of Good Hope" – as the blue plaque on the building now declares. His wife gave her name to a town which withstood a famous siege in the South African War. The house and its owners are described in a *Short Account of the Victoria Park Trust, Manchester*, published in 1937 on the centenary of the opening of the Park. The estate comprised four acres of garden, a large man-

Summerville.

sion, deserted stables, a yard, and a field, sold later for building. Fine trees and many huge glorious rhododendron-bushes graced the garden, whilst apple and pear trees, which had not been pruned for ages, attracted the attention every autumn of passing youngsters, who made frequent sallies over the walls to help themselves to tempting fruit. I used to climb several of these trees, as neighbouring cats often did, to become stranded high up in their branches. The stables and the roof of the big house later became a very familiar playground. It was possible to climb out of a second-storey window and walk along a ledge which gave access to the gulleys and roof of the whole building. When I began to take an interest in the new science of 'Wireless', as it was then called, and possessed a Wireless Telegraphy Licence (cost: ten shillings), I was able to erect aerials between the chimney stacks and neighbouring trees. On one occasion, accompanied by a friend, tightening the supporting wire whilst aloft in a big apple tree, we succeeded in pulling down a large chimney-pot to which an aerial was attached, much to our surprise and the annoyance of my father.

The stables proved a splendid recreation-ground for small boys, who could ascend to the first floor, where no doubt stable-boys were once accommodated. The way up was novel: a series of holes in a vertical wooden upright fastened to the wall into which you inserted your hands and feet as you climbed. On that floor the fodder and hay for the horses must have been kept. There were also rooms for the grooms. Some of the downstairs windows were broken, but it was not long before my friends and I saw to it that those still intact presented a uniform appearance.

At the age of five I was sent to 'Ashford', a private dame's school in Clarence Road, Longsight, kept by a formidable lady called 'Miss Knight'. Here the pupils had chalk and slates for 'sums' and 'copy-books' for writing and spelling. Each morning we sang Mrs Alexander's boring hymn, 'All things bright and beautiful'. We also had religious instruction, from which my father rescued me, when I began to dream rather too vividly about the raising of Lazarus. As a boy, I was very prone to dreaming, some of it distinctly unpleasant and taking the form of recurring nightmares. I remember one, in particular, that haunted me. It began with a far-off threatening din, as of a band marching along the corridors of the house and getting gradually nearer and louder until it was on the point of bursting into the room. At this terrifying instant I would suddenly awake in a panic; and on more than one occasion I would flee for shelter to a friendly student's room and climb into bed with him....

My elementary schooling at Miss Knight's passed off, I fear, without any remarkable academic achievement, but I am on record as being "too noisy". I can also recall a habit of dawdling between home and school and vice versa. It was a journey of little more than twelve minutes, but it often took me three or four times that length. There were friends to meet, variations of route to explore, and adventures of one kind or another naturally detained one. Around Guy Fawkes's day, for example, one was usually late getting home, especially if one had indulged in the purchase of 'Chinese Crackers' or squibs, as we called them. These consisted of a bundle of small red cardboard 'cartridges', each with a fuse, which, when lit and detonated at regular intervals, gave great entertainment. One ploy was to place one of these in a backdoor key-hole, light the fuse, hammer on the door, and then skedaddle. Nowadays, squibs are no longer available to frighten the lights out of poor householders. Pocket-money never exceeded 2d or 3d a week, and this I would spend either on liquorice 'telegraph wires' or 'kali-suckers' (a bag containing a sweet white powder which you could draw up through a hollow liquorice 'straw') or on used foreign stamps, the collection of which began to interest me then, as it still does....

Holidays always provided excitement, joy, and wonder. I suppose my first journey by sea was to Ulster in September, 1913. We crossed by the old route from Holyhead to Greenore (long disused), and as we passed along Carlingford Lough, someone on the train to Newry pointed out a curious animal on the sea-shore. From the distance it looked like a big snake, reared up and waving its head. Could it have been a relative of the Loch Ness monster, I wonder? More probably, it was a grey seal. At Warren Point we watched Sir Edward Carson and his 'volunteers' marching along the front. The crowd waved their Union Jacks and expressed in no uncertain terms their utter rejection of 'Home Rule'. My first taste of Ireland was very gratifying. We experienced that friendliness and hospitality of Irish folk which, in later years, living in Belfast so unforgettably confirmed. At Warren Point, in the County Down, I was greatly taken with an Irish donkey, which, in my innocence, I planned to bring back to Manchester: "There'll be plenty of room for it in the garden of Summerville", I thought. We could have had it for ten shillings; but wiser counsels prevailed. I thought it was a give-away at the price!

Most welcome were our family excursions to Disley in Cheshire, then a comparatively small village and not the dormitory-suburb of the big city it has since become. My Aunty Kitty and Uncle Will lived there, the latter travelling up to town by train every morning on his 'contract': he was 'in' non-ferrous metals, his office being in 'The Parsonage', just behind Deansgate. Their house bordered on a wide expanse of meadow and copse in which my companions and I would play to our hearts' content. My aunt cooked the most glorious meals. I rated her apple-pies and rice puddings as unsurpassed and, indeed, unsurpassable. My uncle played his gramophone records with steel needles on an H.M.V. turntable with a large green horn: you had to keep the motor well wound-up to avoid the awful chromatic descent into a bear-garden and growling-pit of Muzac when it ran down. Later, he forsook the gramophone for a pianola, an instrument that played the notes automatically or rather pneumatically, if one kept up pedalling and had properly inserted the large roll of paper with its notes punched in a continuous pattern. These 'mysteries' always appealed to me. My uncle Will, demonstrating his prowess on the pianola, appeared to me to have joined the society of magicians like David Devant, whom I once saw conjuring in the theatre of the great Midland Hotel in central Manchester.

My first visit to Wales was in the company of a friendly Welsh cook who, going on holiday, begged to take me with her to her home near Wrexham. Here I got my introduction to a coal-mine, and marvelled at the revolving wheels of the pit-head and at the realisation that the 'cage' was on its way down, plumbing untold depths. Here, too, I saw and felt the beauty of hill-country and experienced my one and only hunting foray. A local butcher took me for a ride in his trap. When we had gone some way, he stopped the horse, and standing up, he raised his double-barrelled shotgun and aimed at a rook in a field. The bird was hit and he sent me to retrieve the wounded creature. I set out boldly. It had taken refuge in a hedge, I had never seen a bleeding animal before, and as it floundered about in the hedge-bottom, bleeding profusely, the shock made me quite unable to pick it up. I returned to the road, deeply upset, and, I suppose, after that, ever a firm supporter of the RSPCA.

Next year (1914), the family spent Easter at Bournemouth. The guesthouse employed German waiters, with whom I soon chummed up. It was not long before they were all boarding ship for the Fatherland. Two other incidents recur to me: the flight of Graham White's 'plane over the town, and my ducking in a stream running through one of the parks. This happened whilst sailing my little Dutch yawl, which I think my "wicked Aunty" may have given me. I leaned over too far, toppled into the river and had to be fished out, dripping and cold. It was all exciting and great fun, in a world which the coming of the First World War swept away for ever.

Somehow, the outbreak of war in August of this year does not seem to have greatly impressed my youthful mind, but I do recall how the name 'German' soon became an epithlet of disparagement and shame that you applied to your worst enemies at school. One learnt to suspect, and even see, German spies, if not at every street-corner, at least in anyone strange or apparently 'acting in a suspicious manner'. It was not long before Lord Ponsonby's dictum that "Truth is the first casualty in war" was proved correct in almost all walks of life in a country and Press fighting for survival.

When war was declared, my parents had taken a cottage in Bradwell, Derbyshire. We moved in, hoping for a quiet walking-holiday, inhaling the fresh air, and hungry for the sights, sounds, and above all the peace of that most lovely of counties. Its 'Shivering Mountain' (Mam Tor), its delightful gorge (The Winnats), its limestone caves (the Blue John, the Speedwell Mine), and the Dales around Tideswell and Great Hucklow now became familiar places. However, one morning we had an unpleasant surprise. This was the arrival of the local 'Bobby', asking to see my father. At this point I should mention that we were, of course, strangers in the district and often carried binoculars with which to survey the landscape and watch the birds. In addition, my father often wore a Vienna cape which he had been given by a friend on a visit to Germany some years before. It transpired that local people had reported us to the police, thinking that we might be 'German spies', though what possible objects of national importance in that district might be in jeopardy I have not the slightest idea. It was not difficult for father to provide his *bona fides* and the local police-officer departed, satisfied that we were not intent on betraying secrets to the enemy. Actually, the spy-scare was rampant in those early days of the war, and all kind of rumours circulated amongst a credulous and ignorant populace. One that had wide credence was the notion that Russian troops, on their way to assist the Allies on the Western Front had been seen entraining from Scotland to the South Coast, with the snow still visible on their boots!

It was not long before queues for essential foodstuffs and coal were a regular sight on the streets. Margarine was in great demand, in place of butter, and I often went on errands to the local Maypole shop in Stockport Road. All kinds of shortages occurred. I remember, when, on a visit to Miss Anna Philips's house and park at Prestwich, where each summer she invited a number of parents and children, I remarked quite innocently at tea that Miss Philips's strawberry jam had real strawberries in it! As the war developed and disaster struck the troops in combat, the *Manchester Guardian* printed tremendous casualty-lists week after week, which cast a gloom over everyday life. Trenches were dug in Heaton Park to show those in 'Civvy Street' how our men were living, fighting, and of course dying, but the gross reality was hidden from view. The complete absorption of almost everyone with the conduct of the war affected even school-children with patriotic fervour. One of the few students for the ministry in college at this time was a friendly soul, always ready to talk and joke with a small boy. I had grown to like him and admired his stand against the prevalent war-fever: he was a conscientious objector. One day, I persuaded him to give me a 'No More War' badge like the one he usually wore. With this in my buttonhole, I proceeded to Miss Knight's one morning, only to find myself an object of abuse and contumely. One boy grabbed the badge and tried, unsuccessfully, to throw it into the classroom fire. But I recovered it and wore it for a time, even after this assault.

Other events sometimes recur to mind, but perhaps few more vividly than the spectacle in 1917 of the first American troops, landed at Liverpool, marching from Central Station to Belle Vue, where they were to be billeted. Some of them looked far from fit, and I was surprised to see their comrades supporting them and their packs as they moved along the road.

In the summer of 1918, we took a short holiday in Whitby. The war, which in Manchester by now had all the signs of attrition and a kind of ghastly unreality, took on a much more exciting and violent aspect on the east coast. Whitby had actually been bombarded from the sea and was now a naval patrol-centre for the protection of Allied convoys. On the day we arrived there, a 'plane was actually being recovered from the harbour into which it had fallen, drowning the pilot. The quaysides were crowded with M.Ls. (motor-launches) carrying depth-charges for use against German submarines, which used to lurk in-waiting on the landward side for the daily convoys north and south. More than once from the cliffs we watched naval action between destroyers and enemy submarines.

The college had already closed for the duration of the war, there being almost no students for the ministry. Instead, the house had been let to the University as a hostel for university-women. My father had taken temporary charge of a church in Stalybridge, whose regular minister was away in France with the YMCA. We lived in the manse for the best part of a year. The Unitarian church in Stalybridge was well-attended by a largely working-class congregation and possessed, as a subsidiary, a large day-school building (Hob Hill Schools) which its trustees controlled and which on Sundays housed the many children of the Sunday School. This feature of a denominational day-school was quite common amongst nonconformists in Lancashire and Cheshire.

The church was highly institutional, providing social and recreational facilities for all ages, football and cricket clubs, and in the winter mounting a very successful pantomime, as well as concerts and drama at other times of the year.

The large billiard-room was adjacent to a weaving-shed in a factory long since demolished. A hole in the party-wall was of particular interest to me as it permitted a view of what was going on on the other side. When opportunity offered, I used to gaze, fascinated, at the clattering looms, the swift-speeding shuttles and the women-weavers deftly minding these extraordinary machines. Later, in the 'fifties, I was just as enchanted by the operations in a great linen mill in Belfast, and no less possessed by the sound and sight of a loom working in a shed next to our holiday-cottage in Donegal. Could this be a kind of hereditary, subconscious 'memory' of the world of textiles in which my paternal grandfather, father and an ancestor of my mother all spent a portion of their lives?

I had been unlucky enough, during our stay at Whitby, to catch ringworm, a skin-disease that affected my head and made it necessary for me to have treatment at the skin-disease hospital in Manchester. This took the form of exposure to X-Ray, which was applied to my head, killing the hair follicles and eventually rendering me as bald as the back of my hand. Ointment and soft-soap aided the process, but it was gradual and resulted in the interruption of my schooling.

This had its compensations, however. I undertook a course of reading Dickens, Scott, and, more exciting, the adventures of the Scarlet Pimpernel. I also passed my Tenderfoot test and was welcomed into the Scout fraternity by the Rev. John Ellis on his return from France to Stalybridge. I may say that nothing further came of this, since I never again had any opportunity to qualify as a Scout beyond a reading, later, of Baden Powell's 'Rovering to Success'! I have often wondered, in view of what we now know of radiation, whether the X-Rays could have affected more than just the hair of my head, but I cannot say that I have consciously suffered from any adverse consequences. Nor have my friends, so far as I am aware, ever suggested that my conduct was markedly abnormal! Have they, perhaps, been too polite?

2

SCHOOLDAYS

"As we grow older
The World becomes stranger, the pattern more complicated"
T.S. Eliot: *East Coker*

In the summer of 1918, Miss Knight, considering me ripe for promotion, entered me for a scholarship examination held annually by the Hulme Grammar School in Manchester. I recall sitting amongst many other hopeful aspirants in the large hall of that institution and thinking myself an unlikely candidate for academical advancement. However, strange to relate, I did pass the test, and still have the letter from the Headmaster informing my father that I would be admitted, providing he gave an undertaking that I should stay until I was eighteen. No such undertaking was needed. My parents decided, instead, to send me away to a small boarding-school in south Cheshire, where, as the son of a Unitarian minister, I would attract special financial consideration, a fact of which I was entirely innocent all my schooldays. No doubt their decision was also influenced by the consideration that the collegiate atmosphere at Summerville was not really suitable for a lad whose interests would, of necessity, be quite different from those of the students living and working in the College. Doubtless, also, it was considered wise not to run the risk of cosseting an only child!

That it was a right decision I have no doubt whatever, though at the time I was definitely in two minds about leaving home. My sense of adventure prompted me to jump at the chance of a complete change of life, but at the same time I knew I should miss the old landmarks and especially old friends.

However, my departure for boarding-school was delayed until January, 1919 owing to the ringworm incident. I had time to prepare myself for the somewhat traumatic transition from a mixed, private day-

Willaston School, Nantwich, The West Front

school to a single-sex boarding institution, and I believe I was full of expectancy and wonder when my father and I travelled from Stalybridge to Crewe, and thence on the branch-line to Nantwich. At Crewe, we climbed into a compartment full of boys going the same way. One of them, from Sheffield, Laurie Stevenson, belonged to a family who were faithful supporters of our Unity Church there. Alas, he died young, but his sister, Margaret, became a good friend in later years.

Willaston School, Nantwich, was founded by Philip Barker, a wealthy bachelor and Unitarian, who left his house and estate, about a mile from the town, for the erection of "a public school on modern lines'. It was intended, *inter alia*, for the education of ministers' sons, who were admitted on favourable terms. It had opened in September, 1900, but closed after a too brief existence in 1937, owing to financial difficulties, some maladministration, and a lack of wide appeal. Years later, at the suggestion of the Cheshire County Archivist a history of this rather unique little school (as he, and we Old Boys, regarded it) was written by the late George E. Walker, O.W., with the assistance of K. Gill Smith and the writer of these reminiscences, which makes it unnecessary to go into further detail. This history was privately printed and copies were sent to the Archives in Chester, Manchester College, Oxford, the Unitarian College, Manchester and to many *alumni*. Unfortunately, the school, though furnished with fine buildings and ample grounds, was too small to house the number of pupils necessary to make

Mrs Lang Jones ('Ma J.'), July, 1928

it really viable. Starting with twenty-two, it never exceeded seventy scholars. Moreover, though intended to attract the sons of Unitarians, it never proved a sufficient 'draw' within this small denomination and failed to attract a regular stream of boys from other backgrounds.

My first acquaintance with Willaston, accompanied by my father, took the form of admission to the headmaster's drawing-room for what I regarded as something of an ordeal. The Head struck me as a rather peculiar person, silent and withdrawn, an attitude for which his jolly, loud-spoken wife, 'Ma J.', as I learned to call her, did her best to atone. It was a life-long effort, for her husband's taciturnity persisted all my schooldays and beyond, and was accompanied on occasion by quite violent fits of temper. As already mentioned, the X-Ray treatment of my ringworm-infection had left me with little or no hair, though it was beginning to grow again and the light down-covering earned me the nickname of 'Fluffy' with the boys. 'Ma J.' regarded my appearance with undisguised approval. "That is just how we like our boys' hair to be cut", she cried delightedly, and went on to inquire if I liked porridge. Brightly, I replied, "Yes, rather!" For Quaker Oats had been my staple breakfast-diet for as long as I could remember. "You shall have plenty", chuckled the redoubtable lady (whose obituary I was to write many years later). During the next eight years, she kept her promise. But, of course, there is porridge – and porridge; and the Willaston variety, like the soapy cake supplied once a week on Sundays, was often of a repulsive density that not even a coating of treacle could refine. Actually, the provision and cooking of food in my time at Willaston left a good deal to be desired. This was before domestic refrigeration was even thought of, so that in the hot summers of those days meat not seldom 'went off', with fatal results upon tender digestions. The announcement that 'diarrhoea pie' was to be served at dinner made many a sturdy youth blanch with awful presentiment. Only after the Jones's retirement was the regimen properly reformed.

The great flu' epidemic of 1918/19 affected Willaston, as it did the rest of the country, and those who did not fall victims to it, like me, were sent home for about ten days. I was delighted, as I still felt 'a stranger in the midst'... Later in the year, our family returned from Stalybridge to Victoria Park, and my future journeys to Nantwich always began with a stately progress from Summerville to London Road station, as 'Piccadilly' was then called. We travelled in a horse-drawn cab with a large wooden trunk, containing clothes and other 'clobber', trundling over the 'sets' or granite cobbles, which almost everywhere paved the streets of the city at that date.

Surprisingly, my mother kept all of my letters home, from January, 1919 to May, 1921. Reading them, it is easy to see how a first term away from home inevitably seemed an age, and full of horror. The correspondence reflects this, and conveys a measure of misery and disillusionment perhaps natural under the circumstances. "I do not mind the cold showers, and I like the morning drill, but I do not like football every afternoon". Strange this, from one who afterwards went on to play university 'rugby' every winter from 1926 to 1932! The writer continues, "When I play it hurts my joints so.... The letters from home cheer me up". Subsequent epistles show developing self-confidence and a growing appreciation of much that was going on in school and in the outside world. Home-sickness no longer troubled the writer, though the days before the close of term are invariably carefully counted. By November,

1920, we read: "Now I'm having a jolly fine time". On December 2nd, "two gentlemen from Marconi's staff gave a demonstration of Wireless Telegraphy". The boys were able to hear signals from Carnarvon, Seaforth, Hamburg, New York, and Paris, "where the Eiffel Tower time-signals for ships in the Channel... can be heard all over the world". The new and powerful medium of radio soon had some of us enthralled. As an enthusiastic radio-ham myself, this and other like experiences egged me on, and before long, I was spending most of my slender allowance of pocket-money on copper wire, terminals, coils, condensers, crystal-detectors, valves, batteries and so forth. The mystery and excitement of 'Wireless' seemed a cut above Meccano, which had hitherto claimed my sole allegiance!

Sir Alan Parkes, in his autobiography, 'Off-beat Biologist' (1985) and 'Biologist at Large' (1988) has written of his experiences as a boy at Willaston in what I regard as, on the whole, fair comment. He describes the prevailing customs and the rather over-disciplined character of daily life, using at one point the term "a budding Borstal". As an eminent scientist-in-the-making one can appreciate his aversion from what to others – classicists, music-lovers, and humanists – was not without appeal. But there is no gainsaying the fact that the curriculum in its early days was one-sided, at least until 1926, when a chemical and physics laboratory was built. Yes, the endowment of the school was inadequate, the governors badly briefed, and the second headmaster, unfitted for the conduct of a school intended to be run on liberal lines. A good classicist, a fine musician, a clever versifier, his temperament was quite unsuited to the school's proper development and welfare. Amazing as it may seem, this ill-tempered and moody man, shy with parents, strangely romantic, frequently given to sarcasm, and curiously lacking in real sympathy for boys, was given control of a school meant to be a haven and provider of liberal values!

When I arrived at Willaston in January, 1919, the cyclone of military madness which possessed the place under Lang Jones had by no means blown itself out. The cadet corps continued to hold its drills and parades even into 1922. As a junior, I was sucked into these time-consuming activities, marching to and fro, carrying real and dummy rifles, and learning useless evolutions in close and extended order.... Happily, there were other members of staff who nurtured the humane side of our spirits.

The senior master, Albert Tobler (1874–1950) was a Swiss, who

The cricket field at Willaston, Speech Day, 1926, the author opening the school innings against Old Willastonians

taught us French, German, and more importantly, perhaps, a love of Nature. In his time he had been a gymnast and a mountaineer, and conducted more than one party of old boys to the Alps. Near his house he kept bees and poultry, and sometimes in the summer the lesson would be interrupted by a breathless messenger who announced that the bees were swarming. This was the signal for a hectic chase across country, in which a chosen few would happily join – much more exciting than the agreement of French adjectives with the nouns they were supposed to qualify! Mathematics and History were the provinces of Douglas Ross (1882–1982), who also supervised our English Essays. His contribution to the cultural, sporting and social life of the school was remarkable. Games master, producer of school plays, organiser of the chess championship, leader of the Sunday play-reading circle, "the Little Man", as we fondly called him, was a friend to all. He lived to be over one hundred, thus demonstrating the fact that you don't shorten your life by packing it full of activities. On the contrary.

Elizabeth Middleton taught English language and literature and Geography, an able teacher and possessed of a sweet treble voice that combined charmingly with the headmaster's tenor in duets on a Saturday evening. Glen Handley, fresh from H.M. Forces in September, 1921, toiled with us over our Latin proses (he had been a member of Paton's Classical Sixth at Manchester Grammar School), read French, and brought a gust of fresh air and good humour into our close community when he formed a Pierrot troupe ('The Cheshire Cats'), of which I was, happily, one. He left to get married in 1925, and after some years in commerce enlisted again on the outbreak of war in 1939 and was mortally wounded during the retreat of the Highland Division to the Channel coast in 1940.

Though the sciences, apart from botany, were in my time neglected, music, both instrumental and vocal, held a high priority. Visiting teachers taught piano, violin, 'cello, and flute, whilst the Head conducted a small orchestra and the choral society. Every Saturday evening the whole school assembled to sing from 'Gaudeamus', the Fellowship Song Book, or one of the Gilbert and Sullivan operas. Concerts were given by visiting quartets, and recitals by the music staff and others. The almost annual visits of the Arts League of Service, from 1925 onwards, were memorable events. I took piano lessons with Miss Broughton from Crewe, a huge lady who used to pinch my ear when I played a wrong note. Subsequently, I took up the violin with Miss Burrows from Manchester. At her home, off Dickinson Road, there used to gather a small string orchestra on Friday evenings during the winter and this I joined after I left school. At Willaston, we were privileged to meet and hear first-class artists and lecturers, like Cecil Sharpe and Arthur Catterall, and were encouraged in an 'Arts Club', founded in 1922, to read papers on literature, art, and music. In this way we were introduced to a quality of life that carries the transcendent and enshrines "the things that are more excellent".

Rugby football in the winter and athletics and cricket in the spring and summer were compulsory. Only a doctor's certificate exempted. We received little or no coaching, but trained ourselves.... The long jump and the half-mile were two of my favourite 'events' and I raised the records in both, jumping eighteen feet nine inches in 1926 at the age of seventeen. The headmaster seemed pleased with that performance, because it showed an increase of one foot per year's advance since my jump as a junior three years before. (This was the kind of statistic in which he revelled!) As I prepared to take my third jump , standing at the take-off board, he barked, "Have you got nothing in your hands?" I hadn't a splinter. "Take some grass!" he shouted. That was indicative of the amateur way we 'did' our sports, and incidentally the way in which his mind worked. There was something crackpot about him for all his scholarship and musical and poetic abilities. I find that on the same day (5th April, 1926) I ran the half-mile in 2 mins 9 3/5 secs. Douglas Ross, in a letter to my father, noted that "the previous best" time was 2 mins 14 secs and mine was "a very fine performance, considering the comparative roughness of the track". We simply ran around the football pitch on a marked track over which a team of boys had trundled the heavy cricket-pitch roller a couple of times! It was all quite untutored and extempore. However, this particular record had not been beaten when the school closed for good in 1937. Of course, my father was inclined to frown upon my modest athletic achievements, at least officially, especially when I used to return home at the end of the Easter term with several boxes of silver cups. But my mother, God bless her, was only too ready to clean the silver. Looking back, I can see it was rather perverse of him to pretend not to be pleased, since he was himself a keen and doughty tennis-player (with a terrific smash) and a lifelong supporter of the Lancashire County Cricket Club. He also wielded a useful bat and pitched up a very awkward slow ball. I was no great cricketer myself, though I enjoyed the game and used to open the innings in my last season at school.

The game I really favoured was 'Rugger'. My usual position was inside-three-quarter, from where one sees a good deal of the fun. I continued playing throughout my six years at university, though moving to fly-half for two years on the 'A' team and four years on the First XV. In the Christmas and Easter vacations I usually played for local clubs like Heaton Moor and Broughton Park. Later, in Heidelberg (1932–3) I turned out for the 'Rudderklub' once or twice, but the German 'game' was different, indeed almost unrecognisable; so I took up skating on the River Neckar, and in the summer rowing, walking and cycling instead.

Apart from 'Rugger', my main hobby was 'Wireless' (then so-called). I applied for an experimenter's licence and built crystal sets and valve sets, with sometimes quite complicated circuits, for relatives and friends. This was a very time-consuming and pocket-money-swallowing pursuit. At Willaston, a few of us founded a 'Wireless Society' which operated a set in the gymnasium and in the old Cadet corps store-room. The last-named was the scene one midnight of our receiving a signal from an unexpected quarter. Using a single 'bright emitter' thermionic

The Scott-Tagart super-heterodyne wireless set made by the author (about 1922)

valve, I listened to Pittsburgh, Pennsylvania, broadcasting speech and music direct, a very considerable achievement in those days (1925). This could be explained by two factors, namely that we had erected a very good aerial, stretching from the gym across the quad to the main school building, and that, in South Cheshire we were far from any electro-magnetic interference, and I was able to keep the set working just on the sensitive edge of oscillation.

Sundays at Willaston were almost as highly organised as week days. Morning Service, usually conducted by Lang Jones in the Library and later in the Memorial Hall, was followed by a long walk out into the country led by the Head, who set off at a cracking pace. We would arrive back at school tired and hungry. After dinner we were marshalled into classrooms to write home, and then spent a period in the Library reading.

In the evening a favoured few were allowed to take an early tea and sally forth into Nantwich to attend evening service at the Old Presbyterian (Unitarian) Chapel in Hospital Street. This was a pleasant interlude and a much-needed 'escape' into the 'outside world', especially as it afforded contacts with people and ideas different from those met regularly within the school premises. The Unitarian ministers under whom we sat were good scholars and reasonably effective preachers. J. Parke Davies, whose wife used to preside at the organ, later became principal of the Carmarthen College, a training school for Welsh nonconformists ministers. Occasionally he was invited to take service in school. William Carter, an Oxford graduate, philosopher, and student of English literature was totally blind, but his sermons on literary subjects were most informative and attractive. I remember, in particular, his thrilling address on Francis Thompson and 'The Hound of Heaven'. He was a chain-smoker, alas, and died from cancer before his time. Religious Instruction was the Cinderella of the curriculum at Willaston. As I have written about it in the privately-printed history of 'Willaston School, 1900–1937', I will not repeat myself. I turn, rather, to other matters more nearly affecting me.

At half-term, parents would come to visit their offspring, who were able to secure 'exeats' from our autocratic headmaster. Applying for an 'exeat' was almost like petitioning a tribunal for 'income support': you had to 'make a case'.... My mother used to come over from Manchester and take me out to 'The Lamb' or 'The Brine Baths Hotel', where she was staying, and where we could have a heart-to-heart chat and 'a square meal'. The change of diet was an important item in the week-end's celebrations! But above all her attractive and caring self made my day. Every week she wrote to me and I to her. Her deafness, which robbed her of the joys of conversation, which she loved, made her turn to letter-writing. She had the happy knack of remembering anniversaries and conveying her good wishes at the appropriate moment. Her letters to me were a constant source of inspiration as well as information. I have kept many of them down the years. On her death in September, 1940 we received many tributes to her from a wide circle of friends. One ran: "I remember the refreshing pleasure it always was to meet her at Unitarian or Peace Meetings. Hers was indeed a gracious, fragrant, lovable life, shedding light and sweetness in this darkened world".

Mother took her responsibilities as a citizen very seriously. She was a moral-force Suffragette and, in Manchester, an active member of the 'Women's Citizens' movement. Occasionally, as a boy I accompanied her on leafletting rounds in the Victoria park district. A member of the Women's International League for Peace and Freedom, she studied the Covenant of the League of Nations and made a point of reading all kinds of literature on international affairs. When peace was signed in 1919, I walked with her through the city in the peace procession, and more than once took to Mount Street Quaker meetinghouse supplies of cocoa, chocolate and other goods for the starving children in Germany during the inexcusable Allied blockade that followed. As I have already mentioned (page 7), music was her constant joy and solace. At the Brand Lane Celebrity Concerts in the old Free Trade Hall we heard some of the most famous contemporary vocalists and instrumentalists of those days, among them Galli Curci, Chaliapin, Caruso, Clara Butt, Kreisler, Heifetz, Kubelik, and Paderewski. We sat in a front stall for mother's benefit, and on one occasion, when the great Chopin exponent, Vladamir de Pachmann, was appearing, he fixed his eyes on the pretty woman sitting next to me and played to her. Her photograph looks down upon me as I write. It was taken by F.S. Schmidt of Manchester – as famous in the Manchester of his day as Karsh of Ottawa in his. Known as "a photographer of men", he made a few exceptions, among them were Gladys Cooper and my mother.

The Schmidts were neighbours of ours in Victoria Park. Carlo, as his friends called him, had come to Manchester with his brother in 1904. They hailed from Hildersheim, near Hanover, and arrived with nothing but their skills, setting up as portrait-photographers in a studio in Victoria Street. Later, they moved to St Ann's Square and in the next thirty years took portraits of nearly all the Manchester celebrities and prominent visitors to the city. Carlo married a charming woman who was engaged in speech-training and elocution. Nora was a splendid companion and mother. Their son, Rupert, and I became close friends. On Christmas Eve, I was regularly invited to the Schmidts' parties, where I met University professors, BBC officials, members of the medical and legal professions as well as artists and musicians. Amongst their regular guests would be Edward Isaacs, the pianist and founder of the Manchester Mid-day Concerts, and his wife and daughter. Years later in the 'thirties, when working on behalf of Jewish and non-Jewish refugees from Nazi Austria and Germany, I found myself writing several times to a lady in London who signed herself 'Ruth'. Suddenly, she asked me whether I could possibly be "the Jack McLachlan who used to attend the Schmidts' Xmas Parties"... On the death of her father, Edward Isaacs, I wrote to her mother and Ruth replied, "It is pleasant to hear of you again. I think our last contact was in my Jewish Refugee Committee days". She had re-married in 1943 and gone to India and then to Hong Kong, where her husband was professor of Economics at the university. "I was very sad (she wrote) that Mrs Schmidt died whilst I was away."

The Schmidts often received complimentary tickets for the Manchester theatres and took me with them to see actors like Sir Martin Harvey and Fred and Ellen Terry. Carlo was a keen fisherman. I once went with him salmon-fishing on the river Dee beyond Llangollen. As we drove over the bridge there, he was full of happy expectancy: 'the waters were just right!' But, in fact, the flood was excessively muddy and turbulent and we took not a single fish. Returning in the evening, Carlo was loud in denunciation of the state of the waters! he drove home, like Jehu, in high dudgeon. Alas, his temper proved the undoing of the family. My friend, Rupert, who had been sent away to Denstone College and was no great scholar, failed his matriculation, crammed enough to sit again and just scraped through. Then, after failing his medical preliminaries at Manchester, having wasted much of his time, he left the University to become a reporter on the 'City News'. Finally, he left home with a scapegrace cousin in search of Eldorado. This was too much for his father, who refused absolutely to have him back, much to his mother's distress. At Denstone Rupert had at least learnt to shoot, so he joined the Grenadier Guards as a new recruit and took up residence at their depot in Caterham. Here, in 1933, when I was returning from my student-year at Heidelberg, I called to see him. At the guardroom I explained that I was an old friend just back from Germany and asked if I might take him out to tea for a couple of hours. I did not then know that he had assumed another name (it was Slade) but I described him to the duty-sergeant, upon which he exclaimed "You mean the man who lost all his money in the Hatry case?" "Yes", (I replied), knowing the kind of yarn that Rupert would spin, "he's the fellow". I waited, and eventually my friend came marching down the parade-ground, swinging his arms high as only Guardsmen do. At once I saw he was not himself. In fact, he had contracted rheumatic fever and was almost too hoarse to speak. We had tea in a café in Caterham and said 'Goodbye'. It was, I think, the last time I ever saw him. Within a few days he was seriously ill in hospital and spent two years at the Star and Garter Home in Folkstone before being invalided out of the Army. His condition was brought on by the ridiculous custom of swabbing down the dormitory and ordering the recruits to place their bedclothes on the (damp) floor.... The doctor said his heart was permanently weakened and he must be careful not to over-exert himself. Being Rupert, he paid no attention to that advice, but went on dancing, got married, and died before he was forty!

The family photographic business closed down in 1955, two years after Carlo's death. Facing its decline through lack of interest in studio-portraiture and a vast increase in amateur photography, his surviving brother, Theo, wound up the firm and destroyed more than six tons of photographic plates.

Another friend with whom I kept in touch to the end was Fred Bray. He was the son of Manchester City Treasurer, whom I shall always remember as one of the most severe sufferers from migraine I ever encountered. No doubt the city finances even then were a headache! Fred was a crony of mine from the day we met at Miss Knight's, he aged five and I four and a half years old. He went on to Hulme Grammar School and lacrosse, and I to Willaston School and rugby football. We remained firm friends throughout the plundering years. Both of us succumbed to the 'twenties 'wireless' craze, constructing 'receivers' of various kinds and actually transmitting signals (illegally) from his house in Hamilton Road, Longsight, to ours in Victoria Park.... Later, the Brays moved out to 'Easedale', near Disley station, formerly the home of Professor Weiss, pro-vice-chancellor of the University and professor of Botany. They were delighted to find a wealth of alpines and other exotic flowers appearing in the garden during the first Spring of their occupancy, all products of the good professor's gardening enthusiasm. (I often came in contact with Weiss when I was a student and he the senior member of the University branch of the League of Nations Union).

When Fred got married, I was living as a bachelor in Sheffield and went over to Manchester to act as his 'best man' at the Longsight Wesleyan chapel which the Brays attended. I wore an old black jacket which my mother made for my final years at Willaston, and which, by now, must have looked pretty rough, and a pair of dark, striped trousers. I think a white shirt and a black tie, of which I was uncommonly proud, completed the outfit. I must have looked a scarecrow! Fred's fiancée, Flo', proved a splendid helpmate, mother, and encourager of her husband, for he finished up as a qualified surveyor, working for Stafford town and county and settling down at Castle Bank. He was a keen amateur musician and a bit of an authority on Comic Opera and hymn tunes, a lively combination, which gave him and his friends much pleasure. He and his wife had one son, Ted, about the same age as our first-born Peter, and for years the parents on either side made a habit of exchanging presents at Christmas in favour of each others' sons.

Subsequently, Ted got married and was blessed with a daughter,

Catherine. He and his wife booked a holiday in Spain, leaving the baby-daughter at home, and both of them were killed in the Perpignan air disaster on 5th June 1967. Catherine, bereft of both parents, was brought up by Fred and Flo, her maternal grandparents taking little or no responsibility for their daughter's child!

As a small boy, one of the 'treats' to which I looked forward at Christmas was being taken to the Palace Theatre to see the pantomime, where Dorothy Ward and Wee Georgie Wood were the outstanding performers. Miss Horniman's Gaiety Theatre in Peter Street was another regular attraction: here I saw a splendid performance of 'Where the Rainbow Ends'. In the 'twenties, the zoological gardens at Belle Vue were well kept and patronised, but gradually they became run-down, the animal-collection giving way to such entertainments as dancing and grand firework displays, portraying, for example, chauvinistic undertakings like 'The Capture of Peking'.

Later, after the Rusholme Repertory Theatre had been set up, in an old, converted tram-shed, I graduated to more serious theatre-going.

In the 'twenties, Manchester was still 'Cottonopolis', though cotton-manufacture was on its way out. The Royal Exchange building, whose completion had been held up during World War I, was still an important focus for the textile trade. Bales of cloth, cotton and calico, were moved in and out of warehouses by horse-hauled drays. Hackney-carriages and hansom-cabs stood for hire outside Victoria, Exchange, and Central stations, and were the usual mode of travel within the city, if you were laden with luggage. The tram-service was excellent, convenient, cheap, and comparatively fast. It was fun for me and my friends to go upstairs, sit at the front of the trams, talk in loud voices, and imagine we were 'Kings of the castle'! Few motor-cars or powered lorries had, as yet, made their appearance. From Victoria Park to Cheetham Hill, where stood the 'Ice Palace', the journey took little more than half-an-hour. I used to make it, when on holiday, along with Bojidar Tomačevič, the son of a Serbian colonel whom a Presbyterian minister and friend of my parents had brought back from Salonica, where he served with the YMCA. At the Ice Palace I learnt to skate after a fashion, and discovered the thrill of gliding 'on the outside edge' and backwards, which millions can now watch on the 'telly', but which ADT. (our Mr Tobler at Willaston) used to demonstrate during cold snaps in Cheshire, when we seemed to have longer and more severe winters than ever occur nowadays.

Those were the days when five deliveries of letters could be expected, starting at 7.30 a.m. and ending at 5.30 p.m. and one could be sure that a letter posted in the morning would be delivered before evening in Manchester the same day. Postmen, dustmen, and milkmen all came round for their Christmas 'boxes' on, or about, Boxing Day. I don't suppose they were very well paid; not a few were ex-Servicemen on small pensions and they relied on gratuities to make up their pay.

A regular feature of Christmas-time in our family was attendance at a recital of Dicken's 'Christmas Carol'. Bransby Williams and James Bernard were two of several elocutionists who gave recitals of this popular masterpiece. Handel's 'Messiah' also had its annual airing in churches and concert-halls throughout Lancashire and Yorkshire. As a boy, I was taken to these performances and shared in carol-singing and the general festivities. The garden at Summerville looked glorious under snow-conditions and we would bring in holly branches (with berries), laurel, and branches of fir to deck the rooms. The holly and laurel leaves had all to be thoroughly scrubbed and washed to remove the Manchester grime: I can still see my mother carefully wiping every leaf before using it for decoration.... Pollution was a constant menace. The winters seemed long, dark, and were often accompanied by thick ('peasoup') fog. Your eyes would run and the tears make black smudges on your cheeks. For some years an old lady lived in the gate-lodge on Daisy Bank Road, relict of a former gardener. I used to visit her and help her gather dandelions, which she made into delicious dandelion tea.

As I grew older, I accompanied my father on Sundays to Cross Street Chapel in the heart of the city. We would sometimes walk the mile and a half home along Princess Street and Brook Street, passing close to the old home of Mrs Gaskell, the novelist, whose husband, William, had been for over fifty years minister at the chapel where we had just worshipped. (Alas, this "nonconformist cathedral of the North" was destroyed by fire in an air-raid in 1940). We would also pass a pet-shop that invariably slowed down our progress!

Later, in college, I had my own 'pets', namely a dozen Rhode Island pullets, for whom I bought a shed and made a run on some waste ground at the bottom of the garden. Eventually, I erected a second, larger shed and expanded to around fifty head of R.I.'s and Light Sussex hens and half a dozen Indian Runner ducks for a little variety, the last-named purely an economic extravagance. Breeding and rearing poultry proved a curiously satisfying hobby. Friends regarded the venture with amused indulgence. "Of course, he'll lose money on it", they opined. But

I did nothing of the sort. I had a 'captive customer', the college, and utilised a good deal of the scraps available. It made a complete and fascinating change from reading history or theology! After experimenting with clutches of eggs under broody Rhode Islands, I bought a second-hand incubator and a cold-brooder, followed the advice of my old French master, A.D. Tobler, and relied on the almost infallible guidance of *Poultry for the Many*. Needless to say, *my* birds were fed on first-class meal and mixed corn, purchased by the hundredweight, and housed in galvanised bins. I would never have dreamed of feeding them the desiccated corpses of other birds, which factory-farmers have apparently been doing for years. Forty years later, in Cambridge, I preached against factory-farming, on biological and moral grounds. After the Service, Lord McNair, then president of our church, senior Fellow of Gonville and Caius, and a former chairman of the European Court of Justice, told me he entirely agreed with me: as a lawyer and judge, he had sat in judgement on two cases of Factory-farming which (he said) were painful and highly objectionable. In view of recent disclosures and the common incidence of Salmonella poisoning, this whole field of activity, with the commercial practices now indulged in, requires, in my view, most careful appraisal and control, for it really presents a very serious threat to both physical and moral health.

3

SALAD DAYS IN ENGLAND AND GERMANY

"The only wisdom we can hope to acquire
Is the wisdom of humility..."
T.S. Eliot: *East Coker*

I returned from school in Cheshire in July, 1926 with my mind made up. I had just taken the Oxford and Cambridge Higher School Certificate examinations and felt fairly certain I had matriculated. My father made it plain that I should have a free choice in regard to a career and my decision would be final. However, having seen a good deal of the ministry in action and admired many of those who had been students or who came back to the college, I was no stranger to the future that awaited me. I was going into the Christian ministry, not as a career but as 'a way of life'. The only alternative I ever considered was that I should train as a doctor, and sometimes I have wondered whether I might not have done more for humanity, specialising in medicine, than as a preacher and pastor. Upon second thoughts, it would, I now think, have been a privilege to have served in th campaign against cancer.

The Victoria University of Manchester, where my father had preceded me, now became my *alma mater*. I, too, read History and specialised in the modern period. He obtained a First, I a 'top second'. I then entered the Faculty of Theology, working for a degree in Divinity, but at the same time writing a thesis for a Master's degree in Arts. My subject? 'The Curricula of the Dissenting Academies during the reign of George III'. This study of the educational work of the eighteenth century nonconformist academies appealed to me, not merely as an exercise in historical research, but as a step towards restoring the balance between English Dissent and the Establishment. When completed, my father was inspired to expand the work and write the definitive history of the academies from 1662 to 1820. This was published by the Manchester

Manchester University First XV Rugby, 1928–9. Joe Simpson in left bottom corner and author in right, both unable to attend official photographing

University Press in 1931 under the title, *English Education under the Test Acts*. The following year I took a degree in Divinity. Admittedly, I worked hard, but not so hard that I could not enjoy university life as a whole. I have always admired all-rounders and been happy to relax and share in non-academic pursuits and interests. People of different kinds and backgrounds have enriched my life and I have, as far as possible, steered clear of stereotypes. During the six years I spent at Manchester, I met a wide variety of fellow-students. Desmond Heap, reading Law, eventually became chief solicitor to the City of London. Joe Simpson, doing Technology, played rugby for more than one season. He was a huge and fast full-back who often came into the three-quarter line to finish off an attack. As Sir Joseph, he finished up as Chief Commissioner of the Metropolitan-Police. Harry Toft, an old Manchester Grammar School boy, whom I had already met on the school Rugger field, was selected to play for England in the late 'thirties. J.S. Leatherbarrow, reading History, became president of the Student's Union and a Canon of the Church of England. Membership of the University Mountaineering Club introduced me to a number of staff as well as students. These included Harold Gerrard (electrical engineering), Louis Morrell (theoretical mathematics), Wilson Hey (surgeon) and Maurice Linnell (chemist), one of the finest rock-climbers of his day. I joined the University Orchestral Society which used to give concerts of light music on the wards of the Royal Infirmary and at the Ancoats University Settlement. Another useful contact in Manchester was the elocutionist, James Bernard, a tutor of dramatic art at the Royal College of Music and teacher of Robert Donat. His recitals of Shakespeare and Dickens were very popular. Occasionally, he would take services at churches in the Manchester district and I once heard him read the moving passage from the 18th chapter of the second book of Samuel concerning the death of Absolom, with great effect. He was a kind and generous man, with a marvellous voice and memory, who once gave me a lesson on sermon-delivery in Platt chapel. Afterwards, at his home, over supper he presented me with my first cigar (a long one!). It was almost my last, for my head swam so violently that I could hardly walk home.

In 1930, along with a colleague, I joined an interdenominational party of young people on a walking tour through the Black Forest. This was organised by the Council for International Friendship through the Churches, and our expenses were covered by the chairman of the College committee. We walked the three hundred miles from Pforzheim to Müllheim, staying at the recently-opened 'Jugendherbergen', the immediate predecessors of the British Youth Hostels, whose Association was founded this very year and of which I have long been a life-member. It was a mixed party and several of us found ourselves, most mornings, setting out uphill from the hostels carrying two rucksacks, our own and a lady's. Today, such 'gallantry' would be frowned upon by both sexes. We were all impressed by the fine hill and valley scenery, the bitterly cold tarns in which the hardier folk had their morning dip, and the good fellowship which soon developed amongst the thirty or so young folk who hailed from all over Britain. Our leader was the Rev. W.T. Elmslie, a former president of the Alpine Club, who was fluent in both French and German and whom I later persuaded to lecture to the Rucksack Club in Manchester on the Picos del Europe (in Northern Spain) on which he was an authority. Meanwhile, he became engaged to a young lady who had been a member of another party he had taken out that summer. A charming man in his early forties, he confessed to me, in correspondence later, that 'falling in love' at that age was a more disturbing experience (he considered) than at any other! Elmslie became general secretary of the Presbyterian Church in England in 1935, but, alas, was killed by a V-bomb at the Church's offices in London ten years later.

University life suited me well, though I found the college routine somewhat restricting. Had I not enjoyed wide contacts outside the theological course, I fear I should have felt somewhat 'cribbed, cabin'd and confined'. A small and rather introspective community can foster a narrow outlook, unless an attempt is made to look beyond one's immediate environment and become acquainted with ideas and movements that complement or perhaps even contradict what one grows to regard as normal and acceptable. One tended to regard sermon-classes as a necessary evil, but as they were usually held on a Wednesday afternoon, I managed, during the winter, to skip them, as I was regularly selected mid-week, to play rugby for the university.

Two of my contemporaries training for the ministry at this time were women, both excellent students, very conscientious, and spiritually-minded. My father was strongly in favour of the 'ministry of women', but under no delusions about their future. When they completed their courses (normally three years in college) they could only hope to obtain charge of small and struggling congregations. In fact this was what actually happened. Even amongst Unitarians (who pride themselves on their progressive notions) an almost Johnsonian prejudice against women in the pulpit lingers on, especially amongst their own sex, who are, of course, a majority in the churches. One of our women graduated B.D. with credit; the other passed out with a good college certificate; both made good pastors, if not altogether attractive preachers; yet neither ever served large churches and both retired early from the active ministry owing to ill-health. It remains true, however, that Protestant churches in Britain and on the Continent can all boast of excellent women ministers, who have served with acceptance and even distinction.

For many years, students for the ministry from the oldest Unitarian church in the world in former Hungarian, now Romanian, Transylvania came to England for training. I got to know a succession of them. Their country churches have a tradition, reaching back to Reformation times, of faithful service to their peasant people through long years of poverty and persecution. During my student-year abroad (1932–3), accompanied by a fellow-Hungarian student I made a point of visiting Cluj (Kolozsvár) and the Sekler valleys where many of the Hungarian-speaking Unitarian churches are situated. March, 1933 was cold and wintry, and travelling over iced and snowy roads difficult and slow, especially in a farm cart or old coach which the friendly and hospitable local folk made available to us. On at least two occasions since, I have visited Budapest and Cluj.

In 1968 I went to celebrate the 400th anniversary of the Diet of Torda, at which the Unitarian leader, Francis David, pleaded for toleration and a decree securing freedom of speech for 'all ministers of the gospel' was passed. I went again to Transylvania in 1979 to attend meetings marking the 400th anniversary of the martyrdom of Francis David, the founder of the oldest Unitarian Church in the world. At the symposium in the main hall of the college in Cluj I read a paper on the 'Links between Transylvania and British Unitarians from the 17th century onwards'. The Romanian government compelled me to submit a copy of my manuscript to Bucharest for its approval. I resented this interference, but got my own back by employing the Hungarian names for towns and villages in Transylvania when actually lecturing. This caused quite a stir among the three or four Romanian communist commissaries who had been ordered to attend and who sat stolidly in the front row of the audience.

Until recently, the Communist dictatorship in Romania threatened to uproot Hungarian and German minorities, destroying their villages and forcing thousands to become refugees. But the Christmas Revolution of 1989, fortunately, put an end to this madness.

I have purposely omitted commenting on internal college studies and the day-to-day life of theological studies, because these can be of little general interest. On Sundays we were usually engaged in 'supplying' vacant pulpits in Lancashire and Cheshire and even further afield, and we had our adventures. For example, I once arrived at Victoria Station on my way to a preaching engagement and suddenly realised I had not the faintest idea where I was supposed to be going! I had to telephone the college and ask one of my colleagues to consult the engagement list before I could book a ticket! Sometimes one ran the risk of being taken for a student from another theological college (there were several in Manchester) and being conducted to the denominationally *wrong* chapel, if one had not been to the district before. Funny things happened not only on the way to the preaching forum, but also during Services. One of our women students was handed a slip of paper just before the sermon and asked to announce that "There will be a Bull Sale in the schoolroom after Service this morning". Her mind filled with apprehension as she weighed up the possibilities awaiting her. Happily, the occasion proved to be horticultural and not a sale of farming stock!

The McLachlan Library of the Unitarian College, about 1930, Herbert McLachlan standing in front

The college library (over 30,000 volumes) was a valuable collection built up over many years and housed in a handsome new building, opened in 1924. My father spent most of his free time arranging and cataloguing the books, many of which came from old chapel libraries and individual donors whom he persuaded to part with their treasures. It contained both manuscripts and rare editions which he examined and collated. Students were encouraged to help in arranging and cleaning the volumes. One Saturday at lunch a student who had been working there remarked "Doctor, what an amazing number of books that man 'Tome' has written!" The ingenuous comment must have amused the Principal, though outwardly he showed little sign of this. 'First steps' in appreciation of the world of books deserve to be encouraged rather than pilloried.

In July, 1932, after graduating in Divinity and being awarded an honorary research-scholarship by the university, I prepared for a year abroad. The Hibbert Trustees had agreed to fund a year at Heidelberg, where I elected to go, in order to hear lectures in New Testament studies, philosophy, and history. Leaving England in August, I travelled to Strasbourg to attend a holiday-course in German language and literature before crossing the Rhine. Architecturally and historically, the chief city of Alsace is a fascinating place. In the two months I spent there I learnt to appreciate the differences and strong appeal of the two cultures, Gallic and Teutonic, which meet and mingle there. French and

Germans have both endowed the city with numerous fine buildings, and the cobbled streets and squares, the canals and bridges, added a quaint and old-world charm to the place. I was fortunate to have as guide a young architect who lunched regularly at the hostel where I stayed. He insisted on showing me unusual sights, reached in his car, which *I* had to drive! One day, he took me up into the dome of a former German government building and, opening a trapdoor, bade me look out upon "all the kingdoms of the (Strasbourg) world and the glory of them".... Then there was the beauty and dominating splendour of the great Gothic cathedral, one of the highest in Europe, adorned with a famous astronomical clock. Of course I had to make an ascent of that! The friendliness of the people was only equalled by the tastiness of Strasbourg food: hams, cakes, and *pâté de foie gras*. The university was Goethe's old *alma mater* and, more recently, the scene of Albert Schweitzer's activities. It was a privilege even to walk its corridors. The 'Cours pratique d'Allemand' which I followed there concentrated not merely on language but on customs and culture as well. It included visits to places of interest like Colmar, Trois Épées and the Vosges. We gazed with astonishment at the castle of Haut Koenigsberg and at the hunting trophies adorning its walls, and with amazement at the inscription in Kaiser Wilhelm II's private apartment: "Ich hab' es nicht gewollt!" "I never wanted it!" the reference being to the First World War....

The family with whom I was to stay in Heidelberg, the Kaysers (no relation!) happened to be on holiday at their cottage in the Black Forest, so I paid them a flying visit and secured rooms in their house for Dr John Davis, a Rockerfeller scholar, whom I had met by chance in Strasbourg. He was on his way to a year's research at the Kaiser Wilhelm Institute in Heidelberg into the physiology of muscles and associated lactic acid. His wife, Marjorie, was with him, but they had made no previous arrangement for lodgings, so they were only too glad to join me in the Kaysers' lovely home at 9, Bachstrasse, Neuenheim.

The theological faculty at Heidelberg at this time could boast a corps of very distinguished teachers. Amongst these was the New Testament specialist, Professor Martin Dibelius, one of the founders of the new study of the text of the Gospels, *die Formgeschichte Schule* (the Form-history school) which discovered in the Gospels a pattern of literary forms based upon the oral traditions that lie behind the written documents. The form-critics isolated various units which had been shaped by the life of the early Christian community. The study of the origin and history of these units helps to throw light upon the earliest Christian traditions, the life of Jesus, and the beginnings of Christianity. One important result of form-criticism has been to show that the Gospels are *not* biographical accounts but *documents of faith*. This new approach to the New Testament, which was only just beginning to come into prominence in Britain, seemed to me to be of crucial importance, if one were concerned to get at the truths underlying the text of the New Testament.

A second attraction was the liberal-minded church-historian, Professor Walter Köhler, whose lectures on 'The Enlightenment' gathered an enthusiastic crowd of students and whose seminar on 'English Puritanism' proved to be most stimulating. Both Dibelius and Köhler were exceptional in inviting their students to meet them, out of university hours, in their homes and on walks in the Odenwald, the forested hills around the town. In addition, Karl Jaspers lectured four times a week on Immanuel Kant, a course which was very well attended. Jaspers had begun his career as a medical student and professor, and had then moved over into philosophy and psychology. His classes were always crowded and his lectures splendidly organised and delivered. I'm afraid I 'signed on"...., during my first Semester from November to February, to hear more lectures than were good for me, but of course it was tempting to listen to experts on subjects seldom treated so fully or enthusiastically in British universities, so I drank my fill! Very popular was the veteran neo-Kantian, Heinrich Rickert, who delivered his lectures seated in an old armchair. His course on 'Schopenhauer, Richard Wagner, and Neitzsche', which contained first-hand reminiscences of the last-named philosopher, proved a great draw.

I was struck by the number of my German contemporaries who wrote shorthand. I was also intrigued by the freedom with which students moved from course to course, as well as from university to university. It was no exception, for instance, for a chemistry student or some other science student to drop in on a theological course, or vice versa. I recall that a woman 'medical' regularly attended Rickert's lectures with an anatomy compendium open in front of her! I myself took an opportunity to accompany 'medicals' into the anatomy laboratory. It is obviously refreshing to hear lectures which interest you, but upon which you are never likely to be examined. Several aspects of student life in Germany naturally appealed to me. I mention only two here. First and most important at this date (1932) was the full accident and health-insurance-cover afforded to every student for a modest premium included in the university charges. For the first time in my life I was X-Rayed to make sure that I was free from any trace of pulmonary disease; and my journeys to and from the university buildings on bicycle were safeguarded. Secondly, all students carried an identity card which secured for them tickets for reduced admission to concerts, operas, cinemas and the like. No such benefits were enjoyed by contemporary British students.

Heidelberg was, of course, a very pleasant place in which to study. Situated on the river Neckar, sixteen kilometres before it joins the Rhine, a medieval town has burst its originally restricted bounds at the point where the river issues from close-crowding hills. On the north side of the valley lies the famous Philosphen Weg, where one can walk in comfort, looking down on the river and across to the south side where stand the ruins of the splendid Renaissance castle of the Electors Palatine, which still shows signs of its battering by French troops in the late 17th century. Below the castle, the river is spanned by the Alte Brücke, which Góethe claimed to be "more beautiful than any other in the world" – a pardonable exaggeration. At every season, the town has its own particular charm, especially when seen from the hills above. In winter the snow-laden trees of the forests on either side of the river are a wonderful sight, and the frozen river is the scene of great activity: skating, ice-hockey, and other sports engage young and old. In spring the almond and prunus blossoms create a glorious frame for the gold-tinted stones of the old university and castle precincts, whilst summer brings with it activities of a different kind on river and hills, notably sculling, swimming, hiking and jogging along the many tracks that run for miles on both sides of the valley.

Neuenheim, a pleasant suburb opposite the old town, was a favourite residential area for university and professional people, and Bachstrasse was one of several streets dedicated to musicians and composers. Herr Kayser was a garden-architect and his wife, Paula, an artist. Doubtless, before we arrived in the early 'thirties, like many middle-class Germans, they had experienced the financial squeeze which extremely high inflation had exercised upon the national economy. Their fine house and garden must have been something of a liability, and their four children a burden for which they must find additional sources of income, if they were to continue living in the life-style they had hitherto enjoyed. Unwittingly, as I now realise, John and Marjorie Davis and I were benefi-

The Kayser family at Bachstrasse 9, Heidelberg, 1932

ciaries of a situation which eventually brought cataclysmic changes to German society and State. We were to witness these at first hand before we left the country in July, 1933.... Meanwhile, it was a pleasure and privilege to move in with the Kaysers, to admire Paula's 'still lifes' and children's portraits, which adorned the house, and to appreciate the beautifully-designed garden, pool, weeping willows and colourful borders. Not least among the bonuses of Bachstrasse, 9 was the opportunity to become acquainted with their four charming children.

Herr and Frau Kayser were what the Germans call 'fromme Leute', i.e. religious-minded people. They were Protestants, with relatives in high places in the hierarchy of the Reformed State-church of Baden, and their home reflected Christian values in tone and action, but not, I may say, in any insincere or fundamentalist sense. Herr Kayser I regarded as a truly Christian gentleman and the memory of his kindnesses still lingers. The Davises and I lived happily with the family until the end of the year, enjoying their friendship and watching the children grow up. One curious circumstance, however, came to light. The boys' finger-nails never seemed to need cutting, and any scratches on their hands and knees were extraordinarily slow to heal. Dr Davis, who was, of course, an expert on milk, coming from the Dairy Research Institute in Reading, inquired where the milk we were drinking came from. It turned out that it was all heat-treated locally in the Heidelberg corporation dairy, in fact sterilised. Apparently besides killing undesirable bacilli, this process at the same time annihilates the benign ones and destabilises the calcium content. The boys were growing up with inadequate calcium intake and, of course, the vitamins needed for healthy development. Davis suggested that Paula should obtain milk direct from a local farmer, and see what happened. She did, and, lo and behold, there was no more trouble: the boys' nails started to grow normally and all cuts and bruises healed quickly.

Advent and Christmas at Bachstrasse 9 proved to be a dramatic and colourful festival. Advent garlands, candles and other decorations appeared here but also in university rooms. Herr Kayser took us out to his elder daughter's school at Wieblingen, where a special carol service was held by candlelight. On the second Sunday, we all awaited the arrival of the 'heilige Nikolaus' (Santa Claus). In accordance with custom he knocked and was admitted, bringing a sack of apples and nuts 'for the good children' and a switch or rod for 'the bad'. We all received appropriate presents, Marjorie Davis a bunch of marzipan carrots (since she never ate them!), her husband a little bottle of milk, and myself a bag of chocolate money to console me for the fall in the value of the pound sterling. Nikolaus (i.e. Herr Kayser, heavily-disguised), spoke in verse, cleverly composed. On Christmas Eve, after Church at 5 p.m., the family and guests all sat round the Christmas Tree and shared in a little ritual of carols and readings, after which presents were distributed. On Christmas Day, we sat down for dinner with a decorated Christmas goose, sampled the biscuits and baked meats which had been long in the making, and in the evening drank Gluwein (punch) over games. Altogether, Christmas 1932 was a memorable occasion, no doubt specially devised for the benefit of the British guests, but also reflecting the Christian commitment of the parents and the desire to bring up the children in a way that would help them to value the Good News of love and peace which the life and teaching of Jesus vividly proclaimed.

Alas, there were problems that the Christmas festivities really only glossed over. Paula was not a very practical Hausfrau. She hired a peasant girl from the Black Forest, who did all the cooking and housework for a pittance, and we paying-guests eventually realised that we were hardly getting value for money. The only time we tasted real coffee was on Christmas Day. For breakfast the eggs served came from Bulgaria and were frequently far from fresh, so much so that we asked for apples instead. These, too, were of poor quality. The falling-off in the provision of food, combined with the fact that the pound had dropped in value from twenty to eleven marks (due to Britain going off the gold-standard) determined us to find fresh accommodation. We were sorry to leave Bachstrasse 9, where we had learnt much about German family life, sorry especially that we were leaving the family to continue its struggle to maintain a life-style becoming more difficult to maintain in those fast-changing times. But we were forced to economise. The Davises rented an apartment nearby and I moved to a small hotel close to the river at the corner of the Schiffgasse in the oldest part of the town, where I was near the university refectory and could make my own 'high tea' in my room.

Looking back, it is tragic to think what the war did to this family. Already, when I was their paying-guest, bankruptcies and suicides were frequent occurrences, and street violence and social disruption were on their way. Unemployment was reaching a record figure and the National Socialist Party was plotting for power. Alas, Paula Kayser died young, in her early forties, and both her sons, Hans Werner and Konrad, were killed in action. Herr Kayser married again, but both the girls left home, one to be married, and the other to work in London. Paula was spared the harrowing grief of learning that her precious boys were no more.... They and the girls were 'the light of their eyes': 'Unsere vier Kinder', she wrote in a letter to me on 12th March, 1932, when I was negotiating terms with her, "sind die Sonne in diesen schweren bösen Zeiten". ("Our four children are our Suns in these hard and evil times"). It was the period shortly after the Reichsmark had been massively devalued and Germans lost nearly all their savings, owing to galloping Inflation. One day, the cobbler who repaired my shoes opened a drawer and pulled out some pieces of paper to show me. These were some of the devalued marks which he had kept from 'the bad days'. I noticed that they were overprinted several times, not in hundreds but in milliards.

A fellow-student and theologian in Heidelberg was Rudi Seiferling, whom I first met in Professor Köhler's History Seminar. His mother, the widow of a cavalry captain in the first World War, kindly invited me in to meals. Eventually, she offered me a bed-sitter in her flat in Neuenheim, and that was where I spent most of my second Semester. The Seiferling home became my 'home from home'. No one could have been kinder than Rudi's mother was to me. His two sisters could almost have been my own, the younger, Steffi, in particular, being a well-read and thoughtful young lady. It was she who introduced me to modern German literature, and I have to thank her that I began to read the poems of Rainer Marie Rilke.

By now, I was well versed in German university life, and with the coming of Spring and my second and last Semester, commencing in March, I would not make the mistake of attending so many lectures as before. I continued to hear Dibelius on 'The history of Early Christian religion' and 'Jesus', and joined a seminar on Karl Barth's 'Dogmatics', which was interesting, but probably a waste of time (Barth was then an outstanding figure in biblical theology). Speaking of 'time', I was intrigued by the curious custom in German universities of 'academic time'. Lectures actually commenced fifteen minutes *after* the officially announced hour. In my first Semester, I was taken aback by what I regarded as regular bad time-keeping, and startled by the way the entry and departure of the lecturer was accompanied by the stamping of feet! This was, however, the custom, and no mark of disrespect to the professors.

Music played an important role in student-life. The local authority arranged a series of concerts and the town's theatre provided a varied programme of drama and opera. It was a privilege to *stand* through a recital by Furtwängler and the Berlin Philharmonic or see Richard Strauss conduct his own 'Tod und Verklärung'. In the summer, there were Serenade Concerts in the Castle Yard, and in July, just before I left Heidelberg, a magnificent performance of Beethoven's Ninth Symphony. This was, however, spoilt by a political harangue from the Nazi spokesman, Alfred Rosenberg who developed a tirade against the liberal traditions of the University! More than once, a party of friends would visit the Mannheim Opera House, where Mark Twain heard 'Lohengrin', his first Wagner opera in Germany. There I heard 'Siegfried', 'Götterdämerung', and just before leaving for home, 'Die Meistersinger'. All were fine performances, but their great length (6.30 to 11.20 p.m.) rather detracted from their brilliance. For relaxation of a different kind there were cycling trips into the Palatinate and a memorable Whitsuntide tour up the Neckar valley to Heilbronn (with its Rathaus portrait of England's Henry VIII) and on through Swabia to Rothenburg and Bad Mergentheim on the 'Romantische Strasse'.

Lovely as it was, it now became necessary to get away from Heidelberg to escape the increasingly noisome Nazi propaganda which per-

Nazi Brownshirts parading by the River Neckar, Heidelberg, January, 1933, taken from hotel window

vaded university and town during the late winter and the spring of 1933. Nazi students were now interfering with the regular course of university life. The Hitler salute had become mandatory as a daily greeting. Many of the intelligentsia caved in and joined the Party. Jewish professors found their lectures peremptorily cancelled, and the normal placid existence of the town was interrupted by marching Brownshirts demonstrating at all hours of the day. I was present at the burning of Marxist and Jewish books in front of the old university buildings, symbolically intended, no doubt, to be an insult to the past and a statement of 'the new and better' present! The motto carved over the Schurmann Arts Faculty 'To the Human Spirit' was obliterated, and in its place was set 'To the German Spirit'. One felt that society was being dragged back to the Middle Ages! One much-appreciated amenity supplied by the University was the Reading Room, where daily papers, journals, and magazines of all kinds were kept available. However, in March, 1933, newspapers like *The Times* and the *Manchester Guardian* were no longer to be seen. They had been banned by the authorities. Hitherto, I had regularly received the *Guardian Weekly*, posted from Manchester, but this eventually ceased to arrive, except for one issue, which reached me in a roundabout way, via South Africa! The discerning may be able to explain this miraculous delivery....

My friend, Rudi, had by now joined one of the more Nationalist student 'corporations'. It was what was termed a 'Schlagende Verbindung' (a fighting club). This meant it indulged in illegal duelling. Rudi's ambition, as an officer's son, was to obtain a scar (*Schmiss*) on his cheek. Eventually he did so, and returned late one night with a disfigured face and a shirt soaked in blood, His sister opened the door to let him in and, when she saw him, passed out, hitting her head on a table and becoming a second casualty! His mother took it bravely, and, I suppose, felt appropriate pride.... Duelling had been forbidden during the Weimar Republic, but was re-introduced when Hitler took over the chancellorship. This was part of the general preparation for a trial of strength for which the Nazis were grooming the German people.

At the November election in 1932, the Nazi party, previously gathering influence amongst the petty bourgeoisie, small shop-keepers, and unemployed, lost over two million votes, and economic pressures on government and people, for some years oppressive, began to seem less so. Faced with a serious loss of popularity, the Nazi demagogues were compelled to turn to violent strategies. Amongst these was the February firing of the Reichstag, increased mass-meetings and demonstrations, and various forms of intimidation. The Nazi press, headed by Dr Goebbels, began its acute campaign of anti-Semitism, and *Der Stürmer* (Goebbels's paper) increased its circulation by the printing of unscrupulous falsehoods and fear-promoting articles. Nazi leaders and brown-shirted students invaded the lecture-rooms and the Nazi salute and the clicking of heels was a constant obligato. Jewish or part-Jewish professors and students were completely isolated, and the whole tone of university life quickly deteriorated. All students applying for admission or re-admission for the Summer Semester of 1933 were required to fill in a questionnaire as to their origins and ancestry. I recall how objectionable I found being compelled to make a declaration that in my family I had no Jewish relatives on either side.

As the months passed, military training was openly extended to include students and even school-children. I saw youngsters being taught how to throw hand-grenades efficiently. The High Street was hung with swastika flags. From my hotel window I watched parades of Storm-troopers, bands and banners most days. The temperature of excitement was continually stoked up. One by one, all organisations that might have rivalled or moderated the Party plans and popularity were banned, and their newspapers, meetings, use of communication media, and so on, were 'regulated' out of existence. For instance, the office of the Social Democratic Party's local newspaper, which happened to be opposite the Seiferlings' flat, where I was living, was picketed by Storm-troopers three days before the official dissolution of that Party. The take-over of the State and Society was carefully orchestrated and thoroughly executed. Hitler consistently asserted that one must strike opponents early and devastatingly to achieve one's aims. Above all, the lies one told must always be big enough and incredible enough to 'carry conviction' and gain universal currency.

Psychological warfare in peace-time was something new and unbelievably real. It was also demonically evil. A handful of British students remained in Heidelberg, but most of them stayed on to complete their courses, whilst The Americans packed up and left for home. The atmosphere was cyclonic and sullen. Many Germans refused to believe the rumours that were circulating. I discussed the burning of the Reichstag with a number of people; most of them considered it to have been engineered by the Nazis and intended to influence waverers to join their ranks. But the coup succeeded: Hitler was able to assume supreme control.

Professore Köhler, with whom I had become friendly (his wife Elizabeth had more than once invited me to their home) wanted me to spend a second year in Germany to prepare a thesis for a doctorate. The temptation to stay on was great, but in view of the political situation and the possibility of an attractive appointment in Sheffield, I decided to return home. I travelled north *via* Trier, where the 'heilige Rock', the Holy Coat, supposedly worn by Christ before his crucifixion, was on display at the Cathedral. Pilgrims would be coming from all over Europe to visit this and other 'relics', which are only exhibited once every forty years. To go home by way of the old Roman city of Trier, making the journey by boat from Mainz to Koblenz down 'old Father Rhine', and then up the beautiful valley of the Moselle by train seemed to be a sensible conclusion to a memorable stay in Germany. So that way I went, notwithstanding the likelihood of crowds and the uncertainty about where I should spend the night. Scenically, the trip was, as I expected, beautiful. But not less enjoyable was the friendly reception I got in Trier from a family I encountered in a city street, when inquiring after overnight accommodation. I joined the queue outside the Cathedral and duly saw the 'Coat', a garment that appeared to me to be a smock of huge proportions, fit for a burly six-foot policeman rather than a slender young man from Nazareth! The simple faith of pilgrims who make their way to such centres of religious devotion is touching.

My year in Germany was at an end. It proved a turning-point in my life. It certainly accustomed me to all kinds of travel, but more importantly, it introduced me to all kinds of people. I learnt to make easy contact with my fellow human beings, to appreciate the infinite variety of the race, and to recognise once and for all that nationality was a comparatively small and unimportant feature of life, whilst humanity was infinitely more significant and of abiding consequence. Moreover, it infected me with more than a penchant for pilgrimage. I had caught the Wanderlust.

4

SHEFFIELD – THE DIRTY THIRTIES

"The pattern is new in every moment"
T.S. Eliot: *East Coker*

Shortly after my return from Germany, I received an invitation to visit Sheffield, with a view to becoming assistant-minister at the Upper Chapel. I already knew the minister, Alfred Hall, who had been a fellow-student of my father's, was generally well-liked and greatly respected, and had made a name for himself in the city, where he had hitherto spent fifteen years. It was an opportunity not to me missed.

Eventually, a letter came from the Secretary of the trustees, Dr Edward Bramley, offering me the post at £250 a year. Dr Bramley was a leading solicitor in the city, later pro-vice-chancellor and a generous benefactor of the university. I retained my friendship with him to the last. He died eleven days short of his one hundred and first birthday. I still have the letter he wrote me in reply to my congratulations on his becoming a centenarian (see p 88 *infra*).

I was fortunate to obtain comfortable lodgings in Nether Edge with a recently-widowed lady, who was bringing up three step-children and needed to supplement her income. She charged me the modest sum of thirty-seven shillings and sixpence a week, board and lodging, including laundry, and was one of the kindest people I have ever met. Unfortunately, she fell ill some time after I moved in with her and lay in bed for many weeks. Her step-son was a bank clerk, but the two daughters were still at school. She was compelled to engage a house-keeper, but never once did she suggest that I should leave to make things easier for her. The family attended the local parish church, but some time after I left Sheffield and they had removed to Fulwood, her elder daughter asked me to conduct her wedding at the Old Chapel there, where I had been minister from 1934 to 1937. Her brother was a keen outdoor-man and a good musician. He died from cancer, during World War II.

My appointment at Upper Chapel, carried with it responsibility for a small 'school-church' in Attercliffe, in the East End of Sheffield. This was a valuable introduction to conditions of life different from anything I had known before or even imagined. (Years later, the building became a mosque and was burned down in the 'seventies by what was almost certainly an act of arson. Many Pakistanis had moved into the district to work in the steel-works. These have now been demolished and the whole area is "changed; changed utterly", and, as yet, no "terrible beauty is born"!)

Edward Carpenter, an incomer to Sheffield fifty years or more before me, recorded this of the inhabitants: "From the first I was taken with the Sheffield people. Rough in the extreme, twenty or thirty years in date behind other towns, and very uneducated, there was yet a heartiness about them, not without shrewdness, which attracted me". For my part, I can say that, from the first, I was greatly taken with the Sheffield people I met in the early 'thirties, though I found in Attercliffe a gentler and more refined working-class then Carpenter evidently did. Their geniality, kindness, and shrewdness captivated me.

The city of Sheffield originally consisted of a cluster of large villages strung together in an irregular assembly, uphill and downdale. Up to World War II, it retained many of its narrow streets and small steel and cutlery works, though now almost all the big steel works have gone. When I arrived and settled in the city, its heavy industries, forges, rolling mills, and cutlery-fabrication were still active. Workers in special steels and non-ferrous metals were busy exporting wares all over the world. But the shadow of change was already creeping near and threatening firms which had hitherto been household words. First, came a period of trade-depression and unemployment, caused by over-production and the rise of rival producers overseas. Then the unnatural spasm of armament manufacture, before and during World War II, checked the demise of industry, but thereafter contraction was inescapable, and with it vast changes in the character of the place, so that, for example, the largest employer of labour in the city at the time of writing is Bassetts, the makers of liquorice all-sorts! The acres once occupied by Brown Baileys, Hadfields, United Steels, Cravens, Steel, Peach, and Tozer are now, for the most part, wastes.

It was, however, against a background of rising unemployment that my four year's ministry was exercised. I soon became aware of a factor called poverty. The economic situation naturally affected the churches. Raising money for church purposes became difficult. One contemporary Sunday School report stated, "In view of the distressing conditions prevailing in many homes one cannot be surprised at the failure (of children) to bring regular contributions".

To live in Sheffield and to work in the East End was a real education. For the first time, I learnt how 'the other half' of the population existed. I had never come up against deprivation, small means, or poverty before. One of my people, married, with a small daughter, worked in a foundry of 'English Steel'. His wages were twenty-eight shillings a week. The same firm paid its foreign correspondent, a young friend of mine who was a master of at least four languages, and later took a degree at Manchester university, the petty sum of twenty-six shillings a week. Unemployed men received two shillings a week for each child. This drove me to protest publicly at what I regarded as an obscene and immoral policy. To gain experience of 'the real world', I began to do a spot of personal visitation for the Council of Social Service. This took me into houses with no floor-coverings or stair-carpets, no proper bedding for children or adults, and diets which certainly did no comply with nutrition-standards now universally accepted. I was amazed and troubled. I had never been in a pawnbroker's shop, nor had I much idea of the inside of hospitals, workhouses, and the like. But in the 'dirty thirties' I learnt to appreciate the operations of all these, not least the pawn-shops, which were an essential element in the social and economic life of the low-paid working-class. It was common practice for a man to put his best suit into pawn on a Monday morning and fetch it home again, if possible, on a Friday night or Saturday morning. Low wages, sickness, T.B. and general debility affected large numbers of the poor and, of course, the unemployed. I became acquainted with several sad cases of tubercular infection amongst young and old, and visited the wretchedly ill and the dying, whose families and medical advisers – both – were powerless to assist. These were the days before the Health Service and the discovery of modern drugs, especially the anti-biotics.

In this connection, I recall with sadness that one dear old lady living in a well-appointed home on the Ecclesall Road, a member of Upper Chapel whom I was asked to visit, startled me by making a vitriolic attack upon Mr Lloyd George. 'Look at the damage he has done to the country' she cried, 'by introducing the Dole'; 'most of the unemployed were ne'erdowells, anyway'! I felt transported back into the nineteenth century, and that is, no doubt, where some people were still mentally and morally living. This, too, I suppose, was a form of education!

Upper Chapel was the oldest nonconformist place of worship in the city. It was founded by James Fisher, the minister ejected from the parish church (now the Cathedral) in 1662. The present building was erected in 1704, and over the years its members have been leading citizens, master-cutlers, mayors, business people, comfortably-off in a steadily expanding township. Dr Bramley's father, for instance was town-clerk, and his grandfather first town-clerk of Sheffield. Now, the old families were dying out. Members moved – or were moved – away from the city-centre into new corporation estates or pleasant villas in places like Fulwood and Totley. The large Sunday School, in which I taught a class of boys on Sunday mornings, steadily diminished in size, and it became clear that it would not be possible much longer to expect children or adults to maintain attendances of twice a Sunday at a chapel whose members were living miles away.

For the first twelve months of my ministry, I used to cycle all over the city on pastoral visitation. Sheffield is a hilly place, and I soon realised that I could not do justice to the calls upon me; in any event, I often got home drenched with rain. At my mother's suggestion, my father loaned me his small car, a 'Riley Nine' which he seldom used, and I was able to rent the empty garage at 6, Sheldon Road, where I was living, for half a crown a week, another instance of my landlady's generosity.

The city's rural environment must be one of the most beautiful of any urban conglomeration in Britain. Sheffield's 'golden frame' offered me an extra bonus, for I could soon be on the moors in the Derbyshire Dales, on the Pennines (the black Peak), or in the limestone country (the white Peak), by 'bus or car, striking out across grand, wild and lonely spaces like Kinder Scout or Bleaklow or following the course of the wandering waters of the Manifold, Dove, or Wye. I had often walked and climbed in Derbyshire when a student in Manchester. In those days you could book a cheap excursion-ticket to Hayfield or Glossop and return from Edale or *vice-versa*. For a change, I would go out from Sheffield to the gritstone 'Edges' at Burbage, Stanage, Wharncliffe Crags or Laddow, and at this date rarely meet a soul. Now, at week-ends, these rocks are festooned with ropes and colourfully-clad young men and women. Occasionally, I visited an old climber and pioneer of caving, a

Shirland Lane Sunday School Football Team, 1935

retired plumber and decorator, James Puttrell, who had climbed with the Abraham brothers of Keswick. He had a fine collection of rock crystals and fossils in his home. These he bequeathed to the city of Sheffield in 1939.

In May, 1934, the Old Chapel at Fulwood, where for thirty years the Congregationalists held the lease and conducted Services, was returned to the Unitarian trustees. They decided that, after repairs and re-decoration, it should be re-opened for Unitarian Services. The idea was to found a new congregation which would eventually be able to sustain its own minister and fund its own activities. I was put in charge. Meanwhile, the Upper Chapel trustees would pay the minister's salary, but provide no manse. No doubt, they watched this 'investment' with 'Great Expectations', but left the young minister to occupy his own 'Bleak House'. Attached to the chapel was an 18th century manse, but this had been let to a friend of one of the trustees and it was not proposed to disturb her. Hence, when I got married early in June the following year to Joan Hall, my colleague's daughter, I was compelled to rent a house in Fulwood where we could start our married life.

The Fulwood experiment was charged with distinct possibilities. The district was a growing dormitory for people moving out towards the 'green belt', and already some Upper Chapel members were living

Fulwood Old Chapel (built 1738) and village stocks

there. The challenge to found and build a new congregation appealed to me, but there was no disguising the difficulties. When Morning Services commenced at Fulwood and we organised a Sunday School, I soon realised that my time and energies were fully stretched, for I was already responsible for Evening Services and an afternoon Sunday School six miles away in Attercliffe, and both congregations had a structured social life which they cherished. Lectures, play-readings, concerts, an annual sale of work, youth groups, carol parties at Christmas, were then the 'order of the day'. Before long, I became aware of the impossibility of fully satisfying everybody, or myself! I suppose complaints that I was putting in time at Attercliffe that would more profitably be spent at Fulwood was natural, but they were certainly unjustified. Nor did they come from Fulwood folk, but from one or two Upper Chapel trustees, who considered that 'propping up' the Attercliffe Church was really a waste of time and energy. Besides, the Attercliffe folk could only make a very modest contribution to the minister's salary! As far as possible, I was careful to divide my time equally between my two major charges. Luckily, I was on the best of terms with both congregations. At Fulwood, we built up a nucleus of good, middle-class citizens, soon had a small but

Harold E. Fishburn, chairman,
Attercliffe Unitarian Church

enthusiastic choir, and were running a small Sunday School. At Attercliffe I possessed the complete confidence of a congregation which had suffered from controversy at the time of the coal strike (1926), since outcropping had been allowed on ground in Handsworth which was used for sports and recreation. Needless to say, the members were somewhat fearful that they might eventually lose my (part-time) services altogether.

The chairman of the congregation was Harold Fishburn, a baker by trade and a man of a remarkably inventive turn of mind, clever with a lathe, and a compulsive gardener. He could also take a church Service with acceptance, and occasionally help out at the organ. He taught me a great deal about plants and flowers and supplied me with seedlings for our Fulwood garden. Born and bred in Sheffield, Harold knew the city, its history and people, as well as any man alive. He was a mine of information about Old Sheffield and could draw on memories of people and events, which I now deeply regret I did not write down. He and his devoted wife, Edith, made my early years in the ministry very happy. In my mind's eye, I can still see him cheerfully at work in the bakehouse, moving the loaves around in the oven as we discussed matters of church policy and practice. From his garden at Handsworth, to which he and Edith retreated at week-ends, came bouquets of flowers for anniversaries of friends and for all deserving causes. As a young man, he had acted as honorary secretary of the church at Shirland Lane, and then became chairman, an office he held for fifty-six years. Few human beings can have given so freely of his substance and self in the service of a liberal religious faith as he. During World War II he kept the little church going under difficult circumstances, by dint of sheer Yorkshire grit. Towards the end, he suffered a stroke, but soldiered on hopefully. In practically his last letter to me he wrote appreciatively of a sermon I had lent him to read. Its subject was 'Self-forgetfulness'. He concluded, typically, "What a glad world it can be". It is comforting to think that the sports field he had so long cared for and administered was sold eventually for the benefit of the mother-church, Upper Chapel, and now forms one of the largest trust-funds managed by the trustees. "And thus the whirligig of time brings in his revenges".

Fulwood Old Chapel celebrated its 250th anniversary in 1978 and happily continues to hold Services. I wrote a short history of the Chapel, which first appeared in the 'Transactions' of the Unitarian Historical Society, 1937–8 and was then re-printed as a booklet early in January, 1940.

The Attercliffe Church, a daughter of Upper Chapel, was opened in 1901 and intended to attract the more thoughtful among the growing numbers of working-class folk in the neighbourhood of the East End steel works. It certainly had its share of what, in this part of the world, are called 'characters'. For the record, I think it may be of interest to list some of the occupations of the membership in the 'thirties: miner, loco-driver in steel works, foundry-worker, fitter, comptometer – supervisor, shop-assistant, tailoress, house-keeper in doctor's surgery, engine-driver, joiner, haulier, painter-decorator, shop-keeper, baker and pastrycook, lorry-driver. I was pleased to find that many of these took kindly to reading Shakespeare, Shaw, Ibsen, Galsworthy *et al.* in the Play Reading Circle which I founded in the early days of my ministry.

Of the many I remember I mention here only one or two, for one or other particular trait or achievement that sticks in the memory: Florence Troop was a widow and came of staunch Unitarian stock. Her father had worked for 'Squire Nightingale' at Lea Hall, Derbyshire, and, as she herself told me, she was named after 'The Lady with the Lamp'. Mrs Troop was senior stall-holder at the annual sale of work in December and every year used to knit me a pair of grey socks. William Trippet, an engine-driver badly injured in a railway accident, was confined to bed. His proud boast was that it had given him time to read the whole of Gibbon's 'Decline and Fall of the Roman Empire', which I consider something of a feat! Joe Poole, our caretaker, a very pleasant and jovial person, had an 'Indian guide' who gave him advice, comfort, and stamina for his physically heavy work at Brown Bailey's steel-works. Several excellent young women, sisters, sang in the choir and taught in the Sunday School and two young men had charge of a lively boys' football club. For the Christmas sale a bag of potatoes usually arrived from one of the Upper Chapel Brahmins, a gift that was treated with respect and gratitude. It was 'the day of small things'....

Joan and I were married in Upper Church by her uncle, William Hall, Unitarian minister, poet, and leading member of the Manchester Literary Club. It was early June, and we spent our honeymoon in the Lake District. This was the first, and only, time I was able to persuade her to accompany me on a rock-climb, poor lass.... She never insisted on repeating the experience! Shortly afterwards, I received an invitation to succeed my friend and climbing companion, Priestley Phillips, as minister at Stand chapel, Whitefield. The call could hardly have come at a more inopportune moment. We had just settled in our home in Fulwood and been given a good send-off by the three congregations. It would not be seemly to move so soon afterwards, we argued. More importantly, perhaps, the Stand committee could not offer us the use of a parsonage. They were on the point of pulling down their old manse and re-building, and they could hold out little hope that the new house would be ready within the next twelve or fifteen months. Very reluctantly, I turned the invitation down. There was still work to do in Sheffield.

At this time, a strong branch of the League of Nations Union was active in the city, with a very lively secretary, Miss Gertrude Ward. Upper Chapel was affiliated to this, and regular monthly meetings were held in the Vestry to discuss international affairs arising from the previous month's events. Joan, an Oxford graduate in History, became a prime mover in the setting-up of an L.N.U. Youth Group, intended to be a feeder for the senior branch. Public meetings with high-powered speakers like Dame Kathleen Courtney and Sir Norman Angel were held in the City Memorial Hall and the city branch played a leading role in the organisation of the Peace Ballot in Sheffield (1934–5). This took the form of a house-to-house canvas. The petition to the government was finally signed by over eleven and a half million householders. Chapels and churches all over the country were involved in the campaign.

As the threat to world-peace increased, partly because of the failure of the former Allies to give solid support to the League of Nations' policies and constitution, and partly from the growing powers of the Nazi party in Germany, public opinion felt increasing revulsion against war. Pacifist sentiment found an outlet in the Peace Pledge Union, and this held a mass-meeting on January 18th, 1937 in the City Hall. The speakers were Dick Shepherd, Vera Brittain, Canon Charles Raven, and Cecil Wilson, then M.P. for Attercliffe. My wife and I had joined the P.P.U. soon after its formation, so I suppose it was natural that I should find myself taking on the stewarding of this meeting. Joan, meanwhile, received an invitation to address a similar meeting in a Chesterfield cinema, where she occupied the place of the 'statutory woman'. I have to say that throughout my ministry Joan was a tower of strength, very supportive, full of ideas for raising money for church purposes and other good causes, and a very acceptable speaker not only on international affairs and peace, but also during the conduct of public worship. She was, in a word, her father's daughter.

The year 1936 was an eventful one for her and for me: our son, Peter John was born on 22nd August. This event was accompanied by another change in family circumstances: May Roath came to help us in the house. She was a former guide and a member of the Ranger Company attached to Upper Chapel, of which Joan was also a member. They were good friends. May's early life had been a harsh one, since both her parents died whilst she was still a child. She had known deprivation and family tragedy in childhood and youth, but fortunately had been introduced to Upper Chapel Sunday School and was a convinced Unitarian. May soon established herself as 'one of the family', caring in turn for our three children, as if they were her own, and sharing the ups and downs of 'family-life-on-a-shoestring'. She worked and washed, cooked and cleaned, 'minded' and cared for our home and all who were in it, for a handful of pin-money. I think we mustered the magnificent sum of eleven shillings a week, plus board and lodging, but all along we were determined to pay the whole of her national insurance stamps in order to make sure that, in the end, she would qualify for full pension benefit. We were never able to pay her a proper wage, but for her, all that she did was a labour of love.

There were now four of us dependent upon an income which was

Family in Halifax: L. to R. Joan, Peter, Grandpa, May Roath ('Aunty May'), 1941

nominally the same as that which I received when I came to Sheffield in 1933, a single man. I began seriously to consider my position. Clearly, I would have to seek a better-paid post. I was paying rent and rates and telephone charges, with no assistance from the churches. My father weighed in to help with the last-named and promised to pay the premium for an educational insurance for our son. But I could expect little or no increase in stipend. Thus, in the autumn of 1937, when I received an invitation to become minister of the Northgate End Chapel, Halifax, I had little hesitation in accepting and preparing to leave Sheffield. I left the city and its people with some regret but the churches with rather less. I had done my best. I left owing one year and a quarter's rent. Hopefully but fruitlessly, the agent for the owner was good enough to offer me the house for around £800, and to wait until I could find the money to pay him for the arrears of rent. It was not a very auspicious beginning for my Halifax ministry....

5

HALIFAX

'HARD TIMES'

"You must go by the way of dispossession"
T.S. Eliot: *East Coker*

Northgate End Chapel, founded by Dissenters from the Church of England in 1672, had for many years been a centre of liberal Christianity. Like Upper Chapel, it still had a moderately good congregation when I commenced my ministry in the autumn of 1937. Unluckily, it possessed no manse, but, at that date, it offered an opportunity to improve our financial position a little. I was engaged on a stipend of £350 a year, £50 less than my immediate predecessor, who had no family and supplemented his income by writing short stories, syndicated for popular magazines. Looking back, I can now see it was a mistake to accept this reduction, but at the time I hoped it would be possible to work the stipend up a bit. I was not 'money-minded', but full of youthful optimism, and the congregation seemed a kind and welcoming people. In particular, the secretary, Arthur Farrar, himself an enthusiast, was a man who inspired confidence. He owned a first-class draper's shop in the town centre, which he used to advertise as 'The Home for good Drapery', publishing a regular series of amusing verses in *The Halifax Courier* each week, combining poetry with an old-world charm.

Halifax, in the late thirties, was a grey, smoky, and somewhat harshly-featured town, a Pennine product and a typical creation of the Industrial Revolution. In the valley-bottom were textile mills and the largest carpet-factory in Europe, whilst wool-processing, cotton-doubling, wood-working machinery manufacture, box and pattern-making and associated trades climbed the rising shelf of rock, on which the town had settled, to a height of a thousand feet above sea-level. It was cold in

Northgate End Chapel,
Halifax, 1944

winter. A number of our people were engaged in manufactures. Several were shop-keepers, retired, or professional folk. The house to which we moved, in Clifton Road, was a large stone terrace-house with a cellar-kitchen and a minimum of modernisation. It had been occupied by previous ministers, was roomy, but hard to maintain. Its chief advantage was its location not far from the chapel and very near the large open space called The Moor. It was the property of one of the chapel-members, to whom I paid a rent of £10 per quarter.

The 19th century Gothic chapel, built to take the place of the old meetinghouse was a dignified building, with good memorials by Flaxman and others, and possessed an excellent organ. The choir of four paid principals and several others regularly sang anthems and accompanied the unusual liturgies specially composed by a previous minister. The blind organist, Harold Uttley, FRCO, was a first-class musician, of whom I shall have more to say later. Music has an important part to play in services of worship, and the congregation was fortunate in being led by able and dedicated men and women. Musically, the chapel had a fine tradition. Until the mid-thirties, the Halifax Orchestral Society regularly met for rehearsals in the large schoolroom beneath the chapel. Every winter, until the outbreak of war, the monthly Sunday afternoon recitals were a popular attraction. Harold and his wife, Ivy, a fine pianist, performed piano-concertos by Mendelsohn, Grieg, Schumann and others, Harold putting in the orchestral parts on the organ. We also had violin and piano recitals, and an occasional visit from the Halifax String Quartet, of which Arthur Harrison was a member.

I found the chapel sadly in need of repairs. We worked hard to raise money for this purpose and the congregation responded well to various appeals. After a time, the church accounts showed a healthy credit-balance, but some members wondered why there should be such stress upon good housekeeping...

In 1938, I joined the International Voluntary Service for Peace, the pioneer organisation for work-camps in Britain and Europe. Its down-to-earth appeal struck me as imaginative and practical at a time when we seemed once more to be drifting towards war. 'Pick and Shovel Peace-making' was something in which any able-bodied person could enlist and effect better international understanding. Its founder was a Swiss scientist and engineer, Pierre Cérésole, a practical idealist who, after World War I had created 'Service Civil International' as a moral substitute for war. It combined voluntary community-service with a philosophy of love-in-action. I cycled over to the old Shropshire mining town of Oakengates, where a group were working on the 'Charlton Mound'. This was a large spoil-heap left behind by the spent coal-field. It overshadowed the little town. The volunteers were digging the mound and getting it carted away by the local authority to fill an old canal. Eventually, this would leave room for a park, a community centre, a bus station, and a swimming pool. The volunteers on this project shifted 60,000 tons by hand. It was the biggest single task the Service had tackled up to that date. I spent a fortnight there alongside French, German, Czech, Swiss and other nationals. Pierre himself visited the site, to advise on the progress of the work. I had already met and conversed with Albert Schweitzer in Sheffield a year or two before. It was now my good fortune to meet another human being who was a man of peace. Pierre, whose

Piere Cérésole, founder of International Voluntary Service for Peace, on the Charlton Mound, Oakengates

father had been a colonel in the Swiss army and president of the Swiss Confederation in 1873, went to prison for refusing to pay taxes for military purposes. I photographed him outside the sheds where we kept our tools and lived our community life: he reminded me very strongly, in manner and build, of Alfred David Tobler, my Swiss teacher at Willaston. Solid, reliable, he was also travelled and experienced in realms of thought untrodden by ADT. Selections from his private notebooks first published in 1954 revealed a modern 'saint', whose deep, free, and undogmatic inner life fuelled his truly Christian and universalist concern for humanity, and for 'The Eternal', who is at once within and beyond humanity. Years later, I read Dag Hammarskjöld's *Markings*, also a 'diary' of thoughts and faith, which contains the significant sentence: "In our age, the road to holiness necessarily passes through the world of action". In Cérésole's *For Peace and Truth* and *Markings* I found a marvellous confirmation of my own belief that "faith without works is dead" and that religion ultimately means 'love-in-action'.

I remained a member of IVSP for about twenty years, though no longer very active, for when World War II broke out, there were many other calls for human concern and service.

First came the Spanish Civil War. I joined the campaign to send food and medical supplies to the Republican government and its forces, which were being attacked by Italian and German Fascists. It was not easy to persuade Halifax folk to donate soup, tinned food, soap and milk for children in Madrid and Barcelona. With a few honourable exceptions, most of the British press supported Franco and his allies. However, when Nazi planes bombed northern Spain and Basque towns and villages, the British public, despite the official 'non-intervention' policy, realised that something had to be done to rescue at least some of the children from the war zones.

The Basque Children's Committee, whose chairman was Eleanor Rathbone, MP for the Northern Universities, initiated an adoption-scheme to bring children to Britain. By May 1937, over 3,800 had been brought away from the danger of air-raids on the Bilbao region. These were chosen by British doctors and nurses out of 10,000 whose parents begged for their children to be evacuated. They came to a camp in Southampton, and from there were distributed to over 100 homes and centres all over Britain. At this date, it cost only ten shillings per week to support one child. I persuaded a number of my congregation to pay me a shilling a week, and in May 1938 we were allotted Eloisa Rodriguez, a delightful twelve-year old, who was in camp near Keighley. From time to time she visited us in Halifax. Her father had been the socialist mayor of a town in the Basque region and was now living with one of his sons, both refugees, in France. The Congregationalist Minister (Rev. J. Nicholson Balmer), responsible for the children's camp, kept in touch with me and thanked our people for "their generous help... I am convinced (he wrote) that it is the most Christian work of our time".

We continued to support Eloisa until her return to Spain in December 1939. She went back carrying a parcel of clothing for her mother, who more than once wrote to me, and in the early months of the war even sent a telegram inviting our family to take refuge in her home, if the Nazi bombing of England threatened our lives. Such was the 'spin-off' of Nazi propaganda in Franco's Spain! Elo eventually returned to England, became a lady's maid in London, and married an Englishman. We are still in touch, and in January 1979, she and her husband drove up through severe blizzard conditions to attend my late wife's funeral in Sheffield. Her own father died, an exile, in Mexico.

For several years after Hitler came to power, I had interested myself in the plight of Jewish and non-Jewish refugees from Central Europe and was in correspondence with the German Emergency Committee of the Society of Friends. The entry of Hitler into Austria and the application of the decrees against the Jews, non-Aryan Christians and others; the Munich 'Agreement' and the extension of the areas of persecution; the November pogrom in 1938; and finally, the invasion of Czechoslovakia had increased the number of refugees by hundreds of thousands. British government reaction to the problem had been, throughout, niggling, parsimonious, and unsympathetic. Between 1933 and 1938, Britain had admitted only 11,000 refugees, though, by the outbreak of war, the numbers had greatly increased. Those admitted were allowed in on the strict understanding that they would be self-supporting. The dire need to escape from Nazi oppression hardly seemed to dawn on government ministers or officials. Nor were they, apparently, conscious of the pitiable conditions under which many thousands of people existed. To our national shame, we were no longer the haven for the helpless, for which Britain was at one time justly famed. It was left to the voluntary bodies to tackle an international problem of human distress, whose scale was not generally realised. Public opinion was uninformed and unaware that refugees, far from being a liability, could bring skills and knowledge that would benefit the host-country. Writing on 'The Plight of the Refugees' in the autumn of 1939, I stated that, quite apart from economic and national considerations sheer human need "should govern British reactions. Christian charity does not stop to inquire of the wounded traveller on the road whether he can pay his way if he is carried to the inn! It succours him and seeks no selfish advantage. The saving of life has always been regarded as one of the signs of a civilised society. Today, we have more than ample opportunity to prove that our community has still some elements of decency left in it".

The location of our chapel in the centre of Halifax and its suitable premises made it an ideal place for a social club for the refugees then resident and working in the town. Hence we opened up our schoolrooms on Saturday nights for this purpose, welcoming all Jewish and non-Jewish refugees and providing a service, for two or three years, that proved a great boon to its members. Some time in the autumn of 1940 "Refugees from Nazi Oppression" presented a large coloured etching of Rheims Cathedral to the chapel "in deep gratitude for the hospitality

De Vries (Dutch Lawyer) and the author in Prague, December, 1938.

given to them". When the chapel was sold in 1982, the trustees kindly saved this picture and handed it over to me as a memento.

Following the dismemberment of the Czechoslovak Republic under the terms of the Munich 'Agreement' in 1938, many Czechs and German-speaking social democrats left the Sudetenland, taking refuge in Prague and other towns and villages within the 'new' Republic. The Lord Mayor of London set up a Czech Refugee Appeal, and several agencies were established to deal with the flood of displaced families. Miss Rosalind Lee, a leading Unitarian minister, decided to go to Prague, where there was a Unitarian church, founded after the first World War, to offer assistance. She required an assistant who could speak German. I volunteered, and my Halifax congregation granted me leave of absence for several weeks. I left London at the beginning of December and returned at the end of January. From previous visits in 1933 and 1934 I was fairly familiar with the Czech capital, but astonished by

The Charles Bridge, Hradčin, and St Vitus Cathedral, Prague, 1938.

the strange conditions and atmosphere now prevailing. It was like a city under siege. Many felt threatened by an imminent Nazi invasion and were leaving the country for France, Canada, and the United States. There were nightly convoys by train through the Polish corridor, and frightened people besieged the offices of the refugee agencies. It was generally accepted that it was only a matter of time before Hitler would take the whole country over.

Miss Lee and I set up our relief committee-rooms in Krakovska Street, just off Wenceslas Square. It was the home of the editor of the *Prager Tageblatt* who had fled to Paris, and was still occupied (in part) by Diana Rowntree's Quaker committee. We came prepared to provide money, vouchers, clothes and advice to those who wished to emigrate. After a few days, we were joined by a young Dutch lawyer, who proved a pleasant and helpful companion. We had three rooms: a waiting room for all cases, invariably crowded; an outer room for interviews and writing up the details; and an 'inner sanctuary', with telephone, files, papers, where we could interrogate people privately and in depth. The work proceeded morning, noon and evening. Men, women, and children came to see us, an unending stream. We put them in touch with agencies suitable to help them, frightened people, most of them genuinely at risk, and many Jewish, some Austrian, some social-democrats, anxious to escape to the West. One father brought his two boys whom he wished to send away to England. We managed to place them on a convoy through the Polish corridor to Danzig. Both were received by Unitarian foster-parents in England and both later joined the Forces. One actually sacrificed his life by sticking to his damaged aeroplane and steering it clear of a densely populated district in Middlesex. Another lad who had fled to Vienna with his parents and had twice prevented his father from committing suicide, lived on his wits in Prague. I managed to bring him to England with the assistance of Halifax Rotary club, and after a month with us, shipped him from Liverpool to Adelaide through the kind offices of Sir Sydney Jones, a director of the Blue Funnel Line. He was actually on his way to Capetown when the war broke out! His parents, Wilhelm and Marie Fried, eventually came to England on 'domestic visas' and went into service with the actor, Robert Donat. They both wrote to us, expressing their gratitude for our care for their son. Many years later, by a curious coincidence, I got to know Donat's former wife, then married to a professor of music, and was able to ask her if she remembered the couple. She had, indeed, a faint recollection of them. All kinds of folk passed through our hands. Two I recall as 'difficult' cases. There was a young lady who had been an announcer on the Prague German-language radio station, who felt she would certainly be severely punished when Hitler arrived, and there was the elderly lawyer, who stressed the importance of *not* training for the Law in present circumstances, since it was no good to you, if you were compelled to flee your country. He also advised me to collect foreign stamps, as *they* went up in value and currency only went down!

In addition to the heavy case work, I visited refugee camps and soup-kitchens, taking wool and knitting needles for the women and clothes for babies and children. I also travelled to Moravska Ostrava, a city on the eastern frontier over against Poland. Here I met the Protestant bishop of the Czechoslovak Church and distributed alms for refugee clergy who had been deprived of their living by an incursion of the Polish army. One rather poignant excursion I made with members of the Prague branch of the YWCA. We taxied out along icy roads on Christmas Eve to a castle near Prerov where a group of sixty children, who had all been separated from their parents during their flight from the Sudetenland, were temporarily sheltering. In the bitter weather, (40 degrees of frost), it was comforting to find that these children, at Christmas, were in good hands. The YWCA volunteers put on a real Christmas feast, with presents for all, around a large, gaily decorated Tannenbaum.

Christmas day in Prague 1938, was marred for every true Czech by the death of a great fellow-countryman, democrat, and humanist, one of Europe's most noted authors and playwrights, Karel Čapek. The events which had so recently placed his beloved country in terrible jeopardy must have come as a severe shock to one who was a disciple of the founder of the Republic, President Thomas Masaryk. Many believed he died of a broken heart. The sense of bereavement felt by the whole population was second only to that experienced on the death of Masaryk himself, 'the Father of the Nation'. The shops were draped with black crêpe and the windows were full of photographs of Čapek. People felt, as happened when Masaryk died, that "a great democrat had died and with him something of the democracy". One curious episode that struck me as quite bizarre was the activity of a person who held sessions, three evenings a week, baptising terrified Jews into the Christian Church. Lined up on cushions thirty or forty at a time, they submitted to 'Christian' baptism in the hope that this would save them from 'the wrath to come!'. How vain this hope proved became obvious to me when on a visit to Prague in the late 'fifties. My friend and guide, a professor at the University, took me to the old synagogue, possibly the oldest in Europe, and showed me, inscribed on the walls of the newly-built extension, the names of forty thousand Prague Jews, who had been murdered by the Nazis. He pointed out whole families, several of whom he had known personally, three generations of which had been 'eliminated' in Hitler's 'Final Solution'.

Happier memories linger. For example, the day I spent at Salvation Army headquarters distributing clothes and comforts shipped from Britain under the auspices of the Lord Mayor of London's Czech Appeal Fund. From early morning to late evening, I was at the Citadel, measuring and fitting men, women and children for coats and suits, and handing dolls, teddy bears, and games to the children. It was, in its way, a fine international occasion. The commandant was a Dane, his lieutenant a Swiss, and we conversed in English. My lifelong admiration for the social work of 'The Army' has never diminished.

Apart from a visit to the National Opera House to see a performance of 'Aida' and a splendid Christmas Eve meal to which we were invited by the family of the young lady who used to help us in our office, we had little relaxation: one felt extreme pressure to work rapidly as many hours as we could, because the time was short. Little wonder that when, subsequently, I returned home, I was disabled by a severely ulcerated stomach and quite unable to stand upright. I had to preach sitting down in the pulpit, which rather cramped my style! The doctor's physic did me no good, but a colleague's psychological relaxation treatment cured me in less than two weeks! (*See Note on Prague and Czechoslovakia below.*)

It was a relief to be back in England and to take up my Yorkshire ministry once more. There was, however, one snag. There was no sign that the chapel committee would increase the minister's salary. During the war, the Denomination appealed to congregations to pay their ministers a war-bonus, but ours declined to comply with this request, even though the chapel's financial situation had markedly improved. The church treasurer, a widower who owned several properties round about the town, decided to get married again. After the ceremony, his brother, acting as 'best man' came into the vestry to inquire about the fee. "Oh", I said, "one guinea will do", which he gave me without hesitation. Some weeks later, in the school hall, the treasurer expressed surprise "that you charged for marrying me the other week". I was so angry that I replied, "How do you think I live, Mr M? I bought a much-needed pair of shoes with that money!" and left him to think it over. The parsimony of some church folk in England, especially church treasurers, has often been an unnecessary bugbear and caused the loss of not a few ministers over the years.

Yet, notwithstanding unpleasantness of this kind, the Halifax congregation contained its share of interesting folk, hard-working, cultured, even artistic. One or two were gifted writers, whilst at least four were artists, and I have already referred to the musicians. One of our artists was Mrs Elizabeth Fisher Clay. A graduate of Smith College, USA, this charming and rather commanding American lady had come to Europe with her sister on a painting expedition and set up a studio in Paris. She married Howard Clay of Halifax (later Mayor), whilst her sister married another Halifax gentleman and became Lady Fisher Smith. Mrs Clay had given us a very warm welcome in 1937 and continued her friendship throughout our stay. On her death in 1959 she left a houseful of rare and valuable antiques and over 400 canvasses, many of which were sold at Christies nearly fifty years later. As to the musicians, our choir principals were gifted and excellent and we were fortunate in our blind organist and his wife. When the war broke out, Ivy took Harold out into the country to avoid the air raids which were confidently expected. I remember that several of us went over to see how they were getting on, including Eric Harrison, who not seldom played for us in our series of winter chamber concerts. In the field outside the cottage where the Uttleys were staying we staged an impromptu festival, singing Purcell's lovely 'Bell Anthem' for all we were worth! The charm worked. Halifax was never intentionally bombed. Only a 'stray' fell from a German 'plane returning from a raid on Liverpool or Manchester. As a volunteer stretcher-bearer, I was called for duty at the Royal Infirmary that night. The first casualty I carried in was dead.

Eric Harrison deserves a special mention. This Halifax lad became a Fellow of the Royal College of Music, Master of Music at St Martin-in-the-Fields and pianist-in-residence at the University of Cardiff. During the war, he was commissioned in the Royal Air Force, but, after he had (reportedly) "crashed one or two planes" the authorities decided he was rather expensive and it would be better to place him in the typists' pool! No doubt, they thought his finger-work would pay dividends there. After the war, I met Eric several times: at a Balliol College Music Society recital in Oxford, and on a concert tour in Northern Ireland in the fifties, when he visited us and cured a squeaking pedal on our piano by giving it a good dose of blacking. His premature death in August 1970 robbed the world of a warm, vital, and lovable human being and a skilled musician.

At the outbreak of war, our family was enjoying a brief holiday in Wensleydale. We packed up and returned home at once. On the first night, the air raid sirens sounded, and we all trooped down into the cellar and sat, rather uncomfortably, until the all-clear was given. We were now in for a spate of fresh experiences: blackouts, air-raid protection training, food rationing, fire-watching, and getting used to wearing 'tin hats' and gas masks. After the loss of so many buildings in the winter of 1940–41, fire watching became compulsory. I can vividly recall the fire-watching duties for which we were responsible. We had to meet in an old furniture warehouse alongside our chapel in Northgate. Here we would make our way upstairs to the 'fire-watching room' where three or four of us would assemble when it was our turn. If you were lucky, and the mice did not keep you awake, you might get some sleep. We inspected the equipment, stirrup-pumps, water buckets, sand, etc., perambulated the premises, looked in at the chapel, and called it a day. We had walked down through blacked-out streets, and when the government decided to introduce double Summertime and continue it throughout the winter, we also walked home in darkness. It was pretty miserable. However, very fortunately we were never called into action. On one occasion we *were* startled. This was in November when the frost had unsettled a large stone coping on the building in which we were stationed. In the early hours of the morning, it crashed through the roof of the chapel, next door. Was it an unexploded bomb? We waited, and then nipped downstairs to have a look. All was blackness and silence, and remained so. Next morning, we discovered what had happened: ten hours later it would certainly have killed several of the children who met in the Stansfeld Room on a Sunday afternoon.

Of course walking and cycling in complete darkness became an occupational hazard for one engaged in pastoral visitation. I remember once being stopped by a policeman because the front lamp on my cycle appeared to be too bright! It complied perfectly with the guidelines, but coming down fast from the upper part of a hilly town, the dynamo which, incidentally, I had purchased when a student in Heidelberg, was apparently turning over too rapidly, and like many a unit made in Germany was just too good!

June, 1940 brought many soldiers of the British Expeditionary Force to Halifax, rescued from the sands of Dunkirk by 'the small boats'. One afternoon a large party arrived in our road, ostensibly to be billeted in a big house opposite. The captain turned it down, as it seemed to be "full of rats", so the local authority was compelled to find another property in which to billet his men. Whilst they were sitting on the curbs waiting for orders, the neighbours arranged a street party, for the lads had had very little to eat and were tired and hungry. We took four of them into our house and fed them there. One young fellow's feet were so blistered that I dressed them and arranged with the captain for him to be conveyed in the lorry, which was carrying rifles and other kit, to their final destination. A day or two later, we were privileged to entertain a lance-corporal and a private from the beaches of Dunkirk who stayed with us for a fortnight until their unit (of Gunners) was re-equipped.

After Dunkirk came the evacuation of the Channel Islands. Again, a number of refugees were brought to Halifax. The billeting officer, whom I knew, telephoned me to say that he had 'settled' most of the families, but there was a man with two teenage girls whom no one seemed to want. The Ellis family, or rather, a portion of it came to us, carrying three small paper-bags containing their worldly possessions. Mr

Ellis had been a labourer on a tomato farm in Peter Port, Guernsey. They left home with little or no warning. The evacuation of civilians appeared to have been both hurried and disorganised. He had no idea where his wife had been taken nor of the whereabouts of the rest of the family, twelve children in all! We succeeded, later, in locating them, in Wigan and near Nantwich.

I could write a book about our latest guests, and our, and their, mutual education, in life-styles, habits of eating, dressing and sleeping. The man obtained work as a navvy, constructing a parade-ground on the north side of the town. The girls, Beryl and Eunice, soon reached school-leaving age. Where were they to work? They could have earned good wages in a textile mill but the racket of the looms and shuttles terrified them, so they opted for a steam-laundry. They gave us problems. Sleeping in their vests and refusing to eat salads and other health-giving foods were small matters. The worrying one was hygiene, made plain to us very shortly by the spread of 'live-stock' to most of our family. My small son, Peter, discovered "little spiders" on his bed, and my wife and May both found their hair infected. Both girls' heads were infested with lice. On landing at Weymouth they had not been deloused. The local health authority at once sent a nurse to help us out of the difficulty. The cure was radical hair-cuts, washing with soft-soap and disinfectant all round. When at last the rest of the family were located and brought themselves to Halifax, much to the annoyance of the local billeting authorities (for these evacuees then became a charge upon Halifax rates), I managed to secure a vacant Glebe property into which they could be moved. It was in pretty dirty condition, but we organised a party to clean it up. Appealing to members of our chapel and friends, I hired a large furniture van and drove around the town collecting tables, chairs, curtains, carpets and kitchen equipment. Beds, straw mattresses, and bedding were obtained from the Council of Social Service. My wife and May scrubbed and polished, and eventually all was ready for the transfer of the fourteen bodies to their new home, the mother and small children from Nissen huts on the outskirts of the town, where they had been living for some weeks and the father and two older girls from our house. For a time, I kept an eye on them. Soon, another baby was on its way. My wife worked at a clothing depot which received parcels from Canada and the United States, intended for refugees and evacuees, so she was able to obtain a beautiful layette for the expected arrival. Alas, when the baby came, the district nurse reported that only newspaper was available for clearing up the afterbirth and no sign whatever of the contents of the layette! We did what we could to make up for this, but ignorance not seldom prevails over commonsense, and prejudice casts its veto over progress and human welfare. Before long, one of the little girls was severely burned, and another we found to be in an advanced state of 'the English sickness' (as the Germans term rickets). I pleaded with the mother, who was half-French, to permit the child to enter hospital for treatment, so as to save her from being bow-legged for the rest of her life, but to no avail. One has to learn that in a so-called 'free society' parents can condemn their children to suffering and handicap for life, without incurring any punishment, and legally there is nothing to be done. The sins of the parents are, in truth, visited upon the children.

To maintain one's mental and physical equilibrium at this time, it was absolutely necessary to go out on the moors and ramble to places like Luddenden Dean, Hardcastle Crags, and the Brontë country. Occasionally, I would take a colleague rock-climbing at Widdop or Almscliffe Craggs. Our young people held socials and discussions and there were the usual congregational junketings at Christmas, New Year and Easter. By the autumn of 1942, children's toys and games were practically unobtainable, so it was decided to hold a 'Christmas Market' in late November. A splendid display of soft and wooden toys, handbags, pinafores, games, Christmas cards, and presents of all kinds was mounted in the schoolroom. In less than three quarters of an hour the stalls were emptied and one hundred pounds was raised for chapel funds. The organisers modestly expected about twenty!

One important feature of church life at this date I mention, for the record. This is the remarkable and now hardly-imaginable ritual regularly performed each year and by no means unique to Northgate End chapel or Halifax. I refer to the 'Sunday School Treat'. At Halifax the children were taken to a field in Lightcliffe for their 'Summer Treat', a relic no doubt of the desire to give poor children a brief 'holiday', which otherwise many of them would never enjoy. The means of transport provided half the thrill. One, or more, brewers' drays drew up outside the chapel with the horses in their war paint, brasses polished, and plumes nodding. On to these drays were hoisted benches to accommodate the living load, then the children, and the baskets of buns and cakes, the bottles of orange and lime juice and milk, a stove to 'mash' the tea for teachers and helpers, and finally the last-named and the minister, all in their best summer outfits. Then off they started to climb the long, steep road up Beacon Hill and through the Cutting to the Field. On one such Sunday School Treat, I think my last, in 1944, moved by a sense of occasion, I distinctly remember saying to my wife and fellow-teachers, "Folks, you are taking part in a ritual which will shortly become a thing of the past. We are the last of a line!". Though I did not speak the thought, I realised that the whole operation would soon be quite forgotten. After games, competitions, refreshments and excitement of all kinds, we gathered the children together, tidied up the Field, kindly lent us by some philanthropic person, and set out for the town, arriving more quickly and more tired than we had bargained for.

A happy event in 1943 was the birth of our second son, Richard. This took place in the Halifax Royal Infirmary, where our dear friend, Miss I.C. Scott was a physiotherapist and actually saw the baby before the rest of us set eyes upon him. She was a niece of the famous editor of the *Manchester Guardian*, C.P. Scott, and a distant relative of mine by marriage. 'Aunty Scotty', as she was known to us all from this time onwards, was henceforth a regular visitor to our homes in Halifax, Oxford, Belfast, Cambridge and finally Sheffield, whither she journeyed from her home in Anglesey at Red Wharf Bay.

As the war dragged on and the winter black-outs proved ever more trying, we hit upon a way of 'beating the blackout', which, for more than two years, was a great success. 'Let Light in on the Black-out!' was the motto on the circulars we distributed on several Sunday evenings in 1941. I persuaded the chapel committee to agree to a novel experiment. We would invite young people off the streets of the town to enjoy themselves in a 'Sunday Evening Club' at Northgate End Schoolroom. We asked, "Do you ever get tired of the Sunday evening walk around town?" "Do you sometimes wish you could take your girlfriend or boyfriend somewhere light, warm and cheerful?" "Do you like games, light music and entertainment?" The chapel second Service was held on Sunday afternoons, so that from 7 to 9 pm every Sunday the Schoolroom was available for the use of the Club. Members were asked to register (at one shilling each, when they received a membership card) and paid one penny per night 'admission'. It was a great success, and we attracted some fine young folk. By 1943, however, most of the boys had been taken into the Forces, and the girls also had been conscripted, so that the Club's activities ceased at the end of the 1942–43 season. It is sad to reflect that several of the lads who entered the Forces were killed in action and one of our finest youth-leaders was lost holding the bridge at

Arnhem. Years later, when travelling in Holland, I made a point of visiting the British Cemetery there and found his grave, beautifully kept...

As the war continued, the government became increasingly alarmed at what might happen to young people during these disturbed and plundering years. It therefore decided to institute 'Youth Squads' to employ youth constructively in the war effort and keep it out of mischief. I sat on the Halifax Youth Committee which interviewed the young people at regular intervals. My contacts enabled me to organise one squad for the boys and another for the girls. The boys, under my supervision, were employed 'digging for victory' on an allotment, whilst the girls met each week at our house knitting scarves, gloves and pullovers for the Lowestoft Patrol.

Another scheme that involved several members of the chapel was a private arrangement I concluded in 1941 with my colleague at the Unitarian church in Park Street, Hull. This was to bring a number of children from Hull, which was suffering bombardment, to Halifax, 'a neutral zone' (so-called, i.e. not an official evacuation or reception area). We found homes for seven children, chiefly girls, of whom we took two, Kathleen, aged 13, and Barbara, aged 8. Their family's home backed on to the railway bottle-neck which the Germans frequently raided. In the event, these two girls, whose father had been a casualty in the First World War and whose mother suffered from dropsy, stayed with us for nearly three years. Both became *de facto* members of our family and only returned home in 1944, when Kathleen entered the Women's Land Army and eventually married a young farmer in East Yorkshire.

The year 1944 was a climacteric one for our family. I began to realise that there was no way forward for us, if we remained in Halifax. On £350 per annum, paying rent and rates and finding all other expenses steadily rising, I was faced with the unpleasant alternative of leaving the ministry or finding another church which could provide a better stipend and, hopefully, a house. I had been unable to save any money and costs were accelerating. Even a small advance would have been a godsend. My father, at my mother's suggestion, had given me his 'Riley Nine' car to help with visiting, but I could no longer afford to run it or face any repairs. It was eleven years old, and I was advised to sell it for 'scrap'. I did so and received two pounds ten shillings for the car, which was, in our eyes at that time, a small fortune! Our stay in Halifax was always a struggle financially and would have been intolerable, but for the kindness of some of the retailers with whom we dealt. We also had good neighbours, who helped us with clothing for our evacuees and occasional little gifts of fruit and preserves. I also took over a garden plot in the vicinity of the house and 'dug for victory' or, more realistically, to provide our kitchen with fresh vegetables and fruit. During the latter part of my ministry, I had no compunction whatever in spending some time cultivating my garden. Fortunately, I have always enjoyed gardening, so that the knowledge that it was actually helping to 'pay our way' gave me increased zest! We were often hard-pressed to pay for our purchases. On one occasion, I received a summons for non-payment of rates, but somehow hurriedly managed to collect enough cash to forestall the threatened legal proceedings. I recall that my wife, Joan, and May could never go out when their shoes were being repaired, as they possessed only one pair of sound footwear apiece, and had to fall back upon slippers.

When the time came, therefore, I was glad to shake off the dust of Halifax and proceed "to fresh woods and pastures new!"

6

OXFORD – A DON'S LIFE

"Autobiography is necessarily a matter of intervals"
Henry W. Nevinson: *Between the Acts*

The late Spring of 1944 was known as the period of 'the Dim-Out'. This expression referred to the fact that 'Blackout' restrictions were modified, because the Luftwaffe seldom entered British air-space, as the Allies were winning the war. If one moved house, it was no longer necessary to provide complete cover for windows at night. My father had given notice of his retirement from the principalship of the Unitarian College in Manchester, leaving a vacancy which was soon filled by Mr R.V. Holt, tutor and librarian of Manchester College, Oxford. I received an invitation to follow Holt as warden and librarian and teach New Testament studies. We moved into his old house, Number 27, Holywell in late September. Thoughtfully, the College committee enabled me to give early notice to my Halifax congregation, so that I should have at least three months in which to prepare for the new post. This was a crucial decision for me and our family, and we all looked forward to the change, I to academic life, my wife to a return to Oxford where she had studied for her university degree in History, and all of us to the fresh opportunities and experiences which the 'city of dreaming spires' would offer. Our family had grown and we now had two boys as well as our friend and helper, May Roath. The College house was commodious, rent and rate free, and my salary would be considerably more than I received in Halifax. This appointment was a godsend, and could, I suppose, be described (in modern jargon) as a way out of 'a poverty trap'. For it promised the possibility of leading a less anxious kind of existence than the one which had been our lot hitherto. I had managed to keep out of debt, but I was never really free from financial pressures. Members of our Halifax congregation had generally been kind and

College Tower, Manchester College, Oxford

friendly; but few realised what a battle it had been to keep our heads above water. Moreover, the chapel committee made no effort to grant me a war-bonus or pay a modest increase out of the credit balance which I had helped them to achieve. Hence our excitement and relief at the prospect of leaving the West Riding and making a new home in Oxford. "The world might become stranger" (T.S. Eliot), but it would undoubtedly become pleasanter and free from undue worry and care.

Manchester College was founded in 1786 by a body of Dissenters from the Church of England to provide higher education for "young men of every religious denomination, from whom no test or confession of faith" would be required. It has had a peripatetic existence, moving from Manchester to York, back to Manchester, to London, and finally in 1889 to Oxford, where it now has a permanent home. One of its main purposes has been the training of ministers of religion.

Inevitably, the work of the College had been largely interrupted by the War, when the Government requisitioned the buildings in the inter-

The Tate Library, Manchester College, Oxford

ests of the war-effort. There were few students and most of the strictly College operations had to be carried on outside the main buildings, in the Holywell hostels. We had access each day to a temporary dining-room at the end of a corridor near the kitchen, and, for half an hour a day, we were permitted to use the main library which at other times was full of 'Wrens' (Women's Royal Naval Service). They were, we understood, an important component of the forces engaged in preparations for the invasion and occupation of Europe. It was said that every one of the Allied Forces was represented here, except the Russians.

To make room for a typists' pool, large numbers of older books had been removed from the College library to the New Bodleian basement and a 'working library' of several thousand now occupied shelves in two rooms in the old Holywell buildings. Both quadrangles hosted large Nissen huts, erected on solid concrete platforms, whose foundations necessitated considerable excavation (and consequent heavy soil infill at the end of the War). The place was a hive of activity right up to the cessation of hostilities and a colonel of the Marines was in charge of the whole unit. Lectures and tutorials took place in what was later christened 'Warrington house', whilst a temporary office was set up in the room close to the old gate to the Hostel, now no longer in use. This was then the normal entry into the 'College' administration and residential area, and discipline was exercised from here, that is to say, the door was closed and locked from 10 p.m. onwards and opened by the member of staff on duty until 11 p.m., when it was locked for the night. All members of staff shared this duty. My job was to lecture on New Testament subjects, Greek text and exegesis, introduction and theology, and related topics, and to act as Warden of the College hostel, an official post *vis à vis* the University. The Principal, Rev. R. Nicol Cross, was responsible for philosophy and the work of the ministry, and Professor D.C. Simpson taught Old Testament and Hebrew. Later, a fourth tutor was appointed to teach church history and act as bursar. I found my colleagues easy to work with and good friends. We collaborated smoothly and seriously on the board of studies and it was not long before I felt quite at home in chapel, lecture room, and 'dining hall'. One portion of the College buildings that was not occupied by the military was the College chapel. It became for us an oasis of peace. Morning prayers and Sunday services were a valued and spiritually-satisfying respite from the pursuit of learning, in which the fine Burne-Jones and William Morris windows, the carved oak screen and pews, and the magnificent Nicholson organ all played a part. The organist, Harold Spicer, of whom more later, became a close friend. The choir of some sixteen choristers and six men sang an anthem every Sunday, a feature of the chapel services much appreciated by a congregation of both town and gown.

Soon after our arrival in Oxford, our daughter, Elizabeth Jane, was born, and Mr Cross baptised her in the chapel. Her mother had been admitted to the special Government maternity hospital which had been set up in Ruskin College chiefly for women from the London area. The first telegram of congratulations she received was addressed to Mrs McLachlan, c/o 'The Risky Maternity Home', Oxford, a clever (?) misreading of the proper address. As it happened, the maternity service at Ruskin was first-class, a number of the nurses and kitchen staff being expert Austrian and German women, refugees from Hitler.

On 13th May 1945 we celebrated VE Day, the end of the war in Europe, with a special Thanksgiving Service in the chapel. This was attended by all the Service personnel working in the College, as well as by the usual congregation, and it fell to me to give the address. We had won the war, but how, I asked, shall we 'win' the peace? "The challenge of victory was this: to establish in the world the rule of law and the habit of mutual trust among the nations". And I cited the Atlantic Charter, whose signatories aimed to found "a peace which will afford to all nations the means of dwelling in safety within their own boundaries, and afford assurance that all men in all lands may live out their lives in freedom from fear and want". The chapel was full to capacity. We are still a long way from fulfilling this aim.

During the two winters following the end of the war, the weather turned very cold, so some of us went skating in Port Meadow. It was a carefree period, although rationing was still the order of the day. Freed from the anxieties of wartime conditions, some folk turned their minds to consider the state of Europe, whilst others reflected seriously upon the significance of the two atom bombs which had fallen upon Japanese cities. Remarkably, a Jewish publisher, Victor Gollancz, initiated a scheme for sending parcels to the Allied Occupied zones of Germany, entitled 'Save Europe Now'. Food parcels containing solely *rationed* food, purchased with coupons and weighing not more than seven pounds, could be sent to Germany, whilst clothing-parcels containing second-hand clothes, mending materials, books, educational aids, and not more than two pounds of soap might also be sent, by special arrangement. But no coffee, cocoa, tinned soups or other unrationed commodities might be included.

A meeting to rouse the consciences of people in Oxford (and further afield) was held in the Town Hall on 5th December, 1946. Almost predictably, the Bishop of Chichester, George Bell, took the chair, with a strong platform of speakers: Sir Richard Acland, Roger Wilson, Victor Gollancz, Barbara Ward, and John Collins. Joan and I attended the packed meeting. The chairman asked those who promised to send parcels of food to Germany to stand up: nearly a thousand did so. It was the beginning of 'Christian Action', of which John Collins, Dean of Oriel College, was the founder and chairman. The work of reconciliation continued, and the Government was petitioned to speed up the repatriation of German prisoners, thousands of whom were still being held in Britain long after the cessation of hostilities. On receiving a letter from friends in Heidelberg, I cycled out to a Prisoner of War camp near Bicester to visit a young German whose parents were worried about him. He was alright, but desperately anxious to return home. On Christmas Day this year, German prisoners could be seen walking about the town rather disconsolately. A small party of them passed our house in Holywell and I ran after them to invite them in. My wife and May plied them with Christmas fare and coffee, and at their request, I took them round the

College premises. In the chapel I was pointing out the great 'West' window, in which the College's motto is represented by the three figures of Truth, Liberty and Religion, when one of the men turned to me and asked, in the circumstances, almost pathetically, "Which is Liberty?" I was moved, as were the rest of us, in the silence which followed.

The chapel, with its pre-Raphaelite windows, oak furnishings, and splendid organ is one of the finest treasures of the College, but the chancel end is dark. The large stained-glass window facing the congregation admits light which, for long, made it impossible to see the copy of Leonardo da Vinci's 'Last Supper' above the communion table. By one of those lucky chances that occur in life to many of us (I believe), I was able to rectify this drawback.

The Leonardo copy is a memorial to a former town-clerk of Sheffield, Herbert Bramley, whose son, Edward (already mentioned) was an old friend of mine, in fact it was he who sent me my first invitation to enter the ministry in Sheffield. One Saturday afternoon, I happened to be working in my study in the College when the doorbell rang. I was the only person in the building that afternoon, so I went down to open up. Imagine my surprise to find Dr Edward Bramley standing there with a lady companion, whom he afterwards married. He was hoping to show her round the College. When we were in the chapel, I made a point of mentioning the fact that 'The Last Supper' could not be seen from the body of the chapel and that it would be well to illuminate it. Edward agreed, and straightaway asked me to arrange for this to be done. He and his brother, Henry, would pay for it. I lost no time in following up that suggestion. I think this may be considered a case of serendipity, being accidentally in the right place at the right time, and knowing the right person....(see page 53 supra).

In 1947 'Christian Action' held another large meeting in the Sheldonian Theatre, at which Victor Gollancz was the main speaker. He urged the need for Reconciliation in a powerful plea, which coming from a Jew, whose people had suffered so disastrously in 'The Holocaust', carried tremendous weight. I joined 'Christian Action' forthwith.

My first contact with John Collins actually preceded the event described above. It came about in this way. Early in 1945, my old History teacher in Manchester, Professor (later Sir) Maurice Powicke, invited me to dinner in Oriel College, of which he was a Fellow. He then suffered an acute attack of gout, and sent me a note to say he could not, alas, entertain me personally, but his friend the Dean (John Collins) would meet me and look after me at dinner, which he did. I shall always remember the charm and kindness of the man, who, throughout the years of his campaign for justice and peace in Europe and South Africa, represented the conscience of Britain at a time when materialist notions were in the ascendant. Subsequently, Collins joined CND and I heard him speak in the Cambridge Union, in the 1970s, on a motion criticising the construction and proliferation of nuclear weapons. 'Christian Action' was a summons to the full acceptance by Christians of social and political responsibility, a call to serve God as citizens by translating faith into action in public as well as private life. It appeared to me to be in line with the heart of the teaching of Jesus. If this is to be labelled left-wing, then assuredly what the *Manchester Guardian* once called "typical Collins activity" made him a reconciler of the stature of Abou ben Adhem, who asked to be written down as "one that loves his fellow men".

I have already referred to the College's lack of students during my first two or three years in Oxford. Perhaps it was a blessing in disguise, for when the buildings were de-requisitioned (September 1946), much restoration work had to be done and the administrative load increased. After nearly five years of occupation by the Ministry of Works, the repairs, replacements and re-decoration cost the British taxpayer a fortune. I mention here chiefly the library. Several thousand books taken to the Bodleian basement were returned worse for wear, since many of them were old leather-bound volumes which had been unceremoniously bundled into sacks and had their backs broken. Needless to say, I put in a claim for compensation. I also purchased cheaply from the Ministry a large number of shelves which were taken up into the tower and accommodated many of the old books, arranged in chronological order. The Tate library itself was in a shocking mess and we had to bring in specialist cleaners and equipment to get rid of the dust and debris. The fine reading tables, whose tops were covered with buffalo hide, were burnt all over by hot tea and coffee pots placed upon them. They had to be re-covered, but not with buffalo hide! The chapel organ suffered from a 'knock-on effect'. Just before de-requisitioning, large quantities of waste paper and documents of all kinds, which should have been shredded and burnt in the specially-erected incinerator, were carelessly consigned to the central heating furnace. These burnt so fiercely that they raised the temperature all over the buildings to a height that, in the chapel, sweated the leather 'straps' controlling the speaking-notes of the various organ pipes, with fatal consequences: they were all ruined and had to be replaced at the expense of the Universal Provider, the British taxpayer.

By 1947, the College was recovering from its wartime experiences. More students came into residence, some of them from abroad, Holland, Czechoslovakia, Poland and Hungary. One young man, a German refugee from Bonn, Paul E. Kahle, had been awarded a special grant to study for the Honours School of Theology. In the library I began and completed the restoration of thousands of books displaced in the College hostel, the New Bodleian basement and elsewhere, finding several unique and valuable works among them, like an author's presentation copy of a drama by Goethe, which I discovered lying on the floor of the new Bodleian. I also came upon many *errata* in the existing authors' catalogue, and came to the conclusion that it was high time that a properly classified arrangement and a subject-catalogue should be created, to bring the collection into line with other college and university libraries. The College committee agreed, and before long we appointed Miss Emily Blomfield to do this work. She had just finished work on the library of Westminster College, Cambridge. She was eminently suited to work on a specialist collection like that of Manchester College, which contained biblical, philosophical, historical and literary works, the remnants of several Dissenting academy libraries, and many rare volumes, presented by generous benefactors over a long period of years.

We agreed to use a modified 'Library of Congress classification' as more suitable for our purposes than the Dewey Decimal system, and this has been found in practice to be highly satisfactory. It took almost two years to complete the classified subject-catalogue. Meanwhile, I examined our holdings of manuscript material, which had never been catalogued. This contained papers, letters, lectures, and other manuscripts from a wide variety of sources, deposited over many years. I began to catalogue these, assisted by my son, Peter. We found they had never been properly examined, but were, in total, a most valuable corpus for the history of British Dissent. For one portion, the correspondence and papers of the Spanish exile and theological writer, Blanco White (1775–1841), I prepared a handlist. The University of Liverpool Cohen Library contains another collection of papers by White, and European scholars were beginning to take an interest in his writings. Hence, it was important to make our collection easily accessible. I then set out to write a brief history of the library, its origins, growth and benefactions, intending to continue this with chapters on the contents, special collections, early-printed books, rare editions and association volumes. But this remains incomplete, as controversy over the future of the College had begun to gather momentum at the time.

I did, however, succeed in doing the research for a doctoral thesis on 'Socinianism in Seventeenth Century England' which the Oxford University Press published in 1951. My supervisor for this study was the Rev. Canon Claude Jenkins of Christ Church, Regius Professor of Ecclesiastical History. Dr Jenkins was a bachelor, living by himself in lodgings in Tom Quad. I used to visit him fortnightly in term to discuss progress. I owe him a debt of gratitude for the way in which he encouraged me to proceed. He was one of the 'antiquities' of the Oxford scene, but also a kind and lovable person. When we were closeted together in his bookstrewn study, he sometimes appeared to go to sleep and I had a little difficulty to rouse him, but he possessed an acute mind and was a stimulating and cheerful scholar. He had been librarian at Lambeth for many years. On his death in 1959 his very considerable collection of books came by will to St Anne's College, which confirmed my suspicion that he was a sturdy advocate of the higher education of women. I would not have been surprised to find him supporting the "priesthood of all believers", specifically, the cause of women priests. More than once, we invited him to tea in Holywell and it was noticeable how well he got on with our children. He 'sat in' at my graduation ceremony in 1949, for long remained a correspondent, and kindly acted as a referee when I applied for a lectureship in Historical Theology at Keele University some four years later, almost convinced I had made a mistake to move to Northern Ireland.

Manchester College, though attracting few students for theology, did provide some interesting series of lectures, which members of the University were glad to attend. In my time, under its Dunkin foundation, came, for example, Sir Ernest Barker, Professor R.H. Tawney, Baroness Mary Stocks, Dr Betty Heimann, Dr A.C. Bouquet, and Professor J.S. Mackenzie. For several years, the College Visitor was Professor Gilbert Murray, who dined with us in hall, and gave an address in the College chapel. Once, when Dr Murray and his wife, Lady Mary, were our guests for dinner, I happened to be presiding, and introduced the two students who were sitting on either side of our distinguished visitors. First, I introduced 'Mr Long' and turning around, found myself facing 'Mr Short'. I have often wondered what our special guests thought of that curious collocation!

Our Church History tutor, Tom Williams, who came to us in 1947 from a Baptist church in Coventry, was a good fellow, but more interested in politics than religion. He resigned his tutorship two years later and entered Parliament, successfully contesting the Hammersmith South division for Labour. For some time he had been attending Bar dinners in London, was eventually knighted for political services, and subsequently became a circuit judge.

The Principal, R. Nicol Cross, fell ill in 1948. He was unable to participate, during Trinity Term, in the 'International School of Religion' which welcomed students from the Continent and America and two visiting lecturers, Professor van Holk from Leiden and Dr Buri from Bâle, both of whom took their turns in holding seminars and preaching in chapel. Unfortunately, Mr Cross never fully recovered, and resigned on grounds of ill-health, writing his last annual report in June 1949. The dearth of students for the ministry undoubtedly troubled him greatly. In his report, he stated that the College "had seldom enough theologicals to utilise fully its resources. Subsidiary schemes have on occasion been adopted, none of which have been permanent". Probably, one of the chief factors underlying this scarcity was the marked decline of those churches on which, almost wholly, the College depended for the supply of its regular students. The tide of Liberal Religion seemed to have receded; and the beginning of this process could be traced back to the second decade of the twentieth century.

However, in addition to the small number of students coming forward to train for the ministry, another important factor of great concern to the College committee was its deteriorating financial position. Already in 1947 the accounts had shown a deficit of £1,637. Economies were effected, but it became clear that radical changes alone could save the day. After careful consideration, the committee concluded that the College premises were "far too large" so long as the student-body in residence remained so small. Maintenance charges had risen steeply after the War, and it was now estimated that the training of a single student actually cost £3,408 per annum.

Negotiations with the Unitarian College, Manchester were begun, in order to consider some form of amalgamation. Eventually, a liaison scheme evolved whereby the two institutions should in fact be united, and in February 1951 a Joint-committee was set up. However, earlier in 1949, and quite independently, a group of persons interested in purchasing the College and all its assets made an approach to the committee.

They hoped to establish a new foundation in Oxford to be known as St Antony's College. The threat to the future existence of Manchester College in Oxford now became acute. The alumni and other governors were alerted to what was going on, especially when valuers (from Cambridge, of all places!) estimated that the site and buildings might be sold for a sum of around £216,000! A number of influential members of the committee had now come to the conclusion that the College in Oxford should be abandoned and its assets realised, even though the figure was entirely inadequate, even absurd. The new chairman, Professor F.J.M. Stratton (of Cambridge) had already declared his determination to carry through a complete re-organisation. Along with several leading personalities owing allegiance to the Unitarian denomination and its General Assembly, he and a majority of trustees (as the governors were then called) on the College committee were prepared to sell the premises 'lock, stock and barrel'. This phrase came much into use at this time, and was employed by opponents of the scheme as a derogatory term with which to beat the selling faction. The general body of trustees (governors) now found themselves deeply divided between those determined to sell the College buildings in Oxford and come to some arrangement with the sister college in Manchester and those, many of them alumni, who were fiercely opposed to such a move.

Almost contemporary and parallel with this controversy came the departure of Tom Williams for Westminster and the resignation and retirement of Nicol Cross. Dr Simpson had retired earlier, so that I was left as the sole resident-member of the teaching staff. To say the least, the future seemed uncertain. Meanwhile, it was decided not to appoint a successor to the Principal but to ask me to carry on as Acting Principal. Between the years 1949 and 1951, the alumni, old students, organised themselves to remove the chief members of the committee in favour of selling the College by voting only for those who were opposed to such action. This had the effect of paralysing all plans for the sale or removal of the College with, or without, union with the sister College. In the event, the Liaison scheme proved merely a *cul de sac*. It accumulated a hefty deficit in its first two years and the transfer of funds from Oxford to Manchester, which was an essential part of the scheme, was found to be strictly illegal, so that the clumsy attempt to run the two Colleges in tandem was abandoned after less than three years.

For my part, I had come to the conclusion that big changes were necessary to render the institution viable in the years that lay ahead. But the idea that the fine, freehold site in the heart of Oxford, with all its treasures and contents should be sold appeared to me to be utter folly and a policy of despair. I was therefore active in opposition, and continued, during what were very difficult and frustrating days, to teach and carry on the general administration until the winds of controversy should blow themselves out.

In my second Report as Acting Principal (in June 1951) I remarked on the serious decline in the number of applicants to enter the College. In my judgement, this was not merely due to the secularisation of daily life, but also to "the rather grave condition of the Unitarian denomination. Within the past seven years, only four men have come from within this group of churches". I went on to forecast that the College would be compelled to change its character and alter the emphasis which had characterised its existence hitherto. "Research, new courses of study, and other supplemental concerns may have to take precedence of training for the ministry." And I added, "A *new* Manchester College, to reverse the epithet by which it was formerly known, might recover not a little of its *raison d'être*, namely the higher education of lay people as well as 'divines'." Looking back, I now realise that, greatly daring, I had scored a bull's eye. For M.C.O., in the course of three decades, has become, to a large extent, a Liberal Arts College, educating increasing numbers of students, and very few for the ministry. The difficulty has been to awaken many of its supporters to the changing nature and needs of society in the latter part of the twentieth century.

Early in 1951, I was offered the Principalship, but in view of the preceding controversy, in which an ex-president of the General Assembly of our churches had, rather unworthily, suggested that I had objected to the sale of the College purely on grounds of self-interest 'with an eye to an eventual appointment' I had little hesitation in turning the offer down, though expressing my willingness to serve for a time under any new Principal who might be appointed. I continued to teach, to work on the library, arranging the special collections (*Unitariana* and early printed books) conducting services in the chapel, and visiting the congregation. I also gave a terminal course of lectures at Rewley House, Wellington Square, under the auspices of the W.E.A., on "The Title-deeds of Christianity, the New Testament and how we got it". Amongst my hearers were a couple of Jehovah's Witnesses, who kindly gave me as a parting gift a copy of the Witnesses' 'New World Translation' of the New Testament.

I had always taken an interest in the history of science, so, for a change, I offered a short introductory course on this topic to the Oxford University Extension Lecture syndicate. This took me at fortnightly intervals to the pleasant town of Eastbourne, where I lectured in the town hall with projector and slides, beginning with the Greek period and concluding with the scientific revolution of the seventeenth century and its aftermath almost to our own day. It was an exercise of *multum in parvo*, and probably impressed me more than it did my audience. The local representative of the Oxford extra-mural department rejoiced in the name of Mr Pass. He it was who entertained me to an evening meal before the lectures, for which I was grateful, for I travelled down from Oxford, and back on a very late train, on the same day. He was what is called a 'crammer', that is to say, he prepared backward pupils to take their examinations with some likelihood of success. I thought his name augured well for those he stuffed, and even wondered whether he had altered his name by deed poll out of professional pride.

I now recall (by way of postscript) that late in 1948 Professor Stratton approached me to let my name go forward as a possible successor to Dr Mortimer Rowe as Secretary of the General Assembly of Unitarian and Free Christian Churches. Stratton was to become President of Manchester College a few months later. I replied that I was not interested. I had no means of knowing what this meant, but I suspected that it was not unconnected with the fact that my removal from Oxford would mean that the last working and resident member of the teaching staff would be taken off the College books, if I were appointed to the London post. And the way would have been made easier for the closing of the College doors in Oxford. But this is pure speculation. The alumni of the College rallied round, and by carefully selective voting removed the majority of those who favoured the sale (including Dr Rowe) and saved the College for posterity.

In December 1951 I received and accepted a call to the ministry of the First Presbyterian Church, Belfast and resigned my post as tutor, warden and librarian as from 31st March 1952. I had taken the advice of friends that I might find some peace and pleasure away from Oxford by serving the historic Mother-church of Presbyterianism in Belfast, which had suffered considerable damage and loss of property during the War. After an extended vacancy, the congregation was most anxious to effect a settlement. Hence, early in April, leaving my elder son Peter, a boarder in Magdalen College School, we left for Ulster.

So far, I have said little or nothing of our family life in Oxford or of my own individual interests and activities, so I now turn to more personal concerns.

Our home (Number 27) in Holywell stood in a terrace of seventeenth century College houses, opening straight on to the street. It had been occupied by my predecessor and his wife, both of whom must have been valetudinarians, judging from the load of bottles, large and small, that we discovered in cupboards and cellars. It was necessary to ask the local authority to send a large van to remove these and the numerous cardboard boxes and other rubbish that they left behind. An upstairs lounge capable of seating at least a score of people was a feature of the house. It had often been used as a 'meeting room', and Einstein had once addressed a full house in it. For a time, in our early days in Oxford, we held a Sunday School there, and entertained students, staff, and visitors in its comfortable embrace. The only snag was that the coal for the fire had to be carried up two flights of stairs. In those days the hostel rooms next door also burned coal in their grates, all of which had to be brought up by the 'scouts'. Whilst the College was occupied by the Admiralty, I used a bedroom as a study, but later I enjoyed the privilege of a commodious study immediately to the left of the main stairway in the College building.

To have, at last, 'a free house' (and other perquisites such as a garage, and at least one dinner a week 'in hall') was a strange but very welcome experience. Holywell, until the end of the War, was rather a noisy street. Around midnight, a convoy of American troops passed down it every night on its way to barracks. It continued to be noisy until closed to through traffic in recent years. But its convenience for shopping, attending lectures, recitals, and theatre was undeniable. The family flourished exceedingly in 'the city of dreaming spires'. After de-requisitioning, the College quadrangles and garden became an admirable (and safe) playground for the two younger children. Nearby were the University Parks and the River Cherwell, a slow-running stream on which we learnt to punt. In the early days of summer, it was 'paradise', moving slowly upstream through the fresh green tunnel of trees, and occasionally we would punt right up to Cutslow (2 miles north) to fetch Richard and Jane from School. This primary school had a wonderful headmistress and was very popular with the children of dons. Most mornings I would take one or other of them to school on my bicycle, until they became too heavy to manage, and then they travelled by bus or in a car with the children of one of Merton College bursary staff. A river paradise it remained to the day when I held on to the punt-pole a fraction too long, and took a dive into the river, to the astonishment and terror of the young occupants of the punt!

Another enjoyable feature of our family-life in Oxford was the regular Sunday afternoon walk out into the countryside. We would take the tow path along the Thames to Iffley and its charming Norman church, walking back by road. Or we would make for Port Meadow and the tow-path to Godstow and Wolvercote. In the autumn, we took the bus to Boar's Hill and picked blackberries. Another favourite outing was through Marston to Elsfield and Woodeaton Wood, remembering John Buchan (Lord Tweedsmuir of Elsfield) and picking a few bluebells and cowslips on the way. Peter, our eldest, attended the East Oxford Elementary school and flourished under the 'Dalton scheme', which permits pupils to work at their own pace on a selected corpus of work. He invariably finished his week's assignment with a day to spare, which he could then devote to 'further reading'. He went on to take the scholarship examination for Magdalen College school, obtained a place, and relieved me of further school fees. Richard, from Cutslow, followed his brother to East Oxford, and then in 1952 continued in Belfast at the prep. school for the Royal Belfast Academical Institution ('Inst' for short), "the school which our ministers always send their sons to", according to my Irish informants. Our daughter, Jane, was only seven, when we moved to Belfast, where she entered Richmond Lodge School, nearby, and spent the rest of her schooldays happily there.

In 1945, the family temporarily increased in size, when a small Dutch boy, Henk de Haas, joined us. He was one of a number of children, brought to England after the War, to be 'built up' after their starvation in Nazi-occupied Holland. He stayed with us for a couple of months. The following year I visited his home in Utrecht, and, subsequently, when my wife and I were attending a conference in Amsterdam, his mother came over from Utrecht to see us in our hotel. Unfortunately, we were both out, and missed her. Holland suffered severely from foreign occupation: it was a shock to see how many memorials there were in the streets and squares to murdered civilians, shot by the Nazis in reprisals.

Living close to the centre of Oxford was, of course, a bonus, as I have indicated. In particular, for me to be able to walk over to the Bodleian library in five minutes and leave books on the table on which I was working, to return to them later in the day was most convenient. The atmosphere of this great library and its subtle attraction for scholars is, indeed, remarkable. I never think of the hours I spent in it without feeling a huge sense of privilege. Oxford has many physical and aesthetic delights and diversions to offer, of which the beauty of its buildings and streets cannot be the least. The influence of fine architecture upon the human mind and spirit must, I suppose, always be considerable. Such 'silent visual music' can hardly fail to nurture the wings of the spirit. Yet 'the meeting of minds' is probably the most important and characteristic advantage that a place like Oxford affords. Hence the number of 'learned societies' and associations for the cultivation of particular interests proliferates. I joined the Society for Historical Theology which offered a programme of meetings addressed by experts in various theological fields. I was also fortunate to be a member of the Dean of Christ Church's New Testament seminar, which brought together university teachers, old and young. When, after the War, the United Nations Association took the place of the League of Nations Union, I became a member of the Oxford branch, of which Gilbert Murray and John Garnett were leading figures.

The short eight-week term sped by with whirlwind swiftness, possibly because it was so tightly packed with demanding studies and duties. No wonder that the saying was current amongst Oxford teachers: "Comes the Term, when no man can work!" Paradoxically, the oblique reference was true, namely, that teaching and administration swallowed up day after day, leaving little time to the scholar and researcher to pursue his own investigations. Yet the don's life was undoubtedly a privileged one, a somewhat rarified existence. In some colleges a bachelor-don could go on extending his knowledge of a particular theme like a squirrel gathering nuts, forgetting, and almost forgotten of, the world. The Oxford scene, very different from Sheffield or Halifax, was also, alas, infected by a form of intellectual and social snobbery. This would emerge when, having been invited to a College function, say a sherry party, where one met a cross-section of university folk and talked to a number of them, you chanced to meet one or another of your new acquaintances in the street, next day perhaps. But though you might smile at them, they often gave not the slightest sign of recognition. They would walk right past you, as though you were a perfect stranger! How different from Yorkshire or Lancashire, the uncivilised North of

England! Is this, perhaps, what foreigners complain of, the unacceptable face of the English intelligentsia?

Yet one could still make friends amongst scholars and Fellows of colleges. I recall regular visits to Dr L.P. Jacks on Shotover Hill, when the sage would expatiate on religion and philosophy, and recount stories of former worthies whom he had known and valued; to Dr Gilbert Murray on Boar's Hill, Visitor to Manchester College and commemorated by a bronze plaque in the chapel, inscribed with the motto from Epictetus: "Think of me as immortal, and go your ways as immortal, too". Jim Maxwell was a gangling, awkward junior Fellow of Balliol, who often called to see us. We sometimes met in the Bodleian, where he was busy editing one of the less well-known plays of Shakespeare. In the course of time, he became a lecturer at Newcastle University, but before he left Oxford, knowing I was a keen mountain-climber, he gave me his precious copy of the Scottish Mountaineering Club Guide to 'The Isle of Skye', inscribing it to me at 'Christmas, 1949'. Many years later, back in Oxford, I had dinner at Balliol and met him once again, no less shy and retiring than when I knew him thirty years before. A good fellow, still a 'loner', he died some years ago, but I remember his friendly presence with gratitude. I made other good friends in Oxford from whom it was hard to part when we left for Northern Ireland. But one I recall with special affection, the late Harold Spicer, organist of Manchester College for over fifty years.

Harold was one of the friendliest and best-humoured persons I ever met. A small, perky little man, unassuming and cordial, he was popular with students and staff alike and full of quips and quiddities. His musical abilities, capacity for teaching, and services to the art in Oxford were recognised by the University in 1949 by the award of the degree of Master of Arts, *honoris causa*. In that year and for several years afterwards he acted as bursar. It was during this period, when I was acting-principal, that we came into closest contact, since we regularly discussed most college administrative matters and often went in tandem to make purchases. His training of the choristers was always careful and cheerful. From time to time, he gave a series of talks to the theological students on 'Music and Worship'. During the week, he taught music at Smithfield school and subsequently became director of music at Culham College, climbing on to a light motor-cycle, which carried him to and from his classes. His voluntaries, anthems, carols at Christmas, and hymn tunes (several of which he himself composed) were a special feature of

Harold Spicer, June, 1958

services in chapel. Until March 1959, he had a choir of about 16 boys and six men at his disposal. Both my sons were at one time members of that choir. Needless to say, the procession of officiating clergy and choir was a feature of the chapel services which astonished, and even offended Unitarian 'puritans' from outside Oxford who occasionally dropped in on a Sunday morning.

Harold completed a period of fifty years' service on 23rd March 1966. On that day, a special anniversary celebration was held in the Chapel, followed by a reception in the Library. I came over from Ireland to be present, and my elder son, Peter, travelled up from London for the occasion. As a large crowd of friends and admirers was expected, admission was by ticket. It was a unique affair in the history of the College: "Most remarkable evening of my life", wrote Harold to me shortly afterwards. Not only was he a fine musician, he was one of Nature's blithe spirits and gentlemen. Alas, he was becoming deaf, and so decided to retire in December 1969, dying in April 1977.

Some time before we left Oxford for Ulster, my wife, Joan, started to do some supply-teaching, to help with our growing family. It was at May Roath's suggestion, and she readily took on more of the domestic chores to make this possible. Joan was an Oxford graduate with a good degree in History and before our marriage had taught at her old school in Sheffield. From this time on, she valiantly supplemented the family income and made it possible, when we moved to Belfast, for me to run a small, second-hand car which was essential for visiting and very useful on holiday.

In Belfast, she applied for and obtained a permanent post at Kelvin Secondary school, where she taught until 1967 and made a name for herself. When the school expanded and acquired a modern library-building, she became librarian, responsible for book-buying, classification and cataloguing. Before long, she was considered an authority on school-library management and was in demand for talks on the subject. Later, in Cambridge, she also taught full-time at Netherhall School and became Careers' mistress there. Her contribution to our home-economy was invaluable and enabled us to afford good holidays in the West of Ireland and abroad. Looking back, I think it would have been difficult for me to continue in the regular ministry without her help.

7

ULSTER – AN ENGLISHMAN AT LARGE

"So here I am, in the middle way".
T.S. Eliot: *East Coker*

We rose early on the boat that was taking us from Liverpool to Belfast, and walked the deck, to see the new country in which we were about to make our home. It was early April and still a nip in the air. The ferry executed a complete turn, and went in stern first between the marker-buoys, slowly passing the shipyards and factories which make the port at once a fascinating but somewhat forbidding place, especially on a dull, rainy day. But there are compensations. The view to the north and west of the city reveals the hilly framework in which it is comfortably set. Cave Hill to the north and Divis (over 1500 feet) to the west are prominent features, easily seen from city streets. On the south side the Lagan valley is an escape route that for years has been begging to be tidied up and developed as a tourist attraction, if not as a park for the inhabitants of an urban sprawl which owes little or nothing to town planning. There are, however, some buildings of character, a few façades of distinction, a remarkable City Hall (1907), and some twentieth century additions like the Royal Courts of Justice and St Anne's Anglican Cathedral. An eighteenth century church with an oval interior shaped like the prow of a ship, with exquisite galleries and box pews throughout, which John Betjeman once called "the finest example of Georgian architecture in Belfast", was soon to become very familiar. To this, the First Presbyterian Church (1783) in Rosemary Street, in the heart of the city, I was called to minister. It had lost its Central Hall in the German air-raid of May, 1941 and only a small 'minor hall' remained. One of my tasks would be to help replace the Hall, to raise the money to ensure it was a worthy restoration.

Our first days in Belfast were, in a phrase with which we soon became conversant, somewhat 'strange and startling'. We were moving into a house in the rather prosperous suburb of Malone, number 26, Cadogen Park. This had been the manse for at least two of my predecessors. It was large, double-fronted, with gardens back and front, a fairly daunting problem of maintenance, and, in the winter, very cold. Bear in mind, this was before the advent, on any large scale, of domestic central heating. (My successor insisted on central heating being installed, only to find it was too expensive to operate!) Though fond of gardening, I discovered the upkeep of the garden was rather more than I bargained for. There was no garage, and I had been advised by a senior colleague that I would not be able to tackle the rather formidable chore of pastoral visitation of a widely scattered membership, without the aid of a car. I did begin by cycling all over the hilly city, getting very wet in the process, but in the end I was compelled to invest in a second-hand 10 h.p. Morris, which I managed to run around for about four years, continually patching it up and being helped to keep it on the road by a friendly garage owner and his very helpful son. God bless them both! There were no 'car allowances' for ministers in those days, so throughout my ministry in Ulster I was never assisted with the purchase, maintenance or repair of the series of second-hand vehicles I owned.

But to return to those first few days. The ordination and installation service at the church had been arranged for the Thursday morning, three days only after we landed. Imagine the haste and anxiety with which we prepared for this event, awaiting the arrival of our furniture and belongings and trying to clean the house for their reception! We had been told that the cleaning would be done before our arrival, but, alas, it was not. The removal vans were upon us before we could possibly be ready for them, so we just did our best and lived in utter chaos for a fortnight or more thereafter. Someone had been engaged to dig the overgrown garden into some semblance of order. But, again, this was hopelessly inadequate.

So came the Thursday of the solemn Presbyterian installation, which we were all expected to attend. It was a long and trying ceremonial for an exhausted minister and his family to endure, but there was more to come. Luncheon followed at the Presbyterian Hostel near Donegall Square, and at this there were speeches from a whole cadre of worthies. My younger son, Richard, (aged 9) afterwards asked "Why did so many ministers get up and drink lemonade and call it toast"? This went on into the early afternoon, when, at last, we were free to go home

First Presbytarian Church,
Rosemary Street, Belfast

for a brief respite and a cup of tea. Then at 7.30 p.m. we had to be back again for an evening meeting, when the church and the Sunday School would welcome the new arrivals. The Moderator of the Non-Subscribing Presbyterian Church of Ireland joined us on this occasion. Fortunately, I knew him well: we had been in college together. But the senior elder of my new church greeted us at the door with "You are late, and the Moderator is waiting for you"! We then jumped through the hoops of 'welcome' for a second time, and, faint but pursuing, just about managed to stand up and politely acknowledge the kind sentiments expressed by the new team of speakers enlisted for the evening meeting. At long last, the day's proceedings came to an end, and we were permitted to creep back to our untidy home and fall into bed. I remember saying, "Well, if that is what it's going to be like in Northern Ireland, I think we've made a big mistake!"

However, we soon realised that any other experiences of the kind

Interior, First Presbytarian Church, Belfast

could only be less horrific! And this proved to be the case. My ministry in Belfast was the longest in my life, fifteen and a half years, and, though the work was hard and demanding, it was also varied, upon the whole enjoyable, and rewarding.

In 1952 the congregation numbered well over 300, and families were scattered all over the city, some into Counties Down and Antrim. Visiting has always been a high priority in Ireland, and I used to return from calling upon members completely shattered with fatigue. I kept a record of all visits, and was specifically advised to do so by one of my church-officers, who knew his people well: they might complain that "the new man hasn't been to see us yet"! Before I left Belfast in 1967 I had paid a total of not less than 8,600 visits to houses and hospitals. An unexpected difficulty attending this duty at first was the accent. Irish people are, usually, never short of a word, and some enjoy a monologue, if *they* are delivering it. Hence, listening, and trying to make sense of what people were telling me was rather hard labour, and not seldom I was only, with great difficulty, able to keep my drooping eyelids from closing. After six months or so, I became more adept at interpretation of the Ulster accent and idiom, and grew to love them both, so that now, in after years, it is 'music to my ears' when I return to Ulster (or the Republic) or hear an Ulster voice on the phone.

Life in Ulster was more gracious than in England, surprising as that now may seem. As the years rolled by, the kindness and hospitality, and the charm, of the Irish, call it perhaps their 'ancient courtesy', both North and South, deeply impressed me and mine. In the shops and in the streets, we met with generous consideration, with concern and warmth that, alas, are rarely encountered in England today. Strange it is that alongside evident intolerance and bigotry there still exists a fund of humanity and cheerful bonhomie that oils the wheels of intercourse. Again and again, Englishmen who spent some time in Ulster during the War have confirmed this truth. As to organised religion, the position of the minister in Ulster is jealously safeguarded, and attachment to one's church is real and active. Moreover, it was not long before we discovered how much more generous Ulster folk were than English, when it came to financial support for the Church and other charitable causes. This was brought home to me, as we sought to finance the rebuilding of our bombed and demolished church hall.

One attraction of the 'Belfast Adventure' for me had been the challenge to replace the old Central Hall (1886). During the raids upon the city in May 1941, the main hall and offices were destroyed, and all that was left was a small, inconvenient shell of a 'minor hall' in the rear of a levelled waste. Plans for a replacement had been prepared, but the architects had produced an elevation which was what *they* wanted, rather than what the congregation could afford. The war-damage claim could never have been settled on those terms. So we were faced with insisting upon plans that accorded with our proper needs and ability to pay. This meant seriously re-briefing the architects and clearing up the uncertainties about the piling that would be needed on the site.

Central Belfast consists of land literally floating on silt or sleach, to give it another name (i.e. waterlogged mud). Beneath a crust of earth, this sleach goes down for about sixty feet. I learnt a lot about construction-problems during the erection of the new Central Hall. For instance, piling in an area consisting of unstable mud and gravel, like the banks of the River Lagan, presents real complications. The eighteenth century builders of the church (1783) had overcome these by erecting a 'raft' of material to carry its weight. But the completely new building to be

The Central Hall, Belfast

erected alongside the church would be made of heavy steel and concrete and therefore could not be treated in that way. In the event, we decided to pile for posterity, putting in sufficient new foundations to carry yet another storey on top of the three we intended in the first place to build. Some day, our successors may like to 'go one better' and erect a set of offices which will bring them in rents to help meet what, no doubt, will be inflated costs. It is a satisfying thought. The building contract was signed early in 1958 and the piling alone cost £8,000. The building proceeded on a modified plan, which we insisted should include a proper stage and provision for lighting, flats and so on, for the church had an excellent dramatic society, and the architects had originally only given us a shallow platform. Then, to our dismay, the clerk of the works fell ill and died. I then made it my duty to be on the site at least two or three times a week, checking. For six weeks no work was possible at all, because the architects failed to provide the builders with drawings! Subsequently, when the wiring and electrical components were waiting to be installed, the builders still had no information regarding the conduits in which the cables were to be placed, so they went ahead and poured the concrete, regardless! Of course there was a row about the consequences of this, since unsightly plaster infills had to be constructed to cover the electric cables in every room. The consultant engineer would not permit incisions to be made in the ceilings for fear of weakening the steel reinforcement. All this may seem somewhat technical now, but then it became a bread and butter matter to me. At this point I should, perhaps, explain that the minister is himself chairman of the church committee in Presbyterian churches in Ulster and so plays a much more responsible role than is generally the case in English nonconformist churches. In due course, the architects committed several other 'bloomers'. Possibly the worst was the large ornamental window they designed for the main hall, over the entrance to the building. When glazed, the panes of glass cracked within twenty-four hours. Glazed a second time, they cracked again. Clearly the design was at fault. The big London firm who constructed the window actually sent their chiefs over to Belfast to discuss the situation with our church committee. They and the architects tried to fob us off by saying that someone must have placed a ladder against the window to clean it (i.e. more than once!!). This was so absurd and untrue that it only aroused our contempt. The church committee simply refused to accept the window as designed; and after much argument the makers reluctantly agreed to re-construct the window on lines that we suggested, with two main braces across its width to render the whole structure stable. Since we had a hand in designing the new model, not a pane in the window has cracked in over thirty years. So much for architect-designed windows.

The other big mistake the architects made was not to consult the fire authorities. The fire-escape stairs outside the building at the back were eighteen inches too narrow to suit regulations, and every step the whole way down had to be widened to that extent, quite a large welding operation! There were many other infelicities, proclaiming inefficiency and lack of imagination and demonstrating the inability of architects to envisage the everyday needs of the users of the buildings they plan. It is a sad reflection upon the construction boffins that they sometimes seem devoid of foresight and commonsense.

However, at long last, on 7th November 1959, the new Central Hall was opened by the Right Honourable John L. Andrews, M.P. at a cost of £51,000, of which the sum of £37,000 was war damage compensation. It is probably the finest building of its kind belonging to any church in the denomination, comprising a hall on the first floor seating two hundred and fifty or more, a minor hall capable of holding sixty, cloakrooms and toilets, two kitchens, a church lounge, two committee rooms, a caretaker's flat and a vestibule and lift serving all floors. On the ground floor are five shops whose rentals have been a godsend to church finances. Some years later, at my suggestion, the rest of the site, behind the hall, was drained and paved to form a carpark available for the use of members on Sundays and weekdays, when functions are in progress, and by local shop keepers and others during the week. This carpark is also a welcome source of income, but I must add, for the record, that several members of the church committee were only with difficulty persuaded of the need and advantage of utilising in this way the space available.

I have run ahead at this point because the saga of the re-building of the Central Hall was a major feature of the early days of my ministry in Belfast. Needless to say, the question uppermost in the minds of members of the congregation was how the money could possibly be found to pay for the building, when it was realised there would be a shortfall between the cost and the amount of War Damage compensation the church had already secured. What I proposed, and what was agreed by the committee, was that we should make an appeal to our people and our friends and raise a £10,000 building fund forthwith. This would bring all our folk together and, properly organised and managed, would not only service the Hall but unite members in a worthwhile cause. We prepared an attractive coloured brochure, illustrating the building and its character, and putting the case for giving generously, and this we distributed amongst members and friends, asking for donations and pledges to donate over a number of years, and we arranged to visit individuals and families to explain the scheme in detail. When embarking on an appeal like this, one cannot leave anything to chance: it must be planned down to the slightest detail. Publicity is important, and questions must be answered. We did not appeal to people's generosity in vain. Many English friends also responded, and on the day of the opening I was able to announce that we had already reached a total of more than £9,200. More was to come, and shortly after the end of the year we also received from anonymous donors sufficient money to enable us to add the lift, which has been such an aid to elderly and infirm folk coming into the hall.

The possession of such a fine hall in the heart of the city now gave me the idea that it would be good to arrange occasional public lectures on subjects of popular interest. This would make the new hall better known and provide a service to the community. So, for several years, a series of lectures was held each March and attracted not only members of our own denomination but a number of visitors. Amongst the lecturers were Sir Alister Hardy, F.R.S. from Oxford, Brigadier J.C.G. Broadhurst, formerly adjutant to Glub Pasha, commander of the Arab Legion, Mr Leonard Huxley, the Nature conservationist from Scotland, and several leading Unitarian ministers from England and Ireland. I had hoped to engage a speaker on "The Bible in the Light of Modern Knowledge", who was to have been a professor from the Presbyterian Assembly's College, but unfortunately he withdrew, not wishing to enter into controversy that might ensue from a public pronouncement. Just at this time Mr Ian Paisley was coming to the fore as a fundamentalist and bigoted 'Christian' spokesman, and it was, perhaps, understandable that a member of the Presbyterian Establishment did not relish the idea of getting embroiled with him and his intolerant followers.

Turning now to congregational affairs, which normally took up most of my time in Belfast, I think I may say that I was blessed with good health throughout the whole of the fifteen and a half years of our stay. I can only recollect two occasions when I was unable to conduct Services on a Sunday, owing to illness. Sunday was usually a long and trying day. At 10.30 a.m. I conducted a senior class of youths and maidens in my vestry, and stepped straight up to the pulpit for morning service at 11.30 a.m. Back home for lunch, I would often return for a discussion-circle meeting at 4 p.m., followed by a picnic-tea and evening Service at 7 p.m. Some time after 8 p.m. we would reach home, tired out. The morning Service was the peak hour of the day, however, and at this the choir would usually sing an anthem, well-chosen and well-rehearsed. They would also sing an anthem in the evening, or, alternatively, one of our principal singers would sing a solo. First Church possessed a splendid Lewis organ and, for many years cultivated a tradition of good music. A 'music committee', independent of the church committee, was elected annually, and had general oversight of this side of church life. 'Music Sunday' was an annual celebration, at which a classical, baroque, or modern work of some length and importance was performed, to a full house. I recall many a memorable rendering of Bach, Mozart, Handel, Vivaldi, Schubert, and later composers' work. Sometimes the organist would bring in instrumentalists and a school choir, to grace the occasion. An especially enriching experience would be the singing of Eileen Ervine, whose beautiful contralto voice possessed a quite unique range and who was in great demand for concerts and charitable efforts throughout the Province. She was principal for 43 years, to 1967, when I left Belfast, and continued so until the severe handicap of arthritis prevented her regular attendance. The congregation donated a silver cup to the Belfast Musical Festival to commemorate Eileen's great talent and unique services to the church, and in June 1967, at a 'Music Sunday' Service, the church expressed its deep appreciation and presented her with an inscribed gold watch. Twenty years later, I visited her in her bungalow home, where one of her loyal daughters cared for her still.

Another musical event of a different kind found regular place in the church's year, from 1955 onwards. This was the Carol and Candlelight Service on the last Sunday before Christmas. I first mooted the possibility of this to our devoted Sunday School superintendent, James Meneely. I said to Jim, "Do you think we could ask our folk to loan their brass and silver candlesticks for a special Service of carols, to be sung by candlelight? How lovely it would be to light the old church down the centre of the pews, in the window embrasures, and all round our glorious, oak-fronted oval gallery. What do you think"? Jim, a thoughtful fellow and 'one of the best', paused for a moment, and then replied, "Doctor, we should have to go cannily with this one. You know, the very thought of candles in our church might paralyse some of our people! They might think we were apeing the RC's." But, being a man of some imagination, he could see the possibilities of creating a really inspiring Christmas 'happening'. We thought we would 'persuade' the congregation to 'experiment' (to begin with), and I issued an invitation to members to loan their candlesticks. The choir presented a splendid programme of carols, old and new, and members shared the readings. This became a much-loved annual celebration of Christmas, and, in the seventies, a united Service in which neighbours, the Roman Catholic chapel of St Mary's and the Church of Ireland, St George's, continue to share. After a long illness, Jim Meneely died in hospital on 10th December, 1970. There were over 300 people present at the Crematorium. Jim endeared himself to generations of Sunday School children as well as to all the members of the congregation. When the church urgently needed to be re-wired, being a Post Office executive engineer, he undertook the task and called in the assistance of another loyal and devoted member and craftsman, Fred McMurray. These two saved the church hundreds of pounds. I wrote a memorial notice of this humble and loyal-spirited man, my valued friend.

"Apart from his work, where he was both respected and liked, Jim had two great life interests: Masonry and the Non-Subscribing Presbyterian churches. He served both with a single-eyed devotion to their aims and a thoroughness and enthusiasm quite remarkable. A puckish sense of humour and a lively wit endeared him to all who knew him. He was a pillar of the church, serving on its committees and as property-steward from the 1950s onwards. He represented the church on the old Hemsworth Square Managers' Committee, on which the church's interest in the Riddel Memorial School was maintained. Additionally, he sat on the committee of the Belfast Domestic Mission and gave the Mission his loyal support through difficult times. He was a regular figure at denominational gatherings and always willing to help any of our weaker causes in their need. His personal interest in our community never wavered. For years, quietly and unostentatiously, he performed little services for ministers and congregation, like the regular changing of the 'Wayside Pulpit' board or the fitting of an extra light in church or manse, which made life easier for all concerned. For years, he shared responsiblity for the carol and candlelight Service, and, in the mind's eye, one can still see his face beaming with pleasure as, under his direction, the candles were lit one by one. How symbolic of his own life this was, for unconsciously, he lit candles of faith and fellowship in many a heart by his kindnesses. The lantern of a good man's life is inextinguishable, and the flame of friendship outlasts the years."

I have mentioned Jim Meneely's connection with the Hemsworth Square Schools committee on which I used to sit. It consisted of representatives from different denominations whose schools had been taken over by the education department of the city council. It had a say in the appointment of teachers to vacancies. For an 'Englishman abroad' this proved an educational experience. One instance must suffice. As vacancies occurred, applications would be submitted to the schools' committee, who selected their choices and sent these forward to the city education committee for acceptance or rejection. The applicants were encouraged to canvas for the votes of committee members, and this at a time when young people were just sitting their finals' examinations. Northern Ireland congratulated itself on making progress 'step by step' with the rest of Britain, but this was a politician's boast rather than a reality. In the matter of educational appointments it was definitely out-of-step! I appealed to my fellow committee members, and got a journalist friend of mine to highlight in the Press what was happening, in order to discourage canvassing. (It soon got about that no one need call with their references, to wait upon the minister of the First Presbyterian Church.) I succeeded in checking this pernicious custom and getting a memorandum sent to the city Education Committee deploring it. Believe it or not, this body agreed with the principle of 'no canvassing' in general, *but* stated that qualified teachers "might *send* round their respective papers *for inspection* by the members of the local school boards". The art of 'having it both ways' could hardly have been more prettily illustrated.

In 1956, after the Hungarian uprising against the Communist government, numbers of Hungarian refugees began to arrive in Ireland. Camps were set up near Dublin and two centres were established in County Down, one in a large hotel in Bangor and another alongside an army camp near Dundrum. I joined the committee responsible for these people and visited both 'camps' several times. The Northern Ireland centres were considered to be merely temporary places for families who would eventually be accepted in Canada and the United States. In fact, this is what happened; these unhappy people were gradually syphoned off to permanent homes, mostly across the Atlantic. We did our best to make them comfortable, but there could be no possibility of their settling down in Ulster, where there was already high unemployment and a serious shortage of housing.

The following year, I was invited, as an official guest, by the General Synod of the restored Moravian Church to attend the Quincentenary of the Moravian Brethren, the *Unitas Fratrum*, the oldest Protestant Church in Europe. I left Belfast on 21st May and was met next day in Prague station by friends from the Unitarian and Czechoslovak Churches. Very early next morning, I was driven out to Zelesne Brod for the anniversary Synod. This small town is in the heart of the Bohemian glass-making industry, and whilst there we were taken round one of the factories and presented with specimens of their wares. I was struck by the poor refreshments served at these meetings and also by the inefficient organisation, though the welcome for the foreign visitors was warm and genuine. A peculiar feature of our visit was the fact that the Government provided us all with 'pocket money' (200 crowns per day). Evidently, the Communist authorities intended to give a favourable impression of themselves. After the meetings, the visitors from the West were taken on a thousand-mile coach tour through Bohemia, Moravia

Dr Miloš and Rev. Alena Kanák with the author in Prague, June, 1957

and Slovakia, passing places familiar to me, and stopping off at towns and villages with special associations for the Moravian Brethren, e.g. Kralice, Brno, Uhersky Brod, Bratislava, Modra, and Fulnek. At nearly all these places our arrival was greeted by large crowds and an official reception committee. Clearly, the authorities were determined to give us the 'red carpet treatment'. We were expected to attend a meeting and to address the assembled company. Often, arriving very late at our destinations, we were almost too exhausted to speak, and divided the duty between us so that at least half of us could get a meal and some sleep. A week of this tested the stamina of even the most athletic!

We were accompanied on this tour by English-speaking Communist party commissaries, who kept an eye upon us, to prevent our wandering or seeing what we were not intended to see. At last, back in Prague, I slipped off to pay a visit to the British embassy, whilst the main party was taken to a large church for a concert. My absence was duly noted, and when I rejoined the main body I was asked where I had been! I had no intention of satisfying our guardians' curiosity. Next, we were taken to the Hradčin to be given a pep-talk by the Minister responsible for church life in the Republic. Coffee was served, and we were told that all was well with the churches under the aegis of a communist administration. Of course, we had observed for ourselves a very different state of affairs, and had been told just how difficult the government made things for ministers and church organisations in general. After the formal talk, I tackled the Minister about the fact that Professor Kaňák had not been permitted to travel to Oxford earlier that year. He was to have taken a place reserved for him at Manchester College for a short period of study relating to his work on John Wyclif. "You have been talking about the need for exchanges of scholars and information between your country and the West, and yet you have prevented just this in the case of Dr Kaňák", I said. "How can you defend this behaviour"? To say the least, the man was flummoxed. He attempted an excuse, muttering something about 'armaments' but I believe he took the point, for within a few months Dr Kaňák, a distinguished historian, was given a permit to travel, and made his way to Oxford.

The Misses Eliza and Isabella Riddel were wealthy sisters, the last of whom died in 1924, aged 92. Their benefactions were many and generous. To First Church they gave its splendid Lewis organ, and to Queen's University and the Royal Victoria Hospital endowments for research and health-welfare. The Riddel Memorial School (already mentioned) benefitted from their generosity, whilst in 1913 was set up the first hostel for University-women in the city, a pioneering venture in its day and one of the finest establishments of its kind in the United Kingdom. By virtue of my position as minister of their former place of worship, I was a member of the permanent committee of Riddel Hall. When its fiftieth anniversary approached and I discovered how small its financial resources were, I moved to set up a Jubilee Committee to celebrate the occasion and to raise a substantial sum of money to increase the endowment of the Hall, which already had been such a boon to the University and, in particular, to its women-members. It was a cause very near to my heart. The monthly meetings of the management committee, chiefly University people, were always pleasant affairs. Miss Molly Dawson, the warden, entertained us to afternoon tea, after which, in spring and summer, it was a joy to wander round the well-kept gardens and gaze on the vistas which the large estate commanded. The memorial Service to the Riddel sisters in May 1963, just fifty years after the opening of the Hall, was held in First Church. The warden and the head of the house read the lessons and I gave the address. (Some 12 years later, the Hall had to be abandoned through lack of funds for its maintenance, and the assets were given to the University in trust.)

Generally-speaking, the day-to-day life of a minister of religion can hardly be described as exciting. Certainly it does not provide material for headlines, unless the man (or woman) is an eccentric, a fool or a sinner. Newsworthy it may not be, but this does not mean that it is not a busy life. It has its peaks of activity, and also its plains of humdrum duties, and it makes varied and often demanding claims upon both time and thought. Apart from preparation for services of worship, reading and writing, visiting, conducting special services, funerals, weddings and baptisms, the minister is also a citizen and must play his part in community affairs. He is also expected to take his share of denominational responsibilities beyond his own church. By 1962, it became clear that my turn had come to act as Moderator of our small group of churches. At the Synod that year I was elected Moderator for two years. This entailed a large number of extra engagements: conferences, installations of ministers, committees, and unusual and unexpected calls for special addresses and services.

During his period of office, the Moderator is the head of the Church, presides over Synod and several committees, and is officially recognised as the representative of the denomination *vis à vis* the public and the Government. Two invitations came my way; first for my wife and myself to a garden party at Government House, Hillsborough, Co. Down, and second, to a garden party at Buckingham Palace. We accepted the former, since we could travel there in our own buggy. The latter we declined with regret, as we could not afford the fares to London. I still possess both beautifully-printed cards, neatly addressed to 'The Rt. Rev. Dr and Mrs McLachlan' – a form of address proper to a Moderator and his lady during the two years of his Moderatorship. Afterwards, I reverted to 'Very Reverend Doctor' and eventually shed the artificial wings and became plain 'Rev'. Incidentally, in Ireland, as in England hitherto, I was determined to wear a clerical collar only on a Sunday and for weddings and funerals. I was told that the Irish would hardly recognise me as a minister, unless I conformed to the habit of clerical dress. I'm afraid I turned a deaf ear to this advice and wore a tie most of the time. Frequent visits to the hospitals in the city and beyond made me quite well known, and my best mixed Manchester and Oxford accent (!) carried me unfailingly to the wards where my people lay. In any case, I had learned, years ago, to talk myself through any barriers of bureaucracy or suspicion. The recipe is boldness and an air of "I have been here before".

The public standing in Ulster of the small Non-subscribing Presbyterian Church of Ireland, of which the First Church, Belfast is a leading member, was consistently high. Traditionally, its ministers and laity had a fine record of conscientious liberal-religious ministry and continuous civic responsibility. For over two centuries the Non-Subscribers (to the Westminster Confession, i.e. creedless, standing purely upon the Bible interpreted by reason) were known and respected, even though the majority of Christians might not be of their persuasion. Hence they are often called upon to take their place, as a matter of course, in public worship and on ceremonial occasions, whereas English Unitarians have had long experience of neglect and even ostracism. This is partly due, no doubt, to the fact that the Established Church of England holds a special position in relation to the State, whilst in Ireland, since Disestablishment, this is no longer the case. All the Irish denominations are on a more equal footing than are their counterparts in England, and this makes for much better relationships.

As an incomer from England, I soon became aware of this difference. For example, the year after I settled in Belfast I was invited to take part in the official Remembrance Service at the Cenotaph in Donegall Square. Along with church, government, and city representatives, I stood and offered prayer before the laying of wreaths and the sounding of 'The Last Post', a moving experience. Later, I was asked to conduct several broadcast services, one of which was recorded for overseas listeners. In November 1966, I prepared a special service for United Nations Day, which was heard all over the British Isles. Whenever possible, I tried to sound an eirenic and reconciliatory note. For instance, in the church calendar for January 1961, I wrote "Religion is not a matter of words and doctrines. It is primarily a disposition, a way of life. Biblical fundamentalism and intolerant literalism are manifestly anti-religious. They are also dangerous in the context of the tensions of our time." And in November 1966, I reiterated the ethos of our churches and ended, "The point to bear in mind is that Christianity is a religion of the spirit, not a religion of external authority. It is only as the human spirit recognises the spiritual authority of the Master and reflects his faith, hope, and love in everyday life that true religion is born and can flourish, making every day sacred and regarding every human being as a 'child of God'".

It is sometimes said that the churches are too often concerned with their own theological and domestic affairs to bother about social problems. This is untrue. Most, if not all, denominations are well aware of the need for social service and make this an important priority. The Unitarian Union for Social Service was founded as long ago as 1906 and was responsible (in the words of its charter) for bringing "the religious spirit into social service and the spirit of social service into religion". Subsequently, the General Assembly of Unitarian and Free Christian Churches set up a Social Service Department which, in the mid-sixties, surveyed just how the Unitarians were fulfilling this aim. As a matter of interest I sat down and listed the activities of my own congregation in this respect. The result was so encouraging that I wrote an article (anonymously) to *The Inquirer*, (the denominational weekly) of which a commentator wrote: "this congregation (is) making a valuable corporate effort to assist many voluntary associations, and its individual members form a band of social workers far more active than any of the eighty other churches which cooperated in this survey".

Community-service had always appealed to me. When in 1958, on the initiative of the Dublin Lions Club, and in particular of the late Archie Preston, an attempt was made to found a Lions Club in Belfast and I was invited to become a charter-member, I had no hesitation in accepting. Charter Night was 20th February 1959, and I was elected honorary treasurer for the opening period. There were 25 original members, all chosen from professional and business men of good standing. We were fortunate in our first president, Bert Mason, who was largely responsible for the rapid spread of Lions throughout Northern Ireland, and who eventually became International President of the movement. The club grew influential in the city, promoting charitable causes, especially the welfare of the elderly and the young handicapped. It purchased a coach to convey old folk and children to the coast for spring and summer outings and ran 'Meals on Wheels' for pensioners living alone. At Christmas there was always a concert and tea for the old folk and a parcel of goodies for each of them to take home. The club raised money for its useful service-activities in all kinds of ways, and managed at the same time to run social occasions for members and friends that made for good comradeship and solidarity.

The senior cultural club in the city was the Belfast Literary Society. This met about half-a-dozen times each winter at the residence of its president. In keeping with its age and status (founded 1801), each meeting was solemnly announced by a printed invitation, giving details of the event and providing a synopsis of the paper to be delivered, so that members might prepare themselves for discussion, which was usually animated and serious. Generous refreshments were a feature of the meetings. Early in 1962, I read a paper on 'Friedrich Nietzsche and the Spiritual Vacuum of our Time'. Our family had spent a holiday in Sils Maria in the Upper Engadine the previous year and had visited the philosopher's old home, and my latent interest from student days in Heidelberg had been re-awakened. In 1965, as president, I entitled my address, 'A Song of Ascents, or Clerical Climbers, a chapter in the history of Mountaineering'. It was the centenary of Edward Whymper's ascent of the Matterhorn, and lent itself to some research on mountaineering priests and parsons, since two clerics had attempted the summit of the Matterhorn on the same day in 1865, one of them falling to his death. The paper was afterwards published in *Irish Mountaineering*, 1966, the journal of the Irish Mountaineering Club, of which I was a member for a dozen or more years.

Another society whose meetings were always rewarding was 'The Eclectic Fraternal'. This met at regular intervals, winter and summer. It consisted of a number of liberal-minded clergy of different denominations who met in each others' houses to read papers on theological and related topics. The comradeship and friendly exchanges were most welcome and re-assuring in a Province noted for religious divisions and sectarian violence. Leading members were Dean Hughes of Dromore, Dr Frazer-Hurst of Belfast, Dr A.L. Agnew, and (latterly) Rev. Michael Dewar, of Magherally, Co. Down. The last-named acted as honorary secretary and was (as he himself confessed) "probably the most conservatively evangelical member", but recorded his indebtedness to those of more 'Liberal' traditions "who are always so much more amiable than those whose theological 't's' and 'i's I cross and dot"! In a farewell letter in 1967, he wrote, "God bless you always on behalf of us all".

Such wider contacts as these (and others) helped to prevent my becoming too inward-looking or provincial in outlook, always a distinct possibility in church circles. Membership of Manchester College Council, which I retained during the whole of my time in Ulster, also kept me in touch with theological developments as well as friends and colleagues in Britain. I travelled over to England for quarterly meetings in Oxford and London and was always present at the Closing Proceedings in June. I also served for two years as Visitor to my old college in Manchester and made a point of attending the annual meetings of the General Assembly. I could thus keep *au fait* with events 'across the water', refreshing old friendships and making new, which served me well, when I subsequently returned home to England.

One fortunate circumstance, for which I shall always be thankful was my friendship with Kenneth* Gill Smith of Evesham and his wife, Ruth. Kenneth was an ex-pupil of my old school, Willaston (1905–9), a solicitor by profession, and a director of, and contributor to, the *Evesham Journal*. His grandfather had founded the paper and his father was, for a time, chairman of the Evesham Borough Library committee and keenly interested in the promotion and maintenance of the Upper-Avon Navigation. Kenneth followed closely in his father's footsteps. Not least among his interests was the Unitarian chapel in Oat Street, of which he was chairman for many years. I got to know him well during my years in Oxford, walking with him and my colleague, Priestley Phillips, who was for a time Unitarian minister in Evesham. When I left Oxford for Ireland, Kenneth told me to consider his home my 'pied à terre' in England. He was as good as his word. For over fifteen years, on almost every visit I made to England I hardly ever failed to spend at least one night as his and Ruth's guest. He was a Worcestershire countryman at heart, kept pigs and poultry, and loved a country walk. Despite defective vision, which made it impossible for him to drive a car, he had an uncanny knowledge of the country terrain. He had cycled most of the roads and walked most of the hills. Full of the local lore, he was a delightful companion on a stroll along the banks of the Avon, which ran through meadows below his house, or up Bredon, along the Malvern Hills, or through Broadway and over the Cotswolds. He could relate many a spicy story of Worcestershire farmers, market-gardeners, and tradesmen, often dropping into the local dialect of 'Evesham and its Vale'. He wrote a useful guide of that title and published it in 1954 under the auspices of the town council and chamber of trade. It was dedicated to the memory of his father, William Gill Smith (1860–1927) "Alderman of the borough, who loved and served Evesham well". More than once, he and his dear wife took me to see a Shakespeare play at Stratford, Ruth driv-

*Kenneth, it was, who made us a present of a young dog, Rob, offspring of his golden retriever, who, for more than eleven years was the faithful companion of our family when the children were growing up. He was killed crossing the Belfast–Dublin road on his way home from an overnight foray. We missed him sorely.

ing us there and I driving home to 'The Orchard'. Finally, in August 1982, my old friend died and I travelled up from Sheffield to conduct his funeral and the town's Service of Thanksgiving. That I could retain a small stake (as it were) in a lovely piece of the English countryside was an uncovenanted mercy that I owed to dear friends, whose companionship and kindness remain a haunting memory. No wonder that another old solicitor-friend, living retired and alone in a Belfast hotel, not one of my flock, whom I often used to visit, more than once wryly exclaimed, when I turned up: "To what fortunate circumstance do we owe this visit, Sir, and how long will you be staying in these parts"?

A good deal of my time in Ulster, especially in the sixties, was taken up with work in the public sector. I considered it important to lend support to progressive movements of various kinds and, in particular, to agencies that were working for peace and international understanding. Soon after coming to Belfast I had helped to revive the city branch of the United Nations Association. This proved to be a fateful decision, and led on to a series of events which I must now describe.

A tragic aftermath of the Second World War had been the huge numbers of refugees and displaced persons cut adrift in Europe and elsewhere, many elderly, many handicapped, and all living in temporary and unsuitable accommodation. They formed an intractable problem. A number of younger politicians and others came up with the idea that a vigorous attempt should be made to address this problem and put an end to the wretched camps in which so many refugees were living. In short, they proposed a 'World Refugee Year' to raise money *and* the consciousness of people, so that civilised society should make a real effort to remove the stigma of 'the forgotten people'. Before long, David Ennals (now Lord Ennals) the general secretary of the United Nations Association, paid a visit to Belfast. He came to arouse interest and support for the 'World Refugee Year'. The chairman of UNA in Belfast brought Ennals to our house to discuss what should be done in Northern Ireland. For me it was a momentous visit. I could not resist the invitation to head a Northern Ireland Appeal. This extended over several years from 1956 onwards and involved churches, schools, voluntary organisations of all kinds, charities, women's societies, trade unions, mayoral committees, and the like. By the autumn of 1957, well over £17,000 had been raised and in September David Ennals wrote to the honorary treasurer of the local appeal:

> "We have now received from N.I. the sum of £17,346, raised for work among refugees. This is a truly remarkable achievement....and a great tribute not only to the enthusiasm of those who organised the appeal....but also to the support and cooperation of so many members of voluntary organisations and churches. With the exception of London the contribution from Belfast was by far the largest of any city in the United Kingdom and was, in fact, more than 5% of the total sum raised. The response to the appeal has made it possible for some 6,000 refugees in Austria, Germany, Italy and Greece to be found homes and jobs away from the squalor of the camps. With the funds raised in Northern Ireland we have been able to help the physically and mentally handicapped, those suffering from TB, children and young people, whose future was so bleak while they remained in the hutted campments."

It must be said that we had a splendid WRY committee in Belfast, all of whom worked very hard visiting and speaking on behalf of the appeal. Eventually, with the agreement of my church committee, I was appointed part-time Regional Officer of UNA in Ulster, and for three years, until 1960, I travelled all over the Province speaking on international topics and showing slides of UN headquarters in New York, which I visited in 1958. Luckily, I found in the Editor of *The Belfast Telegraph*, Jack Sayers, a sympathetic ear. For him I wrote, from 1957 onwards, a number of articles on the UN and allied topics. Prior to UN Day in October, I made a practice of circularising every RC priest and Protestant minister in Ulster, commending the Organisation to them, asking them to mention it in their Services and prayers, and offering to supply literature and material for addresses on the subject. In response to more than 1200 letters sent out, I usually received around one dozen requests, which I'm afraid does not speak very highly of local concern for world peace and international understanding....at least amongst the representatives of organised religion.

Pleasanter were my contacts with schools and societies. More than once, I spoke on international affairs at Coleraine High School for Girls and at several Belfast schools, addressed women's clubs in town and country, and helped to found a new branch of the United Nations Association in Londonderry.

My most interesting personal contact was with an old lady in her eighties in Keady, Co. Armagh. Miss Margaret Dunlop arranged a tea-meeting to which she invited friends whom she hoped would become members of UNA. She was a doctor's daughter, the elder of two sisters, who lived in a charming old house, 'Annemount', with a large garden, beautifully situated amid fields on the outskirts of the little town. Her sister, Martha, cultivated the garden, whilst Margaret managed the house and public relations! They had been brought up Presbyterians, but Margaret's naturally inquiring mind and penchant for reading had given her the itch to be ever on the look-out for community and philanthropic causes which she might support.

An inveterate letter-writer, from the early sixties to within a few months of her death in 1975, she bombarded me with epistles, most of which I kept, because of their intrinsic interest and the light they shed upon family life in Ulster, just before, and during, the first half of the twentieth century. In March 1962, after my first visit to 'Annemount', she concluded her letter with, "God help you, having me on your list of correspondents"! At almost ninety, she described herself as 'a problem girl'. Her shrewd observations on life, her fund of anecdotes, and her occasional citations from her 'commonplace book' entertained me and mine for nigh on fourteen years. This unusual, brave and questioning soul suffered for over twenty years from severe recurring shingles, for which she tried many remedies, including charms. She fought the good fight and finished the course in an old people's home in Armagh city on 18th March 1975. When I last saw her, she was reading the life of Albert Schweitzer, whom she greatly admired. I think she was one of the most *caring* individuals I ever met: against cruelty of any kind, especially cruelty to children and animals; against the death-penalty; against war; against religious prejudice and violence, and deeply shocked by the 'troubles' which broke out shortly after I left Ulster. She wrote to the Pope about bull-fights; to the Archbishop of all-Ireland about live hare-coursing; to the Belfast papers about bigotry and the maltreatment of minorities and the condition of refugees. "I am a rebel", she proudly told me. "There are many things I just can't swallow." Not for her to see a wrong committed and 'pass by on the other side'. Her description of a Hellenic cruise she undertook in the seventies was hilarious; she hated the snobbery which she then encountered. Her racy accounts of local life and people, family picnics, and the natural setting of life in Co. Armagh around the turn of the century were vivid and unusual.

Margaret's mother lived to be 97 and was greatly beloved by her family of doctor-sons and daughters. "She never preached to us about religion", wrote her filial daughter, "She lived it every day before us".

Building the Old People's Home (for Yugoslav German-speaking refugees) in Wels, Upper Austria, August, 1960

Margaret nearly outlived her, dying at the age of 96 years and four months, modest, thoughtful, courageous, lovable and liberal.

In the summer of 1960, I thought it might be instructive to join a group of UNA volunteers who were working in Austria, building an old people's home for German-speaking refugees from Yugoslavia. I persuaded one of the younger members of the congregation, Wilson Baxter, to accompany me, and before long we arrived at Wels, in Upper Austria, to spend a fortnight on this scheme. There were about a score of us from Britain, a mixed party of young men and women acting as labourers under the direction of an Austrian clerk of the works. The fact that I could speak German and had had experience with International Voluntary Service before the War was an advantage. We were soon busy mixing and conveying concrete and mortar to the site, loading and laying bricks, even placing steel girders in position for the roof, and generally performing the heavy, physical tasks which the construction-industry entails. I remember one day, working on the sunny side of the buildings, knocking off the wooden shuttering from the window frames, with the perspiration pouring from me, when the clerk came round and told me to 'knock-off', to my great relief! It was an education in building techniques that taught us both a lot. On Saturdays, we were seconded to do a half-day's work for German-speaking ex-Yugoslav farmers who were erecting their own houses. The Austrian authorities insisted on their first excavating a cellar, to prove their *bona fides*. We helped with this and then with brick-laying, using the huge hollow bricks common on the Continent. The gratitude of these refugees, who had been kicked out of Northern Yugoslavia because they were German-speakers, was quite touching. I still possess a letter of thanks from the farmer with whom I spent my Saturday mornings. Some years later, when touring Austria with my wife and our companion, I called at Wels and was able to show them the completed old people's home, now occupied, and meet the local Roman Catholic priest who had entertained the UNA volunteers during our stay there. Looking back on this period when we "scorned delights and lived laborious days", I think I can say that both of us gained much from our experiences. The 'refugee problem' became part of our lives. It was no longer merely an item of 'news'. One happy consequence was the contact I was able to make with the Wels branch of Lions International, who organised a splendid dinner in a local hostelry for all our volunteers and expressed their strong desire to form closer ties with Britain.

Two years later, I became chairman of the Belfast branch of UNA and was closely associated with a second campaign to raise funds. This time it was for the 'Freedom from Hunger Campaign", an early attempt to tackle starvation and underdevelopment in several countries of the Third World. The Northern Ireland Council of Social Service called a meeting to launch the movement. The Earl of Antrim was elected chairman, and Mr G.B. Newe and I agreed to become vice-chairmen. Mr Denis P. Barritt, a leading Quaker, was appointed full-time organising secretary. Dr Stuart Hawnt, then Director of Education for Belfast, chaired an educational advisory group. The project in which Northern Ireland was asked to interest itself was an irrigation scheme in Mwea-Tabere in Kenya. 'Christian Aid' and 'War on Want', schools and many organisations were roped in to assist, and two flag days were held. The Campaign exceeded its target of £100,000 and, in addition, affiliated organisations raised another £20,000. The practical result? One thousand five hundred acres of dry and barren land were converted into an area capable of supporting 350 families. I was asked to represent the N.I. effort at a Progress Committee meeting at the Central Hall, Westminster on 25th November 1964. Mr J.M. Nicholson (our assistant-secretary) and I went over to London, and were introduced to His Royal Highness the Duke of Edinburgh. This effort was, of course, on a much larger scale than the 'World Refugee Appeal' and commanded more influential support, but again, it showed that the people of Northern Ireland only had to understand a pressing human need in order to give generously and repeatedly.

Internationalism continued to claim my attention. The following year, 1965, was the twentieth anniversary of the signing of the United Nations Charter. UN Day fell on Sunday, 24th October, and the year had been denominated 'International Co-operation Year'. It was therefore decided to mark the occasion by holding a united act of dedication in the Ulster Hall, led by the Belfast Choral Union, the Ulster Singers, and several other choirs. Dr Havelock Nelson agreed to conduct and Mr Edgar Boucher to play the organ. More than eight hundred people of different Faiths attended. Readings were taken from the Scripture of six different Faiths and I was asked to give the address. This was an affirmation of support for the ideals of the UN, conceived as a modern expression of the love and service to mankind which all the higher religions profess to inculcate. The welfare of mankind was the aim of the specialised agencies of the UN, and it was the duty of all to strengthen the forces of peace and to attack, not each other, but the true enemies of humanity: injustice, poverty, disease, national selfishness and pride, abuse of power, and the hatred and intolerance which set people against people.

It is certain that a Service of this kind had never before been held in Belfast. We were breaking new ground, but the cultivation of these sentiments and their growth in Ulster was to be slow, especially amongst the older generation, and it is to be feared that organised religion was not yet in a position to take the lead.

The BBC, for its part, did its best. It arranged a special Act of Worship for UN Day, broadcast on the Home Service. This I conducted, and in the Notes intended for the Press and internal information, the official comment ran:

> "Dr McLachlan is widely known for his humanitarian views and has devoted much of his life and work to human rights and the ideals of the United Nations. One of his objects in Northern Ireland has been to unite all religious faiths and denominations in common support of the UN."

In Northern Ireland at this time there was no branch of Amnesty International, the Human Rights organisation founded by the London lawyer, Peter Benenson. My son, Peter, drew my attention to this organisation shortly after its foundation and I joined immediately. In conjunction with Professor George and Mrs Brenda Dick, a number of friends set up a branch in Belfast. Several university men and women came to its support. In our group, of which Brenda was the honorary secretary and I the chairman, there were four doctors and three barristers. Two of the doctors held chairs at Queen's University and had already been associated with the World Health Organization. We tried to enlist the support of churchmen of all colours. But, again, they appeared to be too busy and hesitant to ally themselves with "a voluntary organisation (of this kind) in spite of its worthy objects" (the words of Dr W.J. Philbin, the Roman Catholic Bishop of Down and Connor in a letter to me). The timidity, even unconcern, of some ecclesiastics when humanitarian organisations solicit their support, has always amazed and disappointed me.

We adopted several 'prisoners of conscience', in accordance with Amnesty custom. These included one in Greece, who was being maltreated by the military government of the day, a left-wing doctor who was in jail in Portugal, and a Roman Catholic priest who was held by the Communist authorities in Budapest. We wrote letters on behalf of these and other 'forgotten men and women', whose only 'crime' was that they were opposed to their governments upon conscientious grounds. We were also determined to raise money for the general work of Amnesty. Our first big effort was an Art Sale, to which we invited artists in Ulster to donate pictures. I was able to secure a large room in Riddel Hall where we could display the canvases and entertain all those invited to wine and cheese. The sale was conducted on the lines of an 'American Auction' and netted well over £400.

Just before I left Belfast, in September 1967, we arranged a Concert in the Whitla Hall of the University in aid of Amnesty. On this occasion, Dr Havelock Nelson and members of the Queen's Music Society were of great assistance. We invited Bernadette Greevy, the Dublin contralto, to give the recital and she was accompanied by Dr Nelson. It is good to recall the generosity of the two artists and the University authorities, who made no charge for the use of the Hall. Altogether, in my experience, I have found artists and musicians rather more sensitive to humanitarian appeals than the professional representatives of religion. A sad thought.

As the year 1967 sped by, I was approached by friends in Cambridge to consider the possibility of moving back to England. The minister of the Memorial (Unitarian) Church in Cambridge had died, and this left an attractive vacancy. The idea of leaving Ulster had not occurred to me, though all our children had, by this time, left home. Peter, after graduation at Oxford, had entered the Northern Ireland Civil Service, worked for a time at Stormont, and was now administrator of the National Youth Orchestra in London. Richard had graduated at Trinity College, Dublin, proceeded to York for a crash course in Administration, and then worked in Enfield as a local government officer. Jane, after graduating in Social studies at TCD had gone to Toronto for wider experience in social work, returning later to the London School of Economics and a post in London. Thus there were no family ties to keep us in Ulster. I felt I had probably stayed long enough in Belfast to warrant a move to less strenuous activities. So I paid a visit to Cambridge in April and discovered that the decision really rested with me. Back in Belfast, we held a family powwow and decided that the time to return home had arrived.

As soon as the news became public, I received many expressions of regret and goodwill from a wide variety of people and organisations. I quote only one of the kind letters that I received. John E. Sayers, editor of *The Belfast Telegraph* wrote:

> "My dear Doctor, I am one of the very great number of people in and out of your own Church who have read with a sense of loss of your impending departure from Northern Ireland. The thought first in my mind is that we can so ill afford to be without such a leader. But, at the same time, I am sure that a change to the congenial atmosphere of Cambridge must be something of a reward for all your unsparing work here. I shall remember warmly your great liberality of mind and your world-wide outlook, in keeping with the greatest traditions of your Church. Please be assured that you have helped to set an example that we shall strive to follow. Yours sincerely, John E. Sayers".

The *Belfast Newsletter* more than once referred to my leaving the city, e.g. on 13th September:

> "Dr John McLachlan, who has been one of Ulster's most energetic churchmen for more than fifteen years, leaves Belfast at the

end of this month. His departure is described by everyone who knows him as a great civic loss."

My farewell Sunday on September 24th was a moving affair. It followed a meeting in the Central Hall, whose rebuilding had been such an important feature of the early years of my ministry. At this, members of the First Church expressed their appreciation and made a presentation. In many ways I was sorry to be leaving, but I have learnt that there are times when big decisions have to be made, and this was one of them. The religious–political tensions, so long endemic in Ulster society, had always troubled me and I had supported every effort to bring the two communities, Protestant and Catholic, together, in mutual toleration and respect. Forces inimical to this were, however, emerging. A bigoted and politicised religious fundamentalism was raising its head and threatening to produce chaos, whilst, on the other hand a new impulse was being given to Irish nationalist fervour by the human rights movement. New initiatives were needed. The year before I left, in April 1966, a fresh attempt was made to bring Christians of both communities together at the Corrymeela Centre in Ballycastle. Captain O'Neill, the then prime minister, made the theme-speech on 'The Ulster Community'. Other speakers followed. It was noteworthy, however, that three out of the five were not Ulster born. One was a Canadian, another a Scot and I an Englishman with Scottish ancestry. I spoke on 'Northern Ireland and the World Community', trying to lift people's eyes to the larger scene in which world-history was being made. Remarkable and indicative of Ulster's ills were the confessions of young people present at that conference. They had never met their opposites until now! In many cases, the Roman Catholics and Protestants simply had no idea what those of different communions looked like or thought! So far, each had remained completely isolated in their own ghettos.

Two years later, the explosion, which the chairman of the small Liberal party in Ulster had told me was predictable, and which only required the lighting of the already-laid touch-paper, occurred.

Shortly before we left Belfast, my next-door neighbour, Robert McCall, the BBC Controller in Northern Ireland (1956–66), a Scots-Australian and a very good friend, had recommended my appointment to the BBC Religious Advisory committee. This was for a four-year term. I joined the committee, but soon realised that conservative forces were in the ascendant. There would be no liberalising of processes or programmes if they could help it! It was the same picture in the political field.

The year 1968 had been designated by the United Nations as 'Human Rights Year' and, before leaving Ulster, I had been invited to deliver the 'Essex Hall Lecture' for 1968 and to address the problem of human rights. Essex Hall is the headquarters in London of the General Assembly of Unitarian and Free Christian Churches and stands on the site of the first avowedly Unitarian congregation gathered in 1774. Many distinguished people have contributed to the series over the years, and its delivery is deemed one of the leading events of the annual meetings of the Assembly. I prepared a script entitled, 'Human Rights in Retrospect and Reality'. I was actually at work on this on the 12th of July 1967, when my wife, Joan, May Roath and I drove down to the calm and beauty of Dundrum Castle in County Down. Here, overlooking the sea and away to the 'Mountains of Mourne', we could escape the noise of the drums and fifes of the Orange marches on 'the Glorious Twelfth'. Briefly, I summarised the nature and development of human rights, touched on the philosophy and religious practices underlying democratic systems, discussed the importance of the UN Charter as a step forward towards human welfare, and concluded with an appraisal of the Declaration of Rights of 1948, its meaning for mankind and its linkage with peace and justice for all. I wrote:

> "The defence and promotion of human rights is also the defence and promotion of peace and security. The struggle for human rights constitutes a fundamental element in the campaign for peace.
>
> Fear and prejudice still divide mankind. But in the closely articulated world of our day the human mind must stretch itself to adapt to the very revolutionary material changes that are taking place. Man's spirit needs to grow into line with the vast development of science and technology. At present, most of us are walking about "in worlds unrealised". We cannot afford to do this much longer. Hence the pressing task of the next decade is to educate our minds and discipline our spirits to grasp the import and opportunities of an interdependent world-society. We have to create a community which understands that the purpose for which peace is really desirable and should be strenuously sought after is that it offers the possibility for human personality to fulfil itself, to attain life that is not merely existence, liberty that gives wings to thought

> and spirit, and happiness that is real well-being, because linked with the welfare of others." (p.23)

When we left Cadogan Park in September 1967, I dug up most of my Irish roses and transferred them to the boot of my car. Apart from memories, I would have those to remind me of fifteen and a half years in Belfast, and the many happy (and unusual) experiences that came our way in beautiful Ireland. As I write, twenty-two years later, I can look out from my study-window and see roses from Dicksons of Hawlmark (Newtownards) which remind me of happy days and dear friends, not a few of whom have passed 'into the world of light'. My family and I greatly enjoyed our time in Ireland, our freedom of movement within the Province, our holidays in the West, Donegal, Galway, Achill Island, Connemara, Clare, Kerry and West Cork. But probably, most of all, we remember the kindnesses and hospitality we received from so many people, North and South, town and country, over the years, and last, but not least, the privilege of serving not only our churches but the community at large in small matters as in great. "A minister's duty", wrote the late Dr Frazer-Hurst in his fine autobiography, *The Bridge of Life* (1962) "can never be fully discharged within narrow ecclesiastical boundaries". To this I say a fervent 'Amen'.

8

LAST POST – AT CAMBRIDGE

"And so each venture is a new beginning."
T.S. Eliot: *East Coker*

Returning to England after a long absence proved 'a new beginning'. It was not the England we had left in 1952, nor was the religious scene the same. I was prepared for a secularised society, but hardly for the 'retreat from the churches', the flight from faith, which had taken place, and was accelerating, it seemed, the decline of organised religion.

It took about three years for me to realise just how far our own small group of churches had lost ground. But from 1970 onwards I had ample opportunity to 'test the denominational water' and I found it cool, and getting progressively cooler. The steady loss and closure of many of our chapels and the extreme shortage of students for the ministry boded ill for the future.

Nevertheless, I was looking forward to what would probably be my last active ministry, and realised my good fortune to be going to a denominationally-conscious and influential congregation in a university city where possibilities of growth no doubt existed and there was a goodly company of men and women welcoming our family home.

We arrived in Cambridge on 28th September 1967, with only a portion of our luggage, as our crossing from Ireland coincided with a dockers' strike. Moreover, the removers' men, having suffered delay, refused to empty the vans unless they could be assured of overnight expenses. It transpired that there was a serious lack of liaison between the Blackpool firm and its Birmingham colleagues, who were responsible for unloading. But members of our new congregation came to our rescue. The Induction Service, conducted by old friends, was a happy and helpful one, whilst the welcome meeting which followed, and to which the mayor of Cambridge had been invited, was, on the whole, low key and

The Memorial (Unitarian) Church, Cambridge

appropriate. It was somewhat unusual from the fact that two representatives from my old church in Belfast had come over to support us and bring greetings and good wishes. To our delight, our two sons, Peter and Richard, now both in London, turned up and gave us the feeling that we had, indeed, come home.

My first service in the Memorial Church took place on Sunday, 8th October. When I entered the church, I was startled to find that the whole congregation rose in their seats, a practice to which I never really became accustomed, and one that the hardy puritan tradition of Ulster Protestants would have spurned as inappropriate. That said, it must also be recorded that, on the whole, Irish Protestants do treat their ministers kindly and are often really generous to them, no doubt not caring to be outdone by Roman Catholics who, they hold, are far too obsequious and indulgent to their priests.

The Memorial (Unitarian) Church was built in 1928 with money donated by Mr G.W. Brown, 'a man of business', in memory of his daughter, Jean Millicent (1888–1921), who, I believe, was drowned in the River Cam. In style, it is classical after Christopher Wren and, though comparatively small, is well-proportioned and beautifully furnished with oak panelling, reading-desk and pulpit. The marble dais, reached by steps up into the apse, can present something of a hazard to anyone unfamiliar with the layout, but the risk of a fall is compensated by the beauty of this end of the church and by the cleverly-concealed lighting which accords with the canons laid down by the architect, Ronald P. Jones, one of the Unitarian patricians of his day. I found my rock-climbing experience helped my balance as each Sunday morning I negotiated the polished marble steps in full view of a standing assembly!

For many years, the congregation had enjoyed distinguished leadership and represented a leading intellectual and liberal-minded group amongst British Unitarians. The change from Belfast was challenging, but rather less satisfying devotionally because of the lack of a choir and good choral music. However, an accomplished musician presided over the small but pleasant-voiced pipe-organ in the gallery at the rear, and his services always contributed immensely to what otherwise might have been merely a 'hymn-sandwich' Service.

The congregation contained an interesting mixture of university and townspeople. University fellows, school-teachers, retired professional and business folk, personnel from the American air force base at Alconbury, and a regular sprinkling of visitors from Canada and the United States. Also we were never short of a few undergraduates, coming and going. I refrain from mentioning any by name, but cannot forget how many talented and public-spirited men and women of liberal views composed this community.

I was now in East-Anglia and could take to cycling again! From De Freville Avenue, where we occupied a detached house with a pleasant garden at the rear, I could spin into the town in a few minutes. In no time, one could be across the river and over Midsummer Common or Jesus Green to Trinity Street and 'The Backs'. At peak traffic periods a cyclist could usually beat the cars, especially at the roundabouts, which Cambridge planners had obviously constructed in a mood of the triumph of hope over reality. There were, though, considerable hazards, especially when heavy traffic circulated through or around the town, presenting a vicious threat to cyclists (of which there were many) and not seldom causing injury and sometimes fatalities. I must add, however, that the only time I was knocked off *my* machine was in Trinity Street by an undergraduate whose brakes, apparently, did not exist: he toppled me from behind!

Of course, it was convenient to be near London. But there was a price to be paid. I was hauled, willy nilly, back into the stream of denominational affairs. Committees and other engagements began to take up a good deal of time. Essex Hall, the Unitarian headquarters, became once more very familiar, whilst a new venue, for meetings, though formerly for study, was Dr Williams's Library in Gordon Square. I had spent many hours there, years before, on research, but now I was called upon to act as a trustee of the founder, the 18th century nonconformist minister, who left his large estate for the benefit of Dissenting ministers and students and founded a valuable library, and a girls' school in West Wales. Dr Williams's trustees had to be nominated and 'sworn in' at a curiously archaic ceremony intended to impress all concerned. I suppose it was my nearest approach to Masonry! I regarded the trustees' quarterly meetings, followed by a good dinner garnished with finger-bowls, old silver, not so old wine, and a very peculiar trimming, roly-poly pudding, served by express order of the Founder, as probably my closest approximation to a London club. Of course, we had to 'sing for our supper', that is to say, serve on committees, and I considered I earned my keep. But these were truly pleasant occasions, especially when the chief guest was someone like the historian Elizabeth, Lady Pakenham, whose father had been president of the General Assembly of the Unitarian churches and who had something precious to say.

It was, you may say, convenient to be near London for other reasons. The Festival Hall concerts, the Royal ballet, a play, a musical, or an exhibition of pictures at the Royal Academy or the Tate were great temptations, to which I succumbed more than once. I was able to indulge my interests in music, archaeology, and art. The Tutankhamen Exhibition at the British Museum took me back years to my schooldays, when on Sundays Lang Jones used to read us the accounts of the discovery by Howard Carter and Lord Carnarvon of the burial treasures at Luxor. The Turner and the Constable Exhibitions at the Tate and the display of Goya's canvases at the Royal Academy were equally fascinating and stimulating.

But Cambridge had its aesthetic attractions, too. Most of the colleges had their musical societies, and there were regular chamber-music recitals in the Music Faculty's building and often, at lunchtime, in the Fitzwilliam Museum. This unique art collection was a constant attraction to which we always took our visitors. I joined the Friends of the Fitzwilliam, who organised lectures and excursions to galleries in London and elsewhere, published occasional illustrated papers, and made donations which enabled the Museum to purchase items which otherwise it could not afford. Residence in Cambridge also brought us close to our children. Peter lived at first in Marylebone, and, after his marriage, in West Wickham. Richard was in Enfield, and Jane, after a period abroad in Toronto, settled in South London, and after her marriage, in West Hampstead. We were also nearer to old friends in Ampthill, Evesham, Thetford and South Wales.

Sundays in Cambridge did not entail such heavy duties as they did in Belfast. For a time we held two Services, morning and evening, but the evening service was poorly attended, and it was finally decided to concentrate upon morning worship and to arrange a series of musical recitals on Sunday evenings in winter, instead. These took place in the Carpenter Hall, immediately behind the church. It was the place where Unitarian services were held before the church was built. Our own people supported these recitals which also drew a fair number of visitors. Besides proving a successful and much appreciated series of chamber-concerts, these Sunday evenings provided a platform for young musicians in the Cambridge area, of whom there were many, to play or sing. My son, Peter, was at this time administrator of the National Youth Orchestra, with an office in London, and I was fortunate to have made a number of contacts in both town and university, so that between us there was no shortage of artistes upon whom we might call. I mention only one recital that was arranged but never came off, because of its international aspect. This was to have been a pianoforte recital by Alexander Percy-Holoček, a specialist in the interpretation of Beethoven's sonatas. This young Czech musician, born in 1935, was the son of a well-known opera and symphony conductor and had married an English girl who happened to be a friend of mine. He was a member of the Union of Czech Performing Artists and worked as a musical agent dealing with Anglo-Czechoslovak exchanges. He had agreed to play three sonatas, and the programmes had been printed and distributed. But at the last minute his courage failed him. The reason? He feared that the authorities in

Prague might get to know that *he had played on church premises*! He felt that this might affect his chances of continuing his regular work. I intend no reflection upon the young man's decision, but being well-acquainted with the 'hard line' stance of the Czech Communist party, which was viciously anti-religious and Stalinist, I think this incident is indicative of the political situation subsequent to 'the Prague Spring' and the intervention of Soviet Russia in the interests of orthodox Communism and atheism. There was never another hitch in the series of most enjoyable concerts which ran from the autumn of 1968 to the spring of 1976.

In Cambridge, of course, we were able to enjoy a feast of music: concerts in King's Chapel and the Senate House and organ recitals in several college chapels. In 1970, when the Chicago Children's Choir were on tour in England, I booked them to visit Cambridge, staying overnight with members of our congregation and friends. They sang in the Guildhall and we sold enough tickets to more than cover their expenses and send them on their way rejoicing. This was an unusual and striking combination of young voices, which had a direct appeal, was authentically American, and left a distinct impression of their ability, training and enthusiasm.

Specifically ministerial duties, naturally, were a priority, but are unlikely to be of general interest to my readers, so they need not detain us here. A Unitarian minister is expected to prepare carefully for his Sunday duties, and since the sermon traditionally takes pride of place, he usually spends a good deal of time in his study. But special Services, funerals, weddings, anniversaries, and, last but not least, denominational committees and public duties make regular inroads upon his time throughout the year. The special nature of a Cambridge ministry soon became apparent to me. In term, we held 'At Homes' every Tuesday, serving coffee and biscuits from 7 p.m. onwards. To this came undergraduates and, very often, ordinary members of the congregation. It was always a busy evening, with people coming and going and much lively discussion of things new and old. We also entertained numerous visitors, many of them from abroad, Canadians, Americans, Hungarians from Transylvania or Budapest, young couples wishing to get married in the liberal atmosphere of a Unitarian Church, even on one occasion a young student who had come to church to find out exactly what Unitarianism could be. He came with a long list of questions on theological and doctrinal points, and then asked to come back with another list of questions on matters of morality. We would discuss what kind of service those wishing to be married felt appropriate, and tailor the service accordingly. I would never insist upon a rigid form of service, but was always prepared to create new forms to suit different points of view or religious conviction. This flexible approach is usually appreciated by those concerned, especially if the partners come from widely different backgrounds and religious traditions. Some of the happiest and most satisfactory unions have been those in which the young people have taken a really serious view of the precise nature of the form and words of the marriage ceremony.

A regular feature of the Memorial Church's year were the meetings of the Literary and Social Fellowship, held in the church lounge midweek. Coffee was served, and then followed a talk on some topic of general interest, illustrated, perhaps, by slides. In the summer, the Fellowship arranged coach-outings to a 'stately home', a National Trust property, or a historical site. In the winter, a party would travel by coach to London, to a concert in the Festival Hall or to a theatre or ballet. Each year, just before Christmas, the members held a Christmas dinner in the Carpenter Hall, for the provision of which the various members made themselves responsible. Menus were specially crafted, tables decorated, and some kind of entertainment organised. The Carpenter Hall looked at its best on these occasions and remained decorated for a children's party that followed a special children's Service the next day. As always at this season of the year collections were taken for charities, and the sick members of the congregation would be remembered by gifts of flowers and fruit.

The mention of flowers brings me at once to remark on an outstanding aspect of Services in the Cambridge church, namely the flower arrangements. These were always striking and tasteful, and enhanced the beauty of the interior of an already chaste and lovely building.

The ladies who put their hearts and souls into the decoration of the apse, made it a sanctuary and a focal point upon which the eye rested with joy and inspiration. On special anniversaries you could always be sure that the flowers on the altar-table would reflect the importance of the occasion. An unusual decorative element, which added richness to the interior, though modestly hiding from superficial view, were the embroidered memorial-kneelers of four different designs, which incorporated the initials and dates of departed worshippers. The idea was, I believe, that of a lady architect and former member of the congregation, who laid down the designs to be followed and very kindly designed a special kneeler for the reading desk with all our family's initials embroidered on the upper surface. The series of memorial-kneelers is still continued to this day.

From the outset Cambridge presented another challenge when I learnt, on inquiry, that the local branch of Amnesty had actually petered out. It had to be revived and established as a completely new unit. In due course it became one of the most active and flourishing branches in the country. Its members adopted 'prisoners of conscience' in Greece, Rhodesia, South Africa, the Middle East, Russia, and South America, and raised large sums of money for the whole British movement. Knowing how successful had been the Art Auction in Belfast, I suggested that we should hold another similar event in Cambridge. We appealed for donations of oil and water-colour paintings and drawings and persuaded Trinity College to allow us to hold the display in their Old Kitchen and Common Room. Invitations to a wine and cheese party were issued and a grand total of over £650 resulted. This was probably our most successful money-raising effort. Several of our own congregation played an active role in the Cambridge Amnesty group and two were office holders. We hired St Michael's Hall nearly every year for a sale and took a stall in the market place more than once. In August 1975, with some help from Oxfam, we organised a charity walk that took place in November. I cycled the twelve miles round a course east of Cambridge, setting up the direction-signs, and then returned to the starting point to walk it myself. The walkers were sponsored, and raised a considerable sum. Other means adopted to raise funds included garden parties and second-hand book sales, many of the books being review copies in very good condition.

The 'Prisoners of Conscience' for whom we worked were an assorted collection: Peter Nieswand, the *Manchester Guardian* journalist in Northern Rhodesia, and an Iraqi for whom I lobbied at the Iraqi embassy, where the deputy-ambassador entertained me to coffee alongside Peter Benenson, who happened to be there on similar business! At that moment, the embassy officials had no idea who was in charge of the government in Baghdad. On another occasion, two of us visited the Soviet embassy on behalf of an Ukrainian nurse, who had been in prison for twenty years. My colleague, a lady, spoke fluent Russian, whilst I chipped in from time to time, and even dared to suggest that the Soviet treatment of political prisoners was little better than that meted out to their opponents by the Nazis, a remark that made the official very angry; but it was true.

However, it must not be supposed that Amnesty alone engaged my extra-ecclesiastical attention in Cambridge. When we arrived from Ulster the Vietnam War, with all its horrors, was still in progress. The damage to civilians and, in particular, the suffering of children on both sides could not be overlooked by anyone alive to the awful personal consequences. It occurred to me that it would not be inappropriate for the famous university-city of Cambridge to form a committee to raise money for medical and surgical supplies for the benefit of child-victims in both North and South Vietnam. In my innocence, I thought the then vicar of Great St Mary's, the University Church, might be one to whom I could turn for help and sympathy with this project. I therefore called upon this leading churchman to ask for his support in bringing the matter before the Cambridge public. Unfortunately, I received little or no encouragement from him. He fobbed me off with the suggestion that the right person to approach was the Mayor. Rightly or wrongly, he left me with the feeling that the idea of helping children of the 'Communist' North, as well as the South, did not really appeal to him. So off I went to interview the Mayor, who did not hesitate to co-operate, and before long we had an appeal-fund in being and a city bank lined up to receive donations.

In the summer of 1968, Hungarian Unitarians in Transylvania celebrated the four hundredth anniversary of the foundation of their churches, and were joined by fellow-religionists from all over the world. My wife, May Roath and I flew out with the British party to Budapest, via Prague, and travelled on by coach to Cluj-Napoka in Transylvania. This city was the centre of the celebrations. Here Hungarian Unitarianism had its headquarters, a large church, a college for the training of ministers, and a secondary school. Our Hungarian friends gave us a warm welcome, but we were impressed by the poverty and backwardness of the Romanian State and society. Communism seemed to have done little to bring happiness to people in this part of the world. Always open to corruption, the rigid bureaucracy and inefficiency of Romanian daily life seemed calculated to destroy personal initiative and morale. We visited a number of the old Hungarian-speaking churches scattered through the lovely valleys, attending services, rallies, and celebratory dinners. At the last-named, local Party functionaries, who appeared to be inevitably present, made long, propagandist speeches, intended to produce the impression that the Marxist government afforded all the

Christian churches full liberty and toleration, which, in fact, was not the case. They were until 1990, strictly controlled by an arm of government. On one occasion, at dinner, I sat next to an English-speaking Romanian teacher, who told me she specialised in 'the modern English novel'. I offered to send her a parcel of recent paper-backs, if she would send me a translation of the Government spokesman's speech to the assembled company. This appeared to be an apologia and defence of Romanian government policy towards the Hungarian and other minorities in Transylvania. She promised to do so, but (as I half-expected) this promise was never kept.

From the moment when we crossed the Romanian border, we realised we were in a police state. The police had orders to confiscate any religious or political literature that we might be carrying. We were held up almost three hours whilst inquiries and searches went on. Subsequently, at the request of one of my old fellow students, a Hungarian minister who spent two years at our college in Manchester, I mailed copies of Sir Alister Hardy's Gifford Lectures on science and religion (*The Living Stream* and *The Divine Flame*) to Romania. Perhaps I should not have been surprised, but the authorities extracted from the parcel the second volume, dealing with 'a natural history of religion'. Sir Alister's thesis that religion is a basic element of human nature: "what I am calling the divine flame is an integral part of the creative evolutionary process" was evidently quite unacceptable to Marxist materialists, who inspected the contents of the parcel. Sir Alister had kindly given me the copies for despatch to Romania, so that when I told him what had happened, he was as angry as I was.

After our visits to several places of historical interest, including the castle of Deva, where Francis David, the martyred founder of Unitarianism in Transylvania in the 16th century, was imprisoned and died, we returned to Budapest. On our return journey, long lines of troop-carriers and petrol tankers moving into Budapest passed us on their way to invade Czechoslovakia and put an end to the 'Prague Spring'. Orthodox Communists regarded the advent of 'Communism with a human face' as a shocking heresy to be stamped out at all costs. Our official guide in the coach protested that he did not know what was going on, though crowds of people were besieging embassies and government offices, trying to obtain passes out of Hungary before the borders were closed. Our party was due to leave for home within a couple of days, but clearly we could not return the way we had come, via Prague. Fortunately, we were able to change our tickets and arrange to fly out over Austria and via Amsterdam. The American contingent, meanwhile, made a rapid escape in their hired coaches, driving straight into Austria and then through Germany and France. This left the Dutch, French and British delegates to attend a farewell dinner in Budapest and make a less hurried departure.

Sadly, we said goodbye to Professor Miloš Kaňák, from Prague, who would be returning to a city under foreign occupation. He looked quite forlorn as we dropped him off in a suburb of Budapest. However, late in 1969, when I was giving a course of lectures in Boston and Chicago, I found Miloš at Meadville Theological College, Chicago, lecturing to students on Reformation history. The Americans had invited him over and subsidised his stay whilst he continued work on John Wyclif which he had commenced in Oxford at Manchester College and was to complete before his untimely death in 1986. Miloš had been our guest in Belfast in 1955 and I had been his in Prague two years later. He was the greatly-respected professor of church history in the Protestant faculty of the University of Prague, a specialist on pre-Reformation studies and the lives and work of John Wyclif and Jan Hus. We corresponded for over thirty years, and it was largely through him that I was invited over to take part in the quincentenary of the *Unitas Fratrum*, the Moravian Brethren, in 1957. Our family was united with his, not merely by our joint-interest in Reformation and post-Reformation history, but by ties of affection cemented by firm friendship and meetings in Czechoslovakia, Britain, and America. Alena, his widow, continued her ministry in the Czechoslovak National Church, and his son, Bohdan, whom we knew as a small boy, now married and a graduate doctor of his father's old university, was the well-qualified archivist of the Church. Some time ago, Manchester College, Oxford, to its credit, elected Professor Kaňák an Honorary Fellow. It is sad to think that the closing years of this liberal-minded, sensitive and devoted scholar were spent in ill-health under the yoke of a brutal, totalitarian government of Stalinist doctrinaires.

I referred earlier to lectures I delivered in 1969 in the United States. These 'Minns Lectures' were published in 1972 by the now extinct Lindsey Press under the title of *The Divine Image – Religious Humanism from Homer to Hammarskjöld*. Their aim was to discuss the origins and development of a broadly Christian Humanism. Following a suggestion of the late Victor Gollancz, which he once made in Manchester College Common Room, that humanity's great need was a religious humanism or "a more humanistic religion", I attempted to show how the humanist emphasis derives in part from Jesus and also from a stream of undogmatic Christianity which has not received the attention it deserves. Beginning with the roots of Christian humanism within the Bible and in Classical and Renaissance literature and thought, I surveyed 'the Flowering of Erasmianism', the origin and emergence of a humane theology in the 17th and 18th centuries, and, finally, turned to review non-traditional religion and 'the New Humanism'.

My student days in Germany in the early thirties had taught me the absurdity and cruelly deceptive character of any philosophy that idolised man and dogmatically asserted that people could shape and control humanity's development and call it 'progress'. Far better is it to confess that "we simply do not know all the answers". In all humility, we have to come to terms with our mortality and not assume the prerogatives of God, by trying to take the laws of the universe into our own hands. I wrote:

> "The radical fault of anthropocentric humanism, one feels, is not its humanism but its anthropocentric fixation. And the radical fault of traditional Christianity is that it tends to limit the divine activity to a comparatively small area of time and place, whereas revelation, if you wish to call it that, arises rather from a substantial continuum of spiritual energy underlying human life and history.
>
> "Christian humanism....takes in the whole human drama. It lets the world's needs determine its course. It is radical, positive, creative – identifying itself with the sorrows and sufferings of humanity; it is humble but hopeful. It has an open mind on many questions that assail and puzzle contemporary man; but it accepts that man is able to link himself with the forces that make for truth and justice, goodness and mercy; it does not despair of the future, though it is by no means cocksure, and frankly admits that man will have his work cut out to subdue social and international chaos.
>
> Christian humanism pleads for, and works for, a truly, not merely decorative, Christian society. It believes in the abolition of all that is derogatory to man and woman and unworthy of faith in human dignity and destiny. It demands human rights and acknowledges human obligations. Abandoning the absurd claims of dogma and metaphysical systems, it bases its hopes for the future upon the conscience and spirit of man, touched to finer issues by an Inner Light that is the reflection of a 'Light that never was on sea or land'."

I delivered four lectures in the rooms of the King's Chapel, Boston and two under the auspices of the Meadville/Lombard Theological School in the University of Chicago in October 1969. It was then the Fall in New England, a lovely time of the year, and my reception was what one is led to expect from our friendly and hospitable American cousins. Whilst in New England, I preached in Barre, Vermont, where I had been eleven years previously, staying once again with the Rev. John Christensen and his wife, Edith and their family. In Chicago, I preached at the People's Church, whose minister, Dr Preston Bradley, I had known from Oxford days, when he was our guest in Manchester College. At Berkeley, California, I took a Service in the Unitarian church of which our friends Newell and Elizabeth Nelson were members. Elizabeth was the filial daughter of the late Earl Morse Wilbur, the historian of Unitarianism and former principal of the Pacific School of Unitarianism. My father and Dr Wilbur had long been friends. I and members of my family stayed with the Nelsons several times, and they visited us in Sheffield during our retirement. En route for Berkeley, I flew to Phoenix, Arizona to fulfil a long cherished ambition to visit the Grand Canyon, walking from the South Rim and spending a night at the Phantom Ranch. I have described this amazing experience elsewhere.

Whilst in Boston, I was present on the Common on 'Moratorium Day', 15th October, when over 100,000 students gathered to protest against the Vietnam War. Feelings in America against the War appeared to me to be overwhelmingly strong. Many young men made their way to Canada to escape the draft; among them was the son of the Unitarian minister of the Second Church in Boston, whose guest I was for dinner one Sunday. I was struck by the orderly conduct of those who assembled on Boston Common on 'Moratorium Day'. After the speeches and the folk songs and the chanting, they set to and collected all the waste paper and discarded circulars and departed without any commotion. I spoke to one of the many armed policemen present and asked him why the authorities had sent in such large contingents of police. He replied, "You never can tell. You have to be ready for anything". I am inclined to think that the overt prescence of police on such occasions sometimes has exactly the opposite effect to what is intended. It can be counter-productive. I now recall that early in 1968 I conducted the wedding in Cambridge of a fine young American and a lovely Swedish girl, a most handsome couple, who had decided not to go to the United States until the Vietnam War was over.

Cambridge, like Belfast and many other cities, ran a scheme of 'Meals on Wheels' for housebound and handicapped senior citizens, under which volunteers with cars took out hot meals each week. I joined the rota for a time, but dropped out to assist another charity which was attempting to meet a growing need. For some time, groups of men could be seen about the town, aimlessly wandering or sitting drinking spirits on Midsummer Common and elsewhere, obviously homeless, 'down and out'. The foundation of Cambridge 'Cyrenians', organised in 1970 as a limited company, was intended to establish houses for the homeless. There are probably about 200,000 single people in the United Kingdom who are homeless, living in hostels, common lodging houses, night shelters, or sleeping rough – men and women of all ages and, latterly, a large number of young people. All need some kind of support, short or long-term. The Cyrenians specialised in this, and from 1970 onwards owned two houses in Cambridge, one long-stay and the other a short-stay, over-night place. I used to go along taking kitchen, bedroom, and lounge equipment from time to time and relieving the volunteer workers, who tried to maintain the spirit of the place, offering help and friendship. It was not an easy assignment, but I felt it was a humane and worthwhile cause.

Another public duty that has commended itself to ministers over the years lies in the sphere of 'communication', that is to say, contributing short articles to local newspapers. A number of men and women have done this, very often with the encouragement of the press up and down the country, and done it very successfully. The *Cambridge News* for some years carried a 'Thought for the Week', which was much appreciated by readers. This feature was written by local clergymen on a rota which provided variety of approach. I was asked to contribute on a regular basis and did so for a year or two, until the column was discontinued. The Anglican minister who valiantly organised the contributions then told me that the newspaper which, by the way, paid not a penny to those who supplied the copy, never even offered to pay his out-of-pocket expenses, postages and phone calls, etc. for the whole period during which he had been responsible for organising the feature.

Napoleon dubbed the English 'a nation of shopkeepers'. When I look back upon sixty years of active association with public life, and especially on the treatment meted out to ministers of religion *in England* by many of their supposedly caring 'supporters', I am inclined to think there is more truth in that uncomplimentary description than most of us would care to admit!

Denominationally, I was busier during my last ministry than at any other period in my life. The editor of the 'Transactions' of our Unitarian Historical Society fell ill and I volunteered to edit the 1973 issue and carry on, if necessary, until further notice. Unhappily, he died early in the year, so that I continued to edit the journal until 1987, bringing out fifteen issues in all. The work was enjoyable, and kept me in touch with historians of Nonconformity at home and abroad. The post was entirely honorary, unlike some other denominational appointments. I became a life-member in 1929, when I was still a student, and when life-membership cost £5; it is now £50.

Soon after returning from Northern Ireland, I became a member of the General Assembly's General Purposes Committee and Council which took me regularly to London. I also retained my membership of the Committee of Manchester College, Oxford, on which I sat for almost forty years. This met quarterly, sometimes in London as well as in Oxford. Late in 1972, the Nicholson organ in the College chapel was found to require a thorough overhaul. It was decided to move the console over to a sunken well on the opposite side of the chancel and electrify the whole action. To meet the cost of this rather revolutionary change an appeal fund was set up. My brother-in-law, Arthur Vallance, and I volunteered to act as honorary secretaries for the appeal and the late Geoffrey Ramsden agreed to act as honorary treasurer. I approached a number of distinguished musicians, inviting them to sponsor the appeal. In the event, the Queen's Master of Music, Sir Arthur Bliss, Sir Adrian Boult, Mr André Prévin, and the head of the piano manufacturers, Captain Evelyn Broadwood, agreed to do so, and made generous contributions, as did Sir Alister Hardy. To get the work started as soon as possible, the two secretaries provided loans, and when Sir Felix Brunner retired from the honorary treasureship of the college in 1973, he donated a sum of £10,000, of which he allocated £2,000 to the Organ Appeal. The total cost of the rebuild was £9,300.

The college now presents a very different appearance from thirty years ago. It has indeed become a Liberal Arts College, taking in students studying several different disciplines besides theology, and thus, incidentally, returning to its original aims and form. The number of students is usually in excess of seventy and the teaching staff has increased in proportion. I finally retired from the College Council in July 1986, thinking it important that new and younger men and women should take the responsibility of guiding the institution into the years ahead. Latterly, I had acted as liaison between the Council and events in Warrington, where the old Academy building near the bridge across the Mersey, was threatened with demolition. The Warrington Civic Society, the Literary and Philosophical Society, and in particular its two influential members, Dr Paddy O'Brien and Mr Robert Oxley, took a keen interest in its preservation. They appealed to the College Council to support their case and I was asked to prepare a paper for submission to the public inquiry ordered by the Department of the Environment. It is perhaps worth putting on record here the memorandum I wrote in April 1976 at the request of the Council:

> TO WHOM IT MAY CONCERN
>
> "We understand that an application has been made to demolish the Old Academy Building in Warrington, Lancs., under a road-widening scheme and that the Department of Environment has ordered a public inquiry.
>
> In view of this, we should like to make representations, along with others, against such action, in the interests of both local and national history and archaeology.
>
> Manchester College, whom we represent, is one of the heirs of the old Warrington Academy. After the Academy's dissolution in 1786, its valuable Library came to the College, and when the latter moved to Oxford, Warrington friends, in 1897, presented a large stained-glass window to the College Library in commemoration of the Academy, its teachers and governors, and in recognition of the fact that the College was a true successor to the Academy.
>
> Warrington earned the title of 'The Athens of Lancashire' solely owing to the far-reaching influence of the Academy, whose teachers made an epoch-making contribution to the modernising of the curriculum of higher education in this country. Distinguished for learning, they were also noted for their promotion of liberty and freedom of thought. Here, in this first building (the second has disappeared) the new sciences of physics and chemistry and the humane studies of history, geography, and modern languages were pursued for the first time in an institution of higher education.
>
> Warrington was one in a long succession of nonconformist academies, going back almost to the Ejection of 1662 and the beginnings of Dissent. They were designed to provide higher education for men excluded from the universities of Oxford and

Cambridge by religious tests. But Warrington differed from its predecessors in that it aimed to pursue learning and liberty. It was an independent academical foundation (not controlled by any outside Fund) free from State control and ecclesiastical influence, ecumenical in character, and taking students from every part of the British Isles, from the West Indies, and the American colonies. It was the first institution of its kind with such a liberal ethos and aims, and in this way was a forerunner of the modern universities.

The building in which it was first housed is therefore of great historical and archaeological importance. It is a visible sign and token of an educational experiment and ideal of more than local interest and ambience. It, surely, should remain and be preserved as a valuable part of the town's historical inheritance and as a permanent memorial of a chapter in educational history and innovation unique in Britain, for outside Oxford and Cambridge and the Scottish Universities, there was no institution of like eminence.

Signed
President
Principal
Chairman of Council
Hon. Secretaries

Together with other representations, this was successful in preventing the destruction of what has been called "the most interesting house in Warrington". Mr Oxley thanked the college for its support in the following terms:

> "We in Warrington owe a great deal to you for your splendidly constructive response to my letters. All of your suggested references were taken up and a formidable case for the retention of the Academy was presented."

The building made history. It was the first structure in the United Kingdom to be moved in its entirety from one place to another (to make room for a road-widening scheme). An article on it appeared in the journal of the Institute of Building. It was actually moved on rollers about sixty feet from its original site, but it was carefully cradled and restored, and still stands, a witness to the power of properly-organised public opinion to forestall and prevent the follies and carelessness of modern 'planners' and Philistines.

Whilst being closely involved with Manchester College, Oxford, I did not forget my old college in Manchester. For a time I served on the academic committee and acted as Visitor and President. It was always moving to return to 'Summerville', Victoria Park, my old home, and to speak in a building, the site of the old Victorian stables, converted in 1924 into a library and named after my father, 'The McLachlan Library'.

Probably the most hectic year in my life was that which began in the spring of 1971. I was then elected president of the General Assembly of Unitarian Churches. This entailed visiting a great many churches and districts, addressing meetings and chairing conferences. I managed to avoid too many absences from my own church in Cambridge by returning by road on Saturday evenings in my old Ford Cortina, a good secondhand car, which never let me down except on one occasion, later, when I ran into a ditch and filled the exhaust-pipe with mud! I was, however, continually on the move, coping with a long list of engagements, some of which were more important than others, and which, upon reflection, I now feel a president ought not to be asked to fulfil. I am thinking now of two of my successors, who died whilst holding office. The strain is considerable, and one needs to be physically fit and courageous enough to be able to say "No". Whilst, then, continually travelling and speaking, I began to look about me and discover that opportunity was also opening up nearer home. At Bury St Edmunds, there was a fine old meeting house, dating from 1711, with a history going back to 1672. The congregation had seriously diminished, and services had been discontinued. But in the neighbourhood were scattered Unitarians, and it might (I thought) be worthwhile drawing them together and holding at least regular quarterly meetings. I obtained a list of folk who might be interested and prepared to come to occasional Services and visited them. Several members of the Cambridge congregation gave their support, and we began holding Sunday afternoon Services, at first in the meeting-house which the trustees had let to an evangelical body, and then at the home of Mr and Mrs Herbert Bond in Fornham All Saints, who most kindly entertained us to tea after the services. The result was the formation of a Fellowship, which, happily, continues to meet today.

By far the most interesting incident (for me) during my presidential year followed my decision to pay a visit to the Khasi Unitarian churches in north-east India. This small group of native Unitarians in Assam, now Meghalaya, was founded in 1887 by a remarkable Khasi civil servant, Hajom Kissor Singh. He had read, and thought, his way out of Orthodoxy and found himself 'a Unitarian without knowing it'. He made contact with an American minister who gave him somc Unitarian literature which included the works of the Boston preacher, William Ellery Channing. To, his amazement, Singh discovered that Channing was simply teaching what he himself had come to believe. Hitherto, no president of the General Assembly had ventured to go out to India to visit these pioneers. Margaret Barr, a trained teacher and a qualified minister, who came up to Cambridge from Yorkshire and, with typical Yorkshire grit, had made up her mind to spend her life among the Khasi hill-folk, made an independent foray in 1933. She had gone out without any encouragement from the denomination, whose officers were against the idea of a woman living and working in the hills. Eventually, however, she persuaded British Unitarians that she was staying there, founding schools, and training leaders and teachers, and they ought to give her their support and encouragement. The Unitarian Women's League raised money, and before long Margaret had bought some land in the jungle and created a Rural Centre with a school, an agricultural training scheme and a pharmacy, to raise the quality of life for the Khasis, some twelve miles from Shillong, the main town in that part of Assam. From time to time, she gave herself leave to return home to England and report on progress. By 1971, she was having trouble with her eyes and was advised to come back for an operation at Moorfields Hospital in London. She had stipulated, nevertheless, in advance that she would only return, provided someone would accompany her back to India. I offered to do so and to convey greetings from the General Assembly as its president. I had known Margaret ever since she was a minister in Rotherham (1928–33). She had always visited our family whilst on furlough in England and Ireland and had watched our children grow up. We had walked the Derbyshire and Yorkshire moors together and had corresponded for years.

Margaret jumped at the idea of our going out to India together, and I was only too glad to be introduced to Delhi, Calcutta, and the Khasi Hills by a devoted disciple of Gandhi. We left England on 25th October, and before I returned I must have travelled 15,000 miles by air, 300 by rail, 300 by taxi, 100 by jeep, and not less than 80 miles on foot, on this my first visit to India. I got back at the end of November perfectly fit (as I thought), and, within twenty-four hours, went down with gastroenteritis! I have told the story of this visit and a later journey to India I made in 1977 in a tailpiece (see p. 180–196). By this time, Margaret was dead (1973) and I attended the official opening of the 'Kong Barr Memorial Hospital' at Kharang.

In September of the following year, the British Council of Churches held a 'Church Leaders' Conference' at Selly Oak, Birmingham, which

The Observer correspondent called "the most heterogeneous and most highly-powered religious meeting ever held in the history of the British Isles". The Unitarians were offered eight places, but in view of the cost and length of the conference only two delegates were sent. As ex-president of our Assembly, I was one.

Some five hundred persons were present, including many bishops, deans, moderators, and leading Nonconformists, and a strong delegation of Roman Catholics, including their brightest bishops and three mother superiors. It was an impressive gathering. There was much talk about 'new life' and 'new thought', but it all seemed to illustrate only too vividly David Jenkins's remark that "the effect of church work, life, and organisation is largely anaesthetic". No one broke out of the charmed circle of rigid Orthodoxy to examine the theological premises to which many Christians still cling. Speakers admitted the pressing need for changes in ecclesiastical structures, but few were to state boldly the need for *changes in theological attitudes*! Yet, two lecturers did, in some measure, compensate for this.

Sir William Armstrong, head of the Home Civil Service, giving a layman's view of the churches, expressed his disappointment with the lack of progress made in coming to terms with the world of thought and action in which they are set. He stated unequivocally his inability to accept the dogmatic beliefs he had been taught as a boy in the Salvation Army. Happily, he had for a time been associated with a Congregational church "because it had no creed", but he confessed that "for the last nine years" he had never been to an ordinary Service in any church. He implied that it was impossible for him to swallow the largely-accepted teachings of Christianity. Significantly, and sadly, no one took up the challenge of this address.

The then Bishop of Durham, Rt. Rev. Ian Ramsey, spoke on 'The Crisis of Faith'. This was, in my judgement, the most striking utterance of the conference. Demonstrating very forcibly the failure of nineteenth century churchmen to face up to the issues raised by developing science and historical studies, Dr Ramsey said that today there were still far too many Christians who adopted the 'Nelson's eye attitude' in preaching, ignoring scholarship and perpetuating misunderstanding. "Traditional Christian preaching on God, prayer, Jesus, man" and much else needed to be re-examined. "This is not the day (he added) for the mere reiteration of theological conclusions, but for encouraging new attitudes and methods".

The conference did not follow up this lead. The 'crisis of faith' has deepened ever since. Alas, the official advocates of Christianity are still content to hasten slowly, if at all. Their concern with 'internal politics', creeds and dogmas, still cramps them into ghettos, whilst the world moves on regardless. Dogmas divide, but the way of fellowship and love, taught by the prophets of all ages, and shown as life-fulfilling by Jesus and every Christlike soul, unites. For me, one bright spot in the conference was the communion service conducted by the Archbishop of Canterbury, Rt. Rev. Michael Ramsey, assisted by clergy of many denominations. I was sitting in the gallery of the hall where this took place, and who should give me communion but Canon Elliot of Belfast, my former, liberal-minded neighbour, in whose parish I lived for over fifteen years!

The United Nations Association branch in Cambridge was well supported, as one might expect. I served on its executive committee throughout my ministry in the city, taking the chair for speakers like Shirley Williams, Frank Judd, and David Lane, MP for Cambridge, and helping to organise International concerts, Services of All Faiths, and joint meetings with Amnesty International. The honorary president of the branch was the international lawyer, former vice-chancellor of Liverpool University and senior fellow of Gonville and Caius, Lord McNair. He happened also to be president of our congregation, a regular attender, and a man whom we all respected and loved. For several years I used to cycle every fortnight to his home on Storey's Way to have a chat over coffee. We had a great deal in common. He had a distinct liking for Ireland. His father and he had often gone fishing on Loughs Mask and Corrib, and his honeymoon was spent at Derrynane, Co. Kerry, where our family had stayed in the lodge of Daniel O'Connell's old home and my daughter learnt to drive on the sand dunes below the house. Our congregation celebrated Lord McNair's ninetieth birthday at the church on the nearest Sunday morning. He died, shortly afterwards, on 22nd May 1975. He had occupied two law professorships and been president of both the International Court of Justice and the European Court of Human Rights in Strasbourg. A staunch Unitarian, one of his last requests was for "a simple religious service to be conducted by my friend, Dr John McLachlan" and his ashes should be scattered in "unconsecrated ground". What actually happened? The college chaplain called upon me and stated that there would be a (full) service in the college chapel, and would I confine my remarks to "not more than seven

At Lord McNair's Ninetieth Birthday Celebration in the Carpenter Hall, Cambridge

minutes". I declined to accede to this rather impertinent request and said I would probably take at least ten minutes to do some sort of justice to the college's and the nation's distinguished citizen. In the event, the president of Gonville and Caius, Dr Joseph Needham, a distinguished Sinologist and, politically far to the left, read the statutory lesson in the C. of E. burial service, hardly a word of which he could possibly have believed, and which would have been definitely 'out of court' with the deceased. It was unfortunate, and quite needless, but it did not prevent me from giving the address in my own way and at my own speed. The departure from the express wishes of Lord McNair in his Will was most regrettable. I print below the words I was minded to speak.

"There is an African proverb relevant to our purposes today: 'Nobody following an elephant needs to knock the dew off the grass'.

It is quite unnecessary for me to elaborate on the public life and achievements of the distinguished alumnus and Fellow of this College, whose death has brought us together. His long and versatile record is fully documented for all to see – and remember.

Starting life in a solicitor's office in London, Arnold McNair came up in 1906 to read Law in Cambridge, and from that time on, with incidental changes of place and position, he pursued a steadfast course, wedded to the Law and, in particular, to that branch of it that is concerned with 'the things that make for peace'.

Dr Samuel Johnson, a favourite author of his, once said that 'Lawyers know life practically'. This was signally true of Arnold McNair. He combined practicality with a delicate thoughtfulness and a truly whimsical humour, born of a deep understanding of human nature and an appreciation of the interesting vagaries and varieties of human life. Independent in spirit, he was generous and tolerant in personal relations, and of him it might be said that 'Nothing human was entirely alien'.

That such a distinguished lawyer, with a remarkable record at home and abroad, in international courts of justice, and, last but not least, as a successful administrator, should have remained so approachable, modest, and lovable, may be attributed both to nature and nurture. He was justly proud that his grandfather was a Paisley weaver. He loved the West of Ireland, where he often went fishing on the waters of Loughs Mask and Corrib, and where, unforgettably, he spent his honeymoon in County Kerry. Once whimsically, he remarked on this liking for Ireland and the Irish and wondered whether it derived from the fact that his maternal grandmother had died in childbirth and his mother was suckled by an Irish woman!

Wise, he was a very human person, and this trait in him is still thankfully remembered in Liverpool. Only last month I stood in the University Hall which bears his name, and heard how well liked and respected their Vice Chancellor had been. His period of office there covered the difficult years of the last War, but was a triumph of humanity over adverse circumstances. Might not Chaucer's words be applied to him: he was 'a veray parfit gentil knight'?

During his years in Cambridge, both as student and as don, he attended the Unitarian Church, and from 1961 to 1972 was the greatly beloved president of the Congregation. A life-long Liberal and a stout supporter of the United Nations Association, his interest in international affairs was, as you might have expected, fundamentally practical. One instance of this was his lively interest in his Indian law-students, who came to Cambridge in its less regenerate days, and were regarded, on the whole, with something like suspicion. For his part, he welcomed them, and so it was not surprising that in 1931 he was invited to India to deliver the Tagore lectures in Calcutta and elsewhere, a visit to the sub-Continent which he greatly relished and long remembered.

As we contemplate this truly noble life, lived far beyond the allotted span, we can only feel, in the words of Milton, that 'Nothing is here for tears, nothing to wail....nothing but well and fair'. Few men, in their active lives, can have contributed more to British community-life than he, and few will be more kindly remembered.

The words of Rabindranath Tagore himself spring to mind as not unfitting here:

'I have got my leave. Bid me farewell, my brothers.
I bow to you all and take my departure...I only ask for
last kind words from you. We were neighbours for long.
At this time of my parting, wish me good luck my friends!'

So, in these last offices, we pay a tribute of respect and affection to a dedicated spirit, a Scot brought up in England, whose country was the world, a lovable soul and a most excellent friend.

A life such as his, surely, must renew our faith in 'the dignity of man' and give us hope for the future, here and otherwhere..."

We were fortunate in having a very active and knowledgeable UNA regional officer in the Cambridge district, Basil Hembry. He it was who arranged and led a study-tour to Paris to visit the UNESCO headquarters and other places of international importance in the French capital. My wife and our companion-help and I had booked for this before Lord McNair's death, but as it clashed with the date of the funeral, I stayed at home. The following year, Basil Hembry arranged another study-tour this time to Geneva, when all three of us were able to go. This excellent introduction to the headquarters of the specialised agencies of the UN was a great success. Whilst in Geneva, we sought out the memorial which 'the sons of Calvin' erected, in more recent times, to the Spanish theological doctor, Michael Servetus, who was burned at the stake in Geneva in 1553, on account of his Unitarian heresies, and we noted the proximity of a street named after him. The 'whirligig of time brings in his revenges', but erecting monuments to murdered people of conscience scarcely atones for foul deeds. We visited several galleries and museums in this renowned city, so beautifully situated on the edge of its great lake.

Just before we left Cambridge for good, the United Nations Association held its annual meetings in the city in April 1976, which brought the M.P. for Cambridge, David Lane, again into prominence. He had always been an interested and loyal supporter, unlike most of his

Conservative colleagues. It was typical of him that he wrote me the following letter:

> "Dear John
> It is sad that you're about to depart from Cambridge. You and your wife will leave the brightest memories, but you'll be greatly missed. Thank you for so much friendliness and encouragement.
> With warm regards and all good wishes, from us both
> Yours very sincerely
> David Lane"

One other organisation in which I became closely involved and which was very near to my heart, was 'World Development Action'. The committee, set up in 1971, usually met in a room at Great St Mary's, the university church. WDA had a very important educational function, namely, to alert the British public to the new kind of world in which they were living. I became a founder-member and served on the committee until I left Cambridge, taking part in all its campaigns and conferences. We were fortunate to attract the support of a young couple, Hugh and Phyllis Starkey, the latter becoming an outstanding honorary secretary. The vicar of Great St. Mary's by this time, Stanley Booth-Clibborn, was also a moving spirit in WDA, his experience in Africa making his contribution especially valuable. In February 1973, we held a conference in St Michael's Hall, and in the following July several of us drove over to the East of England Show at Peterborough to protest at the damage being done to Commonwealth cane-sugar growers by EEC beet-sugar legislation. Perhaps our most useful piece of work was the preparation of a study on Tea, which showed how little the native producers were getting, in comparison with the wholesalers and retailers handling Tea in Europe. We canvassed members of the public in Cambridge marketplace and found most of them quite ready to pay more for their Tea, provided that the actual pickers in India and Africa obtained higher wages. I was also a member of our denominational committee on World Development, whose active secretary was Dr Sheila Crosskey. It aimed, with some success, at making the Unitarian churches more aware of the inter-relatedness of global problems, in particular, the links between hunger, justice, peace, environmental issues, the education of women, literacy, and economic growth.

When the news of my retirement broke in November 1976, Phyllis Starkey, in a charming letter, conveyed the thanks and good wishes of the Cambridge WDA group. By then we had sold our small furnished home in Linton, South Cambridgeshire, and with the proceeds bought a house on Brincliffe Edge, in Sheffield, where we could see the hills of Derbyshire and be within striking distance of the Yorkshire dales, Lakeland and North Wales. When we told our friends in the South that we were moving to Sheffield, they expressed surprise. Who would want to 'emigrate' to 'the Socialist Republic of South Yorkshire', they exclaimed, and to Sheffield of all places? Of course they did not know the city, one of the cleanest in Europe, with fine parks, art galleries, libraries, a large university, good music, and a far better concert hall than any within easy reach of Cambridge. True, Sheffield had no Fitzwilliam, but it was soon to have a little gem of a gallery, the Ruskin, a fine Industrial Museum, and already possessed historic sites all set in a golden frame of green belt and moorland.

My daughter and her husband and family were living there. She had been married at our church in Cambridge and soon afterwards she and her husband set out to go overland to Kathmandu, and then round the world for fifteen months. My second son, Richard, was teaching nearby in Derby, less than an hour away, and his son, Timothy, my eldest grandson, had been born on 27th March 1975. I was now approaching my sixty-eighth birthday and looking forward to enjoying a little more leisure. I had recently taken a share in writing the privately-printed history of my old school in Cheshire, which the Cheshire archivist had suggested should be recorded. Any further writing, I relegated to my retirement and looked forward to a reduction in the pressure, which had always been a factor in my life, often entirely due to my own restless enthusiasms....

On one particular matter, I was determined to insist: that I should now become an active member of the Rucksack Club, of which I had been a rather passive associate since 1934. For obvious reasons, I was unable to attend Meets of any kind at weekends. So, in September 1976, I celebrated my retirement by walking the West Highland Way with my son-in-law, Jim Monach, and his father, John. But for me the outstanding event in the early part of the next year (1978) was the Easter Meet at Crianlarich, the first of many enjoyable mountaineering Meets, organised each Easter by the Club.

As the year 1975 came to an end, we felt as a family that we ought to 'savour the last rites', as it were, in Cambridge, which for the past ninc years had been our home. On 20th December, we enjoyed our last

Christmas dinner in the Carpenter Hall, whilst on Christmas Eve, all the members of the family foregathered and attended Sung Eucharist in King's College Chapel, where we had often seen and heard the choristers sing the annual Carol Service. Our own morning service on Christmas Day followed, and on Boxing Day we all walked out along the Roman Road over the Gogs. On the 30th we held a farewell party in the manse, which our neighbours in De Freville Avenue celebrated with us. The days raced by, and in April I wrote my last message in the church calender:

> "Dear Friends
>
> Those of us who entered the Unitarian ministry in the early thirties started in a very different kind of world from today's. Looking back, however, we can see that we learnt lessons then that were invaluable. For example, we learnt to appreciate the uncommon fineness of the comman man; the miracle of humanity flourishing even amidst harsh circumstances; the importance of Polonius's advice to Laertes to be, above all, true to one's self, not to trim one's sails necessarily to prevailing winds, but to be loyal to a vision of truth once glimpsed and held in focus.
>
> A minister's job, we came to understand, was to be a friend to *all*, to be accessible to all, to vary one's approach, but never to echo or adopt the opinions of others merely to please or appease; to choose one's priorities and to stick to them, yet speaking always the truth in love.
>
> The task as we saw it was to *lead* and not to follow fashionable trends, to live a full life as a citizen of the place where we settled, but always to bear in mind a dual citizenship of the world as it is *and* the world as it ought to be; to fight against parochialism; to open doors to a world-view of things; and to reach out to a region of the spirit which undergirds and envelops the whole life of man.
>
> The Unitarian ministry has always laid emphasis on its prophetic character and gloried in its freedom. This privilege of our pulpits has been cherished and stoutly defended by ministers and laymen alike. To be able to speak one's mind on a large variety of subjects; to try to measure up to the challenges of the fast-changing years; to serve one's fellows in times of personal crisis and to maintain a reasonably cheerful and optimistic outlook is certainly demanding. Of course, no man is really 'sufficient for these things'. We all have our limitations. We even have our moods. And though this is sometimes forgotten, a minister is also human. Yet he

> usually tries to do his best. I would like to think that I also made that attempt.
>
> In stepping aside from the active ministry, I do so with mixed feelings, regretting most of all, perhaps, the regular and friendly contacts with a lively and caring congregation. It has been a joy and a privilege to be free of your homes, to be party to your happinesses and to share in your anxieties. You have been very kind and undemanding, generous and thoughtful, and I hope that, for my part, I have been able, in some small measure, to be of service to you. To be sure of that would satisfy me deeply.

At the farewell meeting in July, the church presented me with an illuminated address, conferring 'Life Membership', and wishing me good health and enjoyment of my remaining years. We were honoured by the presence of a goodly company, which included representatives of the General Assembly and of several of the bodies in the city, with which I had been connected. We were particularly pleased to have with us the vicar of Great St. Mary's, the Regional Officer of the United Nations Association, and members of Amnesty.

9

SWAN-SONG IN SOUTH YORKSHIRE

"We must be still and still moving
Into another intensity

In my end is my beginning
T.S. Eliot: *East Coker*

Much to the surprise of our Cambridge friends, retirement to Sheffield has proved a real blessing. Quite by accident, we discovered a new and comfortable home. Driving along Brincliffe Edge in order to deliver some 'Amnesty' posters on our way back from Derbyshire to Cambridge, we spotted a large terrace house for sale. The situation was exceptional. It stood on a ridge overlooking a hanging wood that stretched nearly a mile east and west below the road. The lounge bay-window faced south and commanded a distant view of the Derbyshire moors. The gardens, back and front, were manageable, and at the rear, tennis courts gave the house an open outlook over the city. Two storeys and five bedrooms provided space for our furniture and library and two cellars were convenient for a work-bench, a freezer and storage space for tools and garden equipment. I had the house surveyed, put in an offer, which was accepted, and arranged for builders to do the necessary repairs. In due course, electricians, plumbers, and central-heating fitters followed. I was fortunate in being able to effect a quick sale of the small house in South Cambridgeshire which we had acquired three or more years before and had let furnished, so I had ready money. We were also lucky in our painter-decorator. He was a Suffolk man, a splendid tradesman, who kept in touch with us by telephone during the months when we were still living in Cambridge, informing us of the various contractors' progress or lack of it!

July 1976, was one of the hottest summers in recent memory, and not an ideal time for transplanting roses, many of which I had brought from Ireland to Cambridge and was loath to leave behind. I saved all but one of these by using all our washing-up and bath-water, and spent the rest of the summer clearing a neglected garden, building a dry wall and rockery, and levelling a lawn.

In De Freville Avenue, Cambridge, we left behind us some of the best neighbours we ever had, folk with whom we have kept in touch throughout the years. Losing old friends through removal, we have found quite unnecessary, especially if the ties of friendship are cemented by family interests and other common concerns. The advantages of coming to Sheffield were many. The Fens had never really appealed to us. "Too flat and boring" was our unanimous verdict. There were few country walks of any character. Happily, Sheffield is set in a green and golden frame. The Derbyshire moors and dales are on one side, the Dukeries on the other, the Yorkshire Dales within easy reach, and the Howgills and Lakeland not much further off. The city itself is no longer the dirty place it was in the thirties, where one could say, "Where there's muck there's money". It has steadily improved its amenities and living space, is the seat of a fine university, possesses several first-class museums and art galleries, hosts music, theatre, and other entertainments, possesses splendid sports facilities, and is the centre of a warm and colourful community life. Best of all, its people are a kind, caring, and outgoing folk, with whom my daughter and her husband had recently made themselves at home. My second son and his wife and a growing family were living at Derby, less than an hour's distance by road, and soon there would be three more grandchildren in Sheffield, all of whom were born at a maternity ward just below the house where I am writing these lines.

Retirement may be the October of a man's life, but October often provides magnificent weather and opportunities for autumnal activities of a special and enjoyable kind.

You can, of course, go on doing more or less what you have been accustomed to do under reduced pressure. You can do it at your own pace, more slowly than of yore and more easily, because you are now a 'free man' and can apply the lessons you have learnt with a more subtle and, perhaps, detached facility. You may even please yourself a little more frequently as well as others. As a minister of religion, you are no longer expected to fulfil schedules or attend large numbers of committees. It has always struck me as rather comical that the German word for 'committee' is 'Ausschuss' the second meaning of which is 'rubbish'! For, in my experience, not a few committees can be a complete waste of time and their output simply a 'load of rubbish'. This thought – a naughty one – must embarrass a democrat, and I confess it only surfaces occasionally. However, looking back upon a long ministry of nearly sixty years, I feel sure that the fewer the numbers composing a committee are, the better, the more efficient, that committee will be. Possibly, as has often been remarked, a committee of *one* is sometimes the most efficient and satisfactory way of dealing with matters requiring speedy resolution. Possibly, I may here be accused of cynicism, but I wonder if there is not a kernal of truth in the statement?

Another advantage of ministerial retirement is that one is free to join societies or organisations unconnected with church-life, political, social, leisure, or purely aesthetic. Hobbies, for which one had little or no time or strong inclination, when one was fully engaged in professional work, may now engage your attention. For example, you can give time to music, painting, stamp-collecting, photography, walking, or even mountaineering. You are free to undertake excursions into regions hitherto 'out-of-bounds'. And this without suffering from any guilt feelings. You can take holidays when you feel like it, avoiding national occasions, school holidays, and peak periods. You can 'go places' you have long wished to visit at home or abroad: *provided that* you can afford to do so, which is not so easy on a small, fixed pension, though it can be quite exciting managing your affairs so that you *are* able, just, to visit those classical Greek archaeological sites or those centres of Italian Renaissance art or join that unusual botanising trip to the Pyrenees or that more strenuous circuit of Mont Blanc. The last-named only for the very fit!

As a senior-citizen you will enjoy some concessions on travel-fares or theatre tickets. In Sheffield, for instance, one could travel free on bus or train in the South Yorkshire region after 9.30 a.m. until 3.30 p.m. and again from 6.00 p.m. until 10.30 p.m., until the Tory Government rate-capped the city council!

The above are a few of the pleasant 'pros' of retirement. The 'cons' are less enjoyable. You are slowing down! Physically and mentally, you are losing agility. Everything you do takes longer than it did, from dressing to map-reading. You become forgetful, keep losing things, keys, spectacles, articles of clothing, especially gloves, sticks, and umbrellas. Appallingly, you cannot recall names of people or places. Events or happenings in your own experience maddeningly escape recall. Eventually, one's hearing is impaired, and one's eyesight is affected. Small print is anathema and ultimately indecipherable: time-tables, instructions upon medicine bottles and tins of food and labels on pictures are indiscernable. But more, and worse, old friends drop off and old places change out of recognition. It is no good. You are walking the Rip van Winkle trail, and can exclaim with Charles Lamb, "Gone, all are gone, the old familiar faces". An ache of loneliness and regret steals over one at times, and you realise, with Sam Johnson, just how "Superfluous lags the veteran on the stage"....

Yet, for myself, though I have been blessed with a strong constitution and remained fairly fit and active, I have to confess that I move more slowly uphill than was my wont. On a long haul, I get out of breath. It is chastening to lose one's hair (or teeth) and to be regarded by the younger generation as *passé* or, which happened to me in a work-camp, as "that old bloke", or perhaps, out of earshot, "that old fogey".

From 1976 onwards, until well into the eighties, my diaries reveal that I was prevented from getting into my stride and 'doing my own thing' by a steady stream of church engagements, a plethora of committees and some secretarial duties which I found difficult to escape. I was pressed to join the academic committee of my old college in Manchester, and later was elected President. This entailed regular visits to Manchester for a number of years. I continued working for Amnesty for some time after I settled in Sheffield, and was co-opted on the executive of the Hallam branch of the United Nations Association. When the Unitarian Peace Fellowship lost its honorary secretary in 1978, I volunteered to fill the vacancy *pro tem*, hopefully expecting that someone else would soon take over, but no one did, and I continued in that position for five years. One consequence of this was that I was able to superintend an important 'relief project' in India for which the Fellowship's 1985 Lent Appeal was made.

Near Kharang, in the Khasi Hills, a jungle hospital had been built and opened in 1977 in memory of Margaret Barr who worked in that region for over thirty years. In 1971, I had been the last European to see Margaret alive, having accompanied her back to India after an eye operation at Moorfields (see p. 186 ff.). I was also present, later, at the opening of the hospital. Naturally, I was greatly concerned that all water had to be conveyed by hand up a steep hill and felt for some time that it would be feasible, and most desirable, to lead running water up to the hospital. Hence the Lent Appeal for this project. It raised a record sum of £5,535 which was increased by additional moneys, mostly from the Unitarian Women's League, to a total of over £11,000.

Raising the cash was, however, quite the easiest part of the –operation. The scheme entailed protracted negotiations, delays and disappointments. Eventually, we secured the help of an Indian geohydrological team, who went to Kharang and drew up a report and plans for a satisfactory mode of supplying water from a dug well. I knew the site, but had no idea how long and frustrating would be the task of getting the work done to proper standards and to our satisfaction. Controlling progress, overcoming snags, deciding on methods of pumping and electricity supply at a distance of several thousand miles would not have been possible without the long and patient co-operation of our friend, Devison Marbaniang, secretary of the hospital committee and lay leader of the Unitarian churches in the area. In fact negotiations over planning and construction continued for more than six years, but the project was completed and the plant officially opened in 1989. It was a bit of a marathon!

I have written about my second visit to India elsewhere (see p. 187 ff.) Before going there I registered in July 1977 to take part in a 'Toc H' work-project at Little Gidding in Huntingdonshire. This tiny hamlet, eleven miles north-west of Huntingdon, acquired fame in the 17th century as a place of retreat for Anglican churchmen under the leadership of Nicholas Ferrar (1592–1637), royalist and theologian, who founded a community composed of family and friends. Since 1970, when Tony Hodgson and his wife bought Manor Farm with its outbuildings and eight acres of land, it has become the centre of another small community, worshipping in the little church of St John the Evangelist, restored in 1853. Ferrar's grave stands in front of the main doorway. Ever since reading T.S. Eliot's 'Four Quartet's', I had wondered about Little Gidding. The poet's imagination had been stirred by his visit:

> "You are not here to verify,
> Instruct yourself, or inform curiosity
> Or carry report. You are here to kneel
> Where prayer has been valid."

The 'Toc H' work-camp aimed to assist a community "irrespective of race, age, class, or creed" to share thoughts and fellowship, whilst repairing a large barn, building a shippon for the Jersey cows, and weeding and cultivating crops in the surrounding fields. I was no stranger to mixing and pouring concrete or brick-laying, though a little out of practice, so I relished the change and was, in addition, privileged to conduct morning-prayers on one occasion. The only snag occurred at the weekend, when a few 'new boys and girls' joined us. Among them was a serious-minded youth, who leaned over the table at tea one evening and inquired, "Are you saved?" This was the only false note struck during the whole week. I regret to say I did not come up to expectation: I was not 'saved', according to his book. Argument with (so-called) Christian evangelicals is seldom productive of good, so I quietly excused myself and withdrew from the company of 'the rigidly righteous'. Fundamentalism of any kind can be a real disservice to religion, and, historically, has been responsible for more unhappiness and cruelty than many other agencies of evil. A happier side of the fellowship was the meeting with the regular volunteers, from various walks of life, who had come to do a 'job of work' irrespective of race, age, class or creed.

Manchester College, Oxford remained of close concern to me throughout the eighties. I served on its governing body until 1986, the year of its bicentenary. To be asked to preach in the chapel on the occasion of the 200th anniversary of the College's foundation was indeed an honour. The sermon was subsequently printed in *Faith and Freedom* under the title of 'The Spirit of the Place' (Summer, 1986). In this I attempted to summarise and appraise the character of the college, its founders and teachers, and the principles of freedom and undogmatic attachment to 'Truth, Liberty and Religion' which the institution has enshrined and promoted.

Locally, in Sheffield, I joined a group of retired professional and businessmen meeting on most Mondays of the year (*Probus*), contributing talks and showing slides from time to time. My wife and I have also been members of the Sheffield and Peak District branch of the Council for the Preservation of Rural England, the Council of Christians and Jews, and the Mental Health Association.

From 1978 onwards, on request, I paid regular visits to the Old Meeting House at Newcastle-under-Lyme, formerly Josiah Wedgewood's place of worship. The lay-pastor, Denis Malbon, an insurance broker, who gave over thirty years' voluntary service to keep this chapel open, ably supported by his wife Doreen, became good friends of ours. After his death in 1983, my wife and I made more frequent journeys over the Derbyshire and Staffordshire hills on Sunday mornings, driving through a countryside which was beautiful and ever-changing throughout the year.

In 1978, we returned to Ireland for our summer holiday, taking the car and driving via Lisburn, where we stayed with Peter and Jill, to Ballyferriter, Co. Kerry. We were joined there by our daughter, Jane and her husband and two girls. My wife, Joan, was unwell most of the time, suffering from internal pains which the doctors seemed unable to diagnose. We drove back to Ulster and the woman doctor at the Lisburn clinic advised us to hurry home and visit our own doctor. Again, the diagnosis was uncertain, but before long our doctor sent her to the Jessop Hospital for Women, where she was operated upon on 9th October. The surgeon found advanced cancer of the ovaries and other organs; the disease was widespread. She came home after three weeks, and May and I nursed her for nine more, when she entered the terminal nursing home, St Luke's, dying there within eight days, on the last day of December, 1978. This was a sad end to a fine and active life.

Throughout our married life, Joan had been a magnificent support to me in my ministry, full of ideas, and an excellent organiser. She was also a good extempore speaker and a convinced pacifist. Latterly, she had returned to teaching history and other subjects and become a financial mainstay of our home. Indeed, I always maintained that it was Joan who made it possible for us to run a small car. Our grievous loss was, however, mitigated by the fact that May Roath, who had been a Girl Guide and Ranger with Joan and then our loyal helper and 'deputy mother' of all our three children, was still with us – after forty-three years. She had kept house for us for a very long time, since our Oxford days. Perhaps it was not surprising that in July, 1979 May and I were married by my brother-in-law, Arthur Vallance, in the little chapel in Great Hucklow, Derbyshire.

May has had a good deal to put up with since she married me, for I have spent a great deal of my time in my study. From 1973 to 1987 I edited the *Transactions* of the Unitarian Historical Society, and am still trying to keep up with requests for information on historical matters, besides contributing articles to various journals. In 1983 I was elected an honorary member of the General Assembly of Unitarian and Free Christian Churches at its annual meeting in Oxford.

Prior to this I had joined a Dutch foundation set up to publish rare works in the field of Continental Anti-trinitarianism, entitled the *Bibliotheca Unitariorum*, which was incorporated in the Netherlands in 1981.

As a member of the Advisory Council, I have been in regular correspondence with the president, Professor Jan van Goudoever of Amstelveen, and for a time with Professor Robert Dán of Budapest. As the sole British member, I made myself responsible for the British appeal for funds. It was proposed to raise about £10,000 and a figure of £1,000 was allocated to Britain. I circulated a number of trusts and associations and almost reached that target. The first volume of the new series, edited by Robert Dán was *The Defence of Francis David* (1582) by Jacobus Palaeologus, a Greek anti-trinitarian. Foreword and introduction were both in English whilst the text was, of course, in the original Latin, a beautiful facsimile. A second volume appeared in 1988: *De Falsa et Vera Unius Dei Patri, Filii et Spiritus Sancti Cognitione Libri Duo*, first published in 1568 in Transylvania. I corrected and revised the English of the valuable introduction by Dr Antal Pirnát. This sprang several surprises, including the suggestion that religious toleration was not universal in Transylvania in 1568, for Catholics had actually been excluded, and only Protestant denominations enjoyed freedom of worship. The *De Falsa et Vera* was probably the most important Anti-trinitarian work ever published in Transylvania. This facsimile of a rare volume, of which there are only twenty-seven copies in Europe was beautifully produced. A third volume of the series is in course of preparation.

A spin-off from this work was a Colloquium on the study of Unitarianism and related movements, held at Hilversum and Amsterdam in May, 1985. A score of scholars from Poland, Holland, Germany, France, Belgium and Britain attended. It was, alas, the last time I saw that fine scholar, Robert Dán, since he died suddenly on 27th March 1986, a sad loss to Anti-trinitarian studies.

Meanwhile, two events of an international character made bright and memorable our retirement days in Sheffield. The first was the flying visit of the members of an American 'Bethlehem Peace Pilgrimage' in April 1983. This was an interdenominational group and included the Catholic Air Force chaplain who had flown out with the 'planes that dropped the first atomic bomb on Hiroshima. Starting in Seattle on the west coast of the United States, they walked across America, landed in Scotland, and were marching though England and Europe to the Holy Land. I arranged hospitality for them in Sheffield and beyond. They were a jolly crowd of about two dozen, chiefly young men and women, from different walks of life, who represented a more thoughtful and caring America than that often portrayed by press or politician.... I was much moved by conversation with the chaplain, Father George Gabelka, 'Peace Pilgrim from Fenton, Michigan, USA', who stayed with us and who had obviously undergone a complete change of mind and heart as a result of his 'connexion' with the atomic bomb.

In the following year, Sheffield was host to the Warsaw Inter-University Choir. They came in late August, travelling in the opposite direction, from south to north. They were invited to visit Britain by the Corriemeela Choir from Northern Ireland, which had met them at an international music festival in Europe and of which my son, Peter, was a leading member. Originally, they were to have sung in Coventry, but this could not be fitted in, so Coventry's loss became Sheffield's gain. When Peter informed me of the possibility that they could come to Sheffield, I felt it was an opportunity not to be missed. It was agreed that they should sing in Upper Chapel. I got in touch with the large Polish community in Sheffield, and its members, along with members of the United Nations Association, provided hospitality for two nights. On the morning before the concert, in brilliant sunshine, I took them on an outing (they were travelling in their own coach from Warsaw) up the Derwent valley and we ate packed lunches above the top reservoir. Before they left for Dundee and Ulster the following morning, they were given a Lord Mayor's reception in the Town Hall. The president of the Choir expressed their thanks to me for organising their stay in Sheffield: "We enjoyed it very much and we consider it a privelege to have been able to sing for such an appreciative audience". The choir's pleasure, however, was hardly equal to the joy they gave to the Sheffield Polish community and many others who welcomed and listened to them!

Music has meant a great deal to me and my family, all of whom learnt to play an instrument. In Ireland we drove down from Belfast to Dublin every year that Richard and Jane were at Trinity College to hear major works by Bach, Haydn or Mozart in which they were taking part, and we still go over to Derby to concerts by the Derwent Singers or the Cathedral Choristers of which Richard is a member.

Retirement enabled me to fulfil three long-cherised ambitions: 1. to do some writing; 2. to travel; and 3. to play a more active role as a member of the Rucksack Club, of which I have been a member since 1934.

1. Writing

One of my first assignments in retirement, entailing both research and correspondence, related to a case in the Chancery Division of the

High Court. It was brought by the South Place Ethical Society against the Inland Revenue, who had refused to regard the Society as a charity under the terms of the Charities Act of 1960.

At the request of the Society, I wrote an Affidavit and later, some supplementary notes, eventually finding myself commenting somewhat critically upon an Affidavit composed by my old friend, Dr Ernest Payne, on the side of the Attorney General. The preparation of the case went on rather slowly for several years and, in the event, I was not called for cross-examination, which was a relief!

The South Place Ethical Society started in the 19th century as a Unitarian church in London, but its theology and ethos had developed. I argued for the possibility of, and the need for, development in religion in concert with the moral and spiritual development of ideas and the new interpretations of religious experience and attitudes which were possible and inevitable with the passage of time. I affirmed the validity of a broader understanding of religion than that which our predecessors had hitherto embraced. And I illustrated this kind of development from the history of Unitarianism.

The final judgement was that "the study and dissemination of ethical principles and the cultivation of a rational religious sentiment were not objects which were for the advancement of religion(!), but they were charitable as being for the enhancement of education and for other purposes beneficial to the community". (*The Times*, 19 June 1980). Hence, though the Society appeared to have lost charitable status on *religious* grounds, it won such status on *educational* grounds. On the whole, this result could be regarded as a resounding success in maintaining the Society's charitable status, but it did not resolve the religious question. The judge, Mr Justice Dillon, stuck to the time-honoured view that religion is the worship of God, but it may well transpire that, in the course of time, such a simplistic (if one dare use the word in this connexion) idea of religion will be found inadequate to describe human attitudes and views of the world which could be considered perfectly 'religious'. At all events, the case undoubtedly raised, in an interesting form, the question, "What is religion?" and "How is it to be defined?" In fact, what is its essence, meaning and character? Perhaps the judge was only too glad to be relieved of trying to answer such questions by taking refuge with an old and customary convention....

I must content myself here with the bare mention of publications for which I was responsible during my retirement. In 1982, I published a memorial volume to the Rev. A.B. Downing, a colleague whom I had known since the early 'thirties, when he was a youth in Sheffield. I persuaded him to consider training for the Unitarian ministry and was one of his referees. He trained under my father in Manchester and, during World War II, enlisted in the Royal Signals and Intelligence Corps, served abroad, and was mentioned in despatches. For five years, he edited the denominational newspaper, *The Inquirer*, and proved a thoughtful and at times brilliant writer. He had come up from poverty and had all the makings of a fine academic, but, alas, was never destined to occupy a post in either of our two colleges. In later life he suffered from a serious heart condition and died suddenly in August 1980. I called my tribute to him "The Downing Flavour" and included excerpts from his writings over a number of years. It was printed privately and distributed to a large number of subscribers both at home and abroad. It gave me, at least, poignant satisfaction....

Next year, I persuaded my shy brother-in-law, Arthur Vallance, to let me publish a selection of his verses, written during a period of more than sixty years. This appeared in October 1983 under the title 'Lancashire Lyrics and Other Verses'.

This year was also the 250th anniversary of the birth of the great Unitarian minister and chemist, Joseph Priestley, the discoverer of oxygen. From my student days, I had been an ardent admirer of Priestley and possessed an engraving of a miniature of him by John Hazlitt, brother of William, the essayist. I also inherited from my father a black basalt Wedgwood medallion of Priestley, dated 1779. It occurred to me that it would be interesting to bring out a tribute to Priestley in the form of an iconography, for there had been many portraits and engravings of him, during and after his lifetime. The research and preparation of '*Joseph Priestley, Man of Science, 1733–1804: An Iconography of a Great Yorkshireman* occupied the best part of three years. There was a 'fall out' from this activity. I was invited to take part in a BBC Horizon programme by preaching in Mill Hill Chapel, Leeds, the successor to Priestley's old chapel; presenting prizes at his old school in Batley, and lecturing more than once at the Birmingham and Midland Institute on Priestley topics.

The first named 'happening', for that it was, turned out to be a rather bizarre affair. Electric cables lay all over the place and arc-lamps and microphones were much in evidence. I was informed that the Service was also the annual flower-service and children would be in attendance. I delivered an address on the great man in a blaze of light and was in full oratorical flight, when, suddenly, all the special lighting was dowsed and the engineers began noisily dragging their equipment away. No one had warned me of this procedure or of the fact that all that was required was a brief showing of a congregation at worship and a minister in the pulpit! More disappointing, though, was the fact that, on this anniversary occasion the good copy of a well-known portrait of the chapel's most famous minister was nowhere to be seen. Only after careful inquiry was I shown the 'Mill Hill Priestley' locked up in an upstairs room! It was in poor condition, but, happily, it has since been restored and given a place of honour.

During the next three years, I was involved in the production of an architectural survey of chapels and churches in the Unitarian tradition in the British Isles (*The Unitarian Heritage*, 1986). The text of this was written mainly by Judy and Graham Hague. I wrote the chapter on the churches of the Non-Subscribing Church of Ireland, provided some of the photographs, and acted as consultant to the editors. This book owed a great deal to the financial expertise of Rev. Peter Godfrey, who managed to persuade American friends to subsidise its production. It was, luckily, researched and printed not a moment too soon, since many of the older chapels (and some of the more recent) have disappeared or are in poor condition. The long lists of disused and demolished chapels are a sad commentary on the decline of organised religion in Britain.

In 1987 I ceased to edit the *Transactions* of the Unitarian Historical Society, but the following year my successor, Mr Alan Ruston, brought out the annual issue as a 'Festschrift' in my honour and published a bibliography of my *historical* writings (from 1935 to 1987).

2. Travel

During my second year at University, a friend and I cycled to London, crossed to Dunkirk, and then rode down the old Western Front to Dijon, camping *en route*. We finished a three-week trip by taking a train across the central massif and cycling through old Aquitaine from Perigueux to Bordeaux, sailing back to Liverpool on a tramp steamer as the Captain's guests. We cut Paris out as quite beyond our means. Not until my eightieth birthday did I make good this grave omission, or, more correctly, have it made good by kind invitation of our good friends, Peter and Sheila Godfrey in September 1988, a most enjoyable birthday present! For the record, our 1928 tour cost us just ten pounds apiece!

Apart from two visits to India and two to America and holidays in Europe from Norway to Greece, most of our family holidays have been spent in the British Isles. In Ireland, in particular, we grew familiar with the west coast, from Donegal to Kerry, camping or taking a cottage, often for a month at a time. One important exception was our extended stay in New Zealand from October 1987 to March 1988. This was made possible through the generosity of our relatives, Elspeth and Arthur Vallance, who emigrated to Blenheim to be near their son, Stephen, and his family. We toured in both islands, and I managed to make several day-outings on foot in the hills and bush. To record our adventures in that superbly beautiful country would take too long, nor would it be possible here to relate a tithe of the experiences with the people, sights, and sounds of a country that never fails to impress visitors, and which my wife and I will never forget.

3. Mountaineering

When I was no longer required to conduct regular Services of worship, my free week-ends permitted me to attend Rucksack Club walking and climbing meets. In particular, I have enjoyed the 'Easter Meets' in Scotland. Details of those I have attended from 1978 to 1989 will be found on page 202 in the section 'The Delectable Mountains'.

I gave up serious rock climbing about 1950, but continued scrambling, ridge-walking and enjoying 'the mountain experience' throughout my retirement. The recent fashion for 'long walks' appealed to me, though I have sternly resisted the temptation to start fell-running.

Walks in Ireland and in New Zealand were idiosyncratic. In particular, I found bush-walking and river-tramping in the South Island challenging, confronting one with entirely novel problems and experiences. I am not likely to forget the Marlborough Forest Park, in which I had a (lucky) fall and spent two marvellous days and a fantastic night in the heart of the bush with my surgeon-nephew, Steve Vallance. Nor shall I ever forget the Hodder River tramp with the Blenheim Tramping Club, when we crossed the river eighty-eight times, often wading almost up to our waists! The toughness of those 'Kiwis' both men and women, impressed me greatly. No doubt it will surprise those who have never been to New Zealand and ventured into the bush or up the river gorges that I found the 'tramping' (the word regularly used) quite severe. To reach some of the ranges in N.Z. one is compelled to follow the course of rivers, crossing from side to side and frequently wading. Though carrying a large stave to help keep me upright in a strong current, I once heeled over and fell headlong into a river, emerging soaked to the skin. Stripping, I left most of my underwear, etc. hanging on a bush to dry, awaiting my return. Of course, in *that* climate you tend to dry off pretty quickly, and can adopt methods of crossing rivers that in the UK would probably land you in bed with a heavy cold!

I celebrated my eightieth birthday on 8 July 1988 with a happy family gathering in the St George's Hotel, not far from home. And this is, I think, an appropriate point at which to wind up this now overlong narrative?

I conclude with a brief epilogue:

Wrote T.S. Eliot, "In my end is my beginning". I, too, have arrived physically, if not spiritually, full-circle. I am back in Sheffield, where I started as a young, inexperienced bachelor, seeking adventure, nearly fifty-seven years ago. I live within a quarter of a mile of the house I once lived and worked in, now a Pakistani grocer's shop. All things change and are new. I cannot recollect ever having walked along Brincliffe Edge in the thirties, gazing over what I am told were the fields of Nab Farm, now row after row of post-war villas. I suppose I overlooked my immediate environment and thought the Elysian fields were much further away. Much travelled, I must confess I have learnt that beauty and adventure may be found quite close at hand. The British scene contains its full share of wonders and delight. 'Abroad' can lie just round the corner. The 'strange and startling' are all around. Today, I look from my study-window through a leafless wood and can see, on a clear day, the Derbyshire moors, and let my imagination wander. The years of my life, like Banquo's ghosts, in *The Tragedy of Macbeth*, pass before me, but not malevolently. Rather, they nudge me into thoughtful recollection of times past and people known, of poetry and music, flowers and friends, parents and children, history and biography, the wonders of nature and the magnificence of 'the mountain world'. A rich tapestry of colour and sound, ideas and also mystery, has continuously enveloped me, and with the passage of the years has come the sense of belonging to a 'beloved community', confined not to an immediate neighbourhood or nation, but inhabiting a commonwealth of friends.

Francis Bacon despondently wrote, "There is little friendship in the world, and least of all between equals". This suggests that Bacon was not a friendly man. Of course it takes a friend to make friends. Happily, Bacon's experience has not been mine.

I can look back on a life blessed with friends, all along the way. To name them would serve no practical purpose. But I can say this: that a good part of what I have been and what I am I owe not only to family but to friends, old and new, people in many different walks of life, lay and professional, academic and non-academic, in town and country, Protestant and Catholic, British and non-British, members of the great family of nations, especially those who have recognised their kinship and mutual responsibilities. For I have long counted myself 'a citizen of the world', owing my primary allegiance to humanity, and regarding this world – a blue orb swimming in space – as a global village, and, in the words of the world-famed refugee from Nazi Germany, Dr Albert Einstein, as "after all, a very small star".

TAILPIECES

Notes on Prague and Czechoslovakia

"A far-away country .... of whom we know nothing."
(Neville Chamberlain in a broadcast of 27th September, 1938)

I have mislaid the detailed Diary of my 'post-Munich visit' to Prague in the winter of 1938–39, but still have notes of its main contents. What follows is a kind of postscript to what I wrote in chapter 5.

Listening to conversation in the train on my way to Prague in December 1938, I felt I was entering a German colony, an impression confirmed, later, when travelling through Moravia and Ostrava and seeing German troops being conveyed across the country from Vienna to Dresden, no doubt a propaganda exercise to convince the Czech population that 'the end had come'.

Many refugee-agencies were at work trying to rescue people from "the wrath to come"; e.g. The Save the Children Fund, the Quaker Refugee Relief Service, the Social Democrat committee, the Thomas Mann committee (helping German and Austrian writers and intellectuals), P.E.N.; the Canadian Red Cross, HICIM (Jewish Emigration committee), Caritas (a Catholic committee), the News Chronicle Fund. The people who came to our office (the Unitarian Refugee Relief committee) included Jews, Social Democrats, Communists, Catholics (Caritas refused help to Social Democrats and Communists); students, and professional men and women. One girl from Berlin was on the P.E.N. club list: she was writing a thesis for her degree on 'The Pre-Raphaelite Movement in English Art'. On my first working day, I went to the main station to watch a transport of the families of three hundred men who had already left the country. The train was routed through the Polish Corridor to Danzig. Just before Christmas, I spent a whole day at the Salvation Army headquarters, helping to distribute clothes from the Lord Mayor of London's Czech Relief Fund. It was thought only proper that an Englishman should superintend this operation! It was the first time in my life that I had been asked to measure men, women and children for clothes!

Hitler pressed the Czech Government hard: all German, Austrian, and Jewish refugees had to be out of the country not later than 15th January 1939.

In the company of Dr Karel Haspl, I visited four refugee camps: one in Kladno (miners and their families), others in Beránek, Koniček, and a municipal home for old people which had turned its basement into a 'home' for 65 refugees. Food kitchens were attached to all these and we carried wool for the women to knit, but the cry was "Work for the men, please"! It was reckoned that there could be around 200,000 refugees from the Sudetenland in camps and private houses in and about Prague and neighbouring towns and villages. The various churches were doing their best to improvise schemes of employment, but the situation was changing and still confused.

Dr Norbert Čapek, the Unitarian minister in Prague, was murdered by the Nazis in 1942, during his captivity in a work-camp. He was injected with pus, as a form of 'experiment' and punishment, for he was a great Czech patriot. His son-in-law, Dr Karel Haspl narrowly escaped death. I kept in touch with the last-named throughout the war by means of Red Cross messages and with his wife and daughter until 1989, when Bohdana Haspl died. After the war, in 1945, the General Assembly Refugee Committee, of which George Grieve and I were members, initiated an appeal-fund to assist a Children's Home at Jilové, near Prague. This met the needs of orphaned and handicapped children. A Unitarian lady who had been a member of the bursary staff of a Cambridge college was appointed matron of this home. George Grieve went out to Prague and Jilové to superintend the setting up of the Home.

When I was in Prague in 1933, I met a former student of the Unitarian College, Manchester and contemporary of mine, Václav Ziska. On his return home, he became the minister in charge of a church in Pilsen, where I visited him and spoke to his lively congregation. The following year, when Priestley Phillips and I were on our way to climb in the High Tatras, we stopped in Prague and took part in a graduation ceremony at the University. Afterwards, we were dining in the gorgeous Municipal House, when a note was handed to me. I went out and found Ziska very distressed. He had evidently got across with Dr Čapek and was no longer exercising a regular ministry.

During the war, Václav had a very adventurous career as a member of the Czech underground resistance movement. He came to England and preached for me in Halifax in June 1944. He had just escaped from a Hungarian prison in Budapest and had made his way via Yugoslavia, Turkey, Palestine and Syria (with his wife) to join Masaryk's staff in London. He wrote an account of the assassination of Heydrich, the brutal 'Protector' of Czechoslovakia, and the Nazi massacre of the mining village of Lidice (published in London, 1943). In August 1944, he wrote to my father saying he was going to Italy *en route* for Prague, to fetch his son away: he had been drafted into the Hitler Youth. He never found him. Early in 1946 Václav died suddenly, it was said, of heart failure. I understand that he shot himself.... Such was the end of a brave Czech patriot. I retain in my possession the book, *Lidice*, which he dedicated "To my dear friend and colleague, Rev. J. McLachlan, 4.vi.44, Author".

INDIA, 1971 and 1977

Reconnaissance and Recollection

"Old men ought to be explorers"
T.S. Eliot: *East Coker*

For over thirty years, Margaret Barr devoted her life to education in north-east India. She founded schools and a rural centre, near Kharang, for the teaching of handicrafts and agriculture and to provide medical attention for the Khasi people emerging from their jungle and tribal life. (The story is told in her little book, *A Dream come True*, published posthumously in 1974.)

I got to know her in my student days, when she was the Unitarian minister in Rotherham, and I kept in touch with her throughout her life.

As already mentioned, Margaret came to England early in 1971 for an operation on her eyes. Since she needed someone to accompany her back to India and it was the year of my presidency of the General Assembly, I offered to go with her. No president had ever visited the Khasi Hill churches, and I thought it time one did! Moreover, as well as carrying greetings, it would be fitting that an old friend should be with her on her homecoming to the Hills.

We flew from Heathrow to Delhi on 25th October, and stayed a few days with Dr Thompson, medical adviser to the American embassy. I saw as much of Old and New Delhi as I could and also travelled to Agra, the Taj Mahal, and Fatehpur Sikri, Akbar's old capital, some twenty-six miles from Agra. I carried with me two cameras and a tape-recorder, the latter proving very useful in the Khasi Hills. Unfortunately, at Fatehpur Sikri the new camera I was using for the first time failed to transport the film, so that I have no pictorial record of what must be one of the finest achievements in stone of the Moghul Emperors. Akbar lived in his new capital only sixteen years and then had to abandon it on account of shortage of water. It is still notable, nevertheless, for its good

Margaret Barr, Dr Yohann Paul and the author at Udaipur airport, Rajasthan, October, 1971

planning, stately buildings, and for the Buland Damaza ('Gate of Victory'), built in 1602 and bearing the Persian inscription: "Jesus – on whom be peace – said, "The world is a bridge; pass over it, but build no house on it!"'. I was impressed, as are most visitors, by the rare beauty of the Taj.

Train journeys in India make their own appeal. They provide ample opportunities to observe one's fellow-travellers, a motley collection of all sorts and sizes, colours and classes. The platforms exhibit a gaiety and variety of life completely novel to Western eyes.

A day or two later, Margaret and I left Delhi by 'plane for Udaipur in Rajasthan: we were the sole occupants, apart from the crew. We went there to meet Dr Yohann Paul, an Indian educationalist and literacy expert, who had recently adopted Unitarianism. He was also a homeopathic practitioner, but his chief interest lay in the adult-education movement, and he aimed at setting up an organisation for the training of teachers who would go into the villages in tribal country and endeavour to raise the level of literacy amongst the peasantry, who were at the mercy of money-lenders and rapacious entrepreneurs. We spent two days as guests with the Paul family and returned to Delhi, arriving in the middle of a 'black-out' exercise. This was not the only occasion of its kind, for we were plunged into darkness in Calcutta only a few days later. At this time Mrs Gandi's government was extremely jittery about Chinese intentions.

In Calcutta, we stayed at the Ramakrishna Mission in Gol Park. This is a large, imposing building, housing a hall and other meeting rooms, a library and offices, and accommodation for guests and students. Irene Ray, a friend of Margaret's, worked here, assisting with publications representing the tolerant and universalist approach of the Mission, which supports educational and philanthropic activities in different parts of India, not least in the Khasi Hills. In Calcutta, we visited Narendrapur, a large compound some fifteen miles from the city, where there is an ashram, a college and school, and a blind boys' institute. About 1500 boys and youths are boarded and educated here, and there is a teaching and domestic staff of about four hundred.

The large number of blind children in India poses a serious problem. On my second visit, six years later, I actually stayed for some days at Whitefield, near Bangalore, on the campus of the Divine Light School, where John Monach, my son-in-law's father, happened to be teaching. The need for government, and indeed individual, attention to the causes of blindness in India appears to be urgent. I hazard a guess at the causes: the prevalence of dust in the dry climate; lack of early parental care for the eyes of babies; and the very prevalent hosts of flies and other insects which seem to be hovering and crawling over small children's faces.

Whilst in Calcutta, I arranged to meet members of the Sadharan Brahmo Somaj, a reformed and liberal Hinduism founded by Ram Mohun Roy, in their headquarters in Cornwallis Street. Some of the younger members attending the meeting I addressed were anxious to be put in touch with Unitarian youth in England, whilst I expressed the hope that students might be sent for theological training to Manchester College, Oxford, so continuing an old tradition.

From Calcutta, Margaret went on to Shillong, chief town of Meghalaya, the hill state carved out of old Assam, but I took a 'plane for Madras, as I was anxious to meet the pastor and congregation of the

Unitarian Christian church (founded 1795) which was experiencing difficulties in recovering its property, sequestered by a former church secretary. In Madras I stayed four days, interviewing both the senior and junior advocates engaged in litigation on behalf of the church and conducting a Service on the roof of the lay-pastor's dwelling. This was an unusual experience. It took place at night, and was attended by about twenty-five adults and a score of children, all called together at short notice and assembled rather precariously on a slightly sloping flat roof! Needless to say, I had never before spoken on a roof-top and in almost complete darkness.

Once in position, I took care not to move. Nearly twenty years afterwards, I received a greeting from the church secretary, Victoria Merlin Gabriel, warmly urging me to re-visit Madras and be present at the inauguration of an Indian Unitarian Union, at which (I was told) my presence was considered to be "highly desirable". In fact, my next visit took place much earlier, in 1977.

The last stage of my journey to the Khasi Hills took me, via Calcutta, by 'plane to Gauhati in Assam, and thence by taxi to Shillong up a sixty mile long road, desperately in need of improvement. The view from the air of the giant Himalayas, in particular Mount Everest and its neighbours, was spectacular.

Unfortunately, the nervousness of the Government of the day over the Chinese presence in Tibet led to restrictions upon all freedom of movement. My permit only allowed me to stay fourteen days and confined me within a fifteen mile radius of Shillong. This meant I was unable to visit outlying churches, yet I made several useful contacts, and a party of eight senior members of the Jowai church, the largest in the Hills, came down to Shillong to meet me.

More importantly, perhaps, I was able to accompany Margaret to Kharang. Here, some dozen or so miles from Shillong, she had established her Rural Centre. It was necessary to hire a jeep for the first part of the journey as the 'road' was unmade and very rocky. After a bout of haggling with the driver, we set off for Smit over the worst track I have ever travelled in a wheeled vehicle. It was a relief, at length, to find a rocky stream barring further 'progress'. Here, two strapping young women shouldered the heavier packages, whilst the three of us – we had been joined by Devison Marbaniang, the indefatigable lay-leader of the Khasi churches – carried the rest. It took us four hours on foot to reach Kharang, or at least the Rural Centre.

This small settlement of wooden buildings stands in a clearing in the jungle and consists of a schoolhouse, a guest house, a dispensary, a cow shed, a poultry shed, Margaret's home, and the headman Dran's dwelling. Some land had been terraced for cultivation, but the jungle appeared to be encroaching fast. Below, were a small stream and two large pools, in one of which Margaret often swam.

Here, I merely summarise impressions of my first visit to this rather remarkable outpost. At night, the temperature in these hills drops suddenly, which is to be expected since one is actually living at over 5,000 feet above sea level. Shillong Peak, which I climbed with Devison is 6,600 feet high and affords what Joseph Dalton Hooker in his majesterial *Himalayan Journals* (Vol. II, p. 289) calls "the finest view in the Khasia mountains". In Shillong, it is necessary to have a coal fire in one's bedroom unless you want to freeze! In Kharang a charcoal-burner is essential, and if you are wise, you carry this with you from room to room. I well remember what a comfort it was. On my second visit to the Hills, I was given a metal model of this useful apparatus to bring home, but was compelled to ditch it during my rather adventurous transit to and from Darjeeling, to be described later. For light in the evenings, the usual Khasi illuminant is a rushlight. In the otherwise total gloom of a tiny Khasi house it is difficult to see anything at night. At dusk one evening I entered the house of one of Margaret's old pupils, then married to the village handiman and herself a midwife. We drank tea with her and ate the regulation rice-crumpet in almost unrelieved darkness. Meanwhile, a bee had evidently taken refuge beneath the thong of one of my sandals, and as I rose to say farewell and walked a step or two towards the door, I felt a sharp sting. The father of the family examined my foot, extracted the sting and applied a little lime to neutralise the acid. I suffered no further inconvenience, and the next day I was able to inspect the primitive hive in his garden. Outside, at nightfall, the Hills breathe magic. All is quiet, except for the occasional puff of wind through the pines and the call of birds. A chorus of cicadas strikes up on every side, and continues as you walk from one place to another. Along the tracks to Kharang village the fire-flies drift leisurely through the undergrowth; few sights are lovelier than these little 'wandering stars', the minute 'forest planets' of the Hills.

At night, we used to gather in Margaret's house – a small circle of youngsters, then living with their teacher, and a few older girls – singing folk songs and camp songs most tunefully. The Khasis are a musical people and it is interesting to hear how quickly they learn Western songs and hymns. I recorded songs and sounds as we gathered round the charcoal-burner or journeyed through the bush. My first stay in the Hills was short, but I had seen enough to realise the immensity of the task this little lady had set herself, and accomplished. Margaret spent 36 years in India, most of them in the Hills; and now, scattered all over the district, teaching, nursing, and occupying responsible positions, were young men and women who owed the whole of their education to Kong Barr. In Jowai and Shillong she had taught in more than one school, and the Sunderland Memorial School was her foundation. But the Rural Centre, with its school, dispensary, and midwifery service was, I think, her most valuable contribution to the raising of living standards in the area.

On my way home, I stopped off at Bombay and stayed at the Salvation Army hostel in Mereweather Road. I wanted to see something of the second city of India and visit Elephanta and the Ajanta and Ellora Caves. Availing myself of a 'city tour' bus I drove by way of Chowpatty Beach, where cricket was in progress, to the Malabar Hill. This is charmingly landscaped. The park is named after the late P.M. Nehru's wife. On the other side of the road are the 'Hanging Gardens', containing fine topiary work, whilst just beyond the trees stand the 'Towers of Silence', where the Parsee community lay out their dead. As I came down from the Hill, I turned in at the Taraporewala Aquarium, which contains an amazing collection of tropical fish, large and small. Was it a mere coincidence, I wonder, that next door to it a small' café proclaimed in large letters:'Fish 'n Chips'? Could there possibly be a trade-connection?

That afternoon, I took the boat from 'The Gateway of India' quay, where stands the huge stone arch, built to celebrate the visit in 1911 of the King-Emperor George V. From this point, numerous small craft ply regularly to Elephanta Island, six miles away, where 'caves' hewn out of the solid rock display scenes from Hindu mythology. These remarkable 'caves' were carved from the top down, a technique of execution found also at Ellora. The main figure of the god, Shiva, was 18 feet high and 12 feet across, one of the largest piece of rock-sculpture in the world. There are six caves in all, dating from the eighth century. An elephant (in rock) once stood at the approach to the carvings. When it was time to return, I made the acquaintance of an Italian businessman, who was travelling for an American pharmaceutical firm. He was visiting Bombay before going back to Vietnam, of which he painted an appalling picture, especially of the lads of the American army, hooked on heroin and prostitution. We had left our boat at the end of a very long, narrow jetty, upon which now stood literally hundreds of people. It took us nearly three-quarters of an hour to cover one hundred yards. All the time, I expected to hear the splash of some poor creature pushed off the jetty into the sea. The good humour of the Indian crowd, who gave way to us, impressed me greatly. Their patience and forbearance was heroic.

Next day, I flew to Aurangabad, some 250 miles east of Bombay, *en route* for Ajanta and Ellora, which I had been told on no account to fail to visit. On the plane was a young English ecologist who was on his way to Canberra to lecture on conservation. He, too, was bound for the Ajanta caves and the Ellora rock temples. We joined forces, booked in for the night at the Aurangabad Hotel and chartered a taxi to pick us up at 7 a.m. next morning. The hotel was comfortable; we rose early and were on our way at 7 a.m. precisely, each with a packed lunch. The driver, a bearded young Sikh of imposing aspect, maintained a steady speed and covered the 66 miles to Ajanta by 8.30 a.m. The caves, over thirty of them, are hewn out of the side of a curving valley, where the rock is soft enough to be worked. They were discovered in 1819 by a British army officer hunting a panther, and were a major archaeological find. Each is profusely decorated with sculpture and murals. The latter are the leading features. They are the work of Buddhist monks and artists and can only be seen when illuminated by a 500 watt lamp which the guide directs on to the walls and roofs. The scenes depicted are from the life of the Buddha and from town and country life, dating back to between the second century B.C. and the 7th century A.D. After about two hours' viewing, we felt it was time to move to Ellora, a twenty mile journey on the other side of Aurangabad.

At Ellora there are over 34 caves, 12 Buddhist, 17 Hindu and 5 Jain. Each temple is carved out of solid rock; some are three storeys high. The Kailasa, a free-standing temple hewn out of the hillside is a marvel of execution. Dedicated to Shiva and thought to have taken ten lives to create, the effect of these cave-temples is overpowering, and we were suitably exhausted. By 3 p.m. we decided to 'call it a day' and asked our driver to take us back to Daulatabad Fort, opposite which we knew there was a restaurant rejoicing in the sporting appellation of 'The Rock and Feathers Snack Shop', where the proprietess is an Englishwoman famed for her good 'cuppas'. We refreshed ourselves accordingly. The 'plane from Aurangabad to Bombay that afternoon left only about one hour late, which is good for Indian Airlines! At Bombay Airport I took leave of my companion, who went into the city, whilst I awaited the Air India flight, via Kuwait, Geneva, Paris, to London. The day had been filled with food for thought: the charming, humanistic frescoes of Ajanta and the amazing and magnificent rock-temples of Ellora floated in memory and imagination for days to come, deepening the impression that my first visit to India had made upon me of the creative and spiritual achievements of mankind.

Early in February 1977, I found myself for the second time, in India. This was at the request of the Khasi Unitarian Union that a British representative should share the celebration of its ninetieth anniversary. No one at Unitarian headquarters in London seemed anxious to go, so I volunteered. I spent ten days in Shillong, Jowai, and Kharang, visited ten churches, met a great number of people, brought the greetings of the General Assembly and addressed more than one gathering. This time there was no limit to the distance I might travel nor the duration of my stay. I planned an extended tour, to Madras, Pondicherry (to visit the seat of the Sri Aurobindo ashram), Udaipur and beyond into the tribal region of the Bihls; I also hoped to go up to Darjeeling and get a glimpse of the Himalayas.

First, I was engaged in conference with the leaders of the Khasi churches, cementing friendships and gaining an understanding of the expanding work and ambitions of our fellow-religionists. On Tuesday, 15th February, I was present at the opening of the new Kong Barr Memorial Hospital. This is situated on a small hill above the Rural Centre and was built with funds furnished by the Dutch Remonstrant churches. I slept there the night after the opening ceremony, performed by the Finance Minister of Meghalaya, who treated us to a thirty-five minute harangue. No doubt he had his eye on the forthcoming election.... I spoke briefly on behalf of the British churches and as an old friend of the foundress. Lunch was served to a crowd of visitors, and afterwards I walked down to Margaret's old home, which has been kept intact since her death in August 1973. I was anxious to see the memorial erected over the spot where her ashes are interred.

The hospital would have delighted her. Its accommodation is modest but capable of expansion. Back in Shillong and accompanied by Devison, I drove the hospital jeep the sixty-six miles down to Gauhati and caught a train to Jalpaiguri, on my way to Darjeeling. I planned to spend a few days there and was booked in at the Windamere (sic) Hotel. This stands above the town, looking out towards the white wall of the Hima-

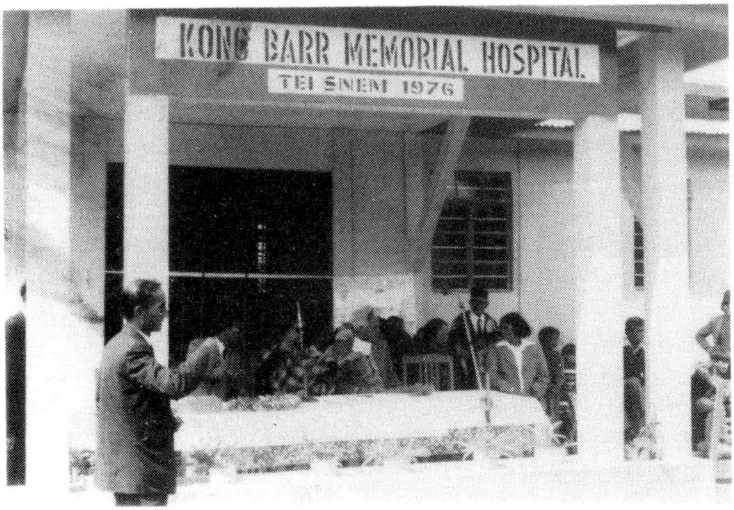

At the opening of the Memorial Hospital near Kharang in the Khasi Hills, 1977

layas. But getting there was something of a problem, since the town was in a 'restricted area'. Ever since arriving in Calcutta, I had been trying to obtain a permit for Darjeeling, first at the Assam government office in Calcutta, then in Shillong, and finally by application to 'Foreigners' Control' in Darjeeling itself. At each attempt I had been foiled by the native Indian tendency to avoid taking responsibility and, if possible, to pass the buck. The Shillong authorities advised me to telegraph the police in Darjeeling, which I did. They replied, "Make every endeavour to obtain a permit from a competent authority", but the problem remained: who was the competent authority? And more to the point, who would act? Someone suggested I could probably pick up a permit in Siliguri, the town in the plain immediately beneath Darjeeling. In the event, I spent the night in the first-class waiting room at New Jalpaiguri, lying on a bench with Hindu and other travellers squatting all around me on the floor.

This town's station was about two miles from Siliguri, where I hoped to obtain a permit. It was 10.30 p.m. when we arrived here, and the waiting room was full of people, bedding down for the night. The police entered and weeded out those who had no business to be there.

Then a strange character circulated, who claimed to be the 'Foreigners' Checking Officer'. His job, apparently was to see than no unauthorised person could proceed further into the Darjeeling district. He informed me that Siliguri could not supply a permit. That had all been altered by a recent government decision. "How could he help me?" he inquired, at the same time quietly asking how much I had given to the coolie who had carried my luggage up to the waiting room. He could, of course, arrange a bond, and then I could go wherever I wanted! However, I did not fall for this. After passing an almost sleepless night, I waited until the 'checking officer' was in the washroom, picked up my bags and rucksack and marched straight out of the station into the midst of a crowd of cycle-rickshaw coolies, who were assembled on the steps. Engaging a likely lad, I told him to take me as quickly as possible to the Hotel Sinclair, an address I had been given, from which I telephoned the manager of the Windamere Hotel in Darjeeling. "Oh, you can get the permit here, all right", he cheerfully declared. "Come up on the service-bus", which I eventually did. The journey by road took about three hours, which is a great deal quicker than the British-built mountain railway, scheduled to take nearly seven!

When I reported to the Tourist office in Darjeeling, they were somewhat embarrassed, especially after a phone call to the local police. But they were kind and sympathetic, as I told my tale of attempts to get a permit. "Go up to the hotel and settle in and rest" they said, for they must have noticed that I was pretty exhausted. Meanwhile, they arranged for me to report next morning to the local police. It turned out that if one came to Darjeeling through Bagdogra airport (down in the plain), one was admitted without a permit. Otherwise it was only obtainable from Calcutta! I mention this to show how bureaucratically-manacled the Indian sub-continent is. Their own people are constantly at the mercy of petty functionaries and ridiculous laws, which make life miserable for foreign travellers as well as the indigenous population. On more than one occasion I listened to bitter complaints about officialdom in India, which gives the appearance of being set up to harass the individual and punish society.

The Windamere Hotel turned out to be a pleasant and homely hospice, where I could have enjoyed myself immensely, had I not had 'a sword of Damocles' hanging over me. Nevertheless, I arranged to join a party early next morning to see the sun rise over the Himalayas from Tiger Hill. If conditions were right we should see Mount Everest from the summit. Alas, all we say was a pale sunrise and a huge veil of dust and mist hanging like a drop-curtain between Tiger Hill and the Himalayan peaks. A small crowd of tourists had assembled on the look-out tower armed with field-glasses and cameras, but it was no use. We had to be content with a visit to the old Buddhist monastery at Goom, its prayer-wheels turning and the monks preparing the ghee-candles. The jeeps brought us back to our hotel, and I ate a slow breakfast and walked over to the Mountaineering Institute, whose director, at this time, was Tensing Norgay, conqueror of Everest. One of its most precious exhibits is the original manuscript of Sir John Hunt's 'Ascent of Everest', whilst another no less dear to a Britisher is the painting of Great Langdale by Howard Somervell, the Everest climber of 1924, who devoted his surgical skills to the people of South India. Somervell died in 1975. I am happy to think I met him and his two sons at the Robertson Lamb Hut in Langdale in 1945, just before they set out to climb Bow Fell buttress.

Following this, I paid my visit to the 'Foreigners' Registration Office' and related my story. By now, I was getting pretty fluent on the subject, perhaps adorning its presentation with effect. The official listened sympathetically and asked me to confirm my flight back to Calcutta four days later, which I did. At his invitation, I then wrote out the whole story of my attempts to secure a permit and he carried the papers upstairs to his superiors. Presently, he returned and said it had been decided to refer the whole case to the Bengal Government in Calcutta, which would mean that I would be out of town before any reply could possibly be in their hands! This diplomatic coup pleased all parties and the senior officer and a colleague joined us for a good laugh over the whole business. I returned to the hotel much relieved. I had been 'given time', but not in a 'lock-up'!

During the rest of my stay in the hill-town, I packed in some interesting experiences: Sunday morning worship at the local church of North India, one of a very small congregation; a visit to the Natural History Museum, a collection created by the British, remaining in much the same condition as it must have been when Independence was granted, labelling, lighting, and housing all out-of-date. The following day there was a splendid view of Kinchinjunga above the dust and heat-haze which so far had hidden the mountain ridges. The Tibetan Refugee Centre stands on a small spur of the hills in the midst of tea gardens, well above the village of Leebong, where "the highest race-course in the world" is situated. For the past three days the Tibetans had been celebrating their New Year with fireworks. Their Self-Help work-rooms were deserted, but as I roamed up and down the terraces I kept meeting Tibetans who have found here, in the border-regions of India, a haven of peace. They seem a happy and pleasant people, even in exile, and quite used to the hills and the altitude, which can be a little trying for anyone coming up from the plains.

Darjeeling stands at 7,000 to 7,500 feet above sea-level, which makes the frequent steep paths and steps amongst the tea gardens rather trying. My stay was coming to an end. My air-tickets (and convenient way of escape) was dated; and so on 23rd February I boarded an Indian Airlines 'bus in the company of a party of Oxfam workers, who had stayed overnight at the Windamere, and we dropped swiftly down to the airport at Bagdogra. Mingling with the other British travellers, I passed through the controls, boarded the 'plane for Calcutta, and flew to Madras. I remember feeling very relaxed at being on my way again, after my 'illegal' trip to the hills!

At Madras, the taxis were all on strike, with the result that everybody piled into the airline bus to the city. There I transferred quickly to a cycle-rickshaw, clutching my luggage and hoping that the little man could really take me the one and half miles to the hotel. This mode of travel, though cheap, is rather nerve-racking. At the Hotel Imperial I arrived unscathed and rejoicing to find Michael and Victoria Gabriel, lay-pastor and secretary of our Madras church, actually waiting for me. It was a warm re-union after six years and we arranged to make the most of the three days of my stay. The church was now in the hands of its legal owners and the process of restoration and re-decoration had begun, though it was sad to realise how much damage it had suffered at the hands of the squatters. The Gabriels persuaded me to spend my last evening with them discussing church affairs, as well as seeing something of the city. Their friendly and charming welcome made my stay a memorable one.

Dr Paul had suggested that, when in Madras, I ought to pay a visit to the Aurobindo ashram in Pondicherry, which is not very far away. I followed his advice and took a bus to the former French enclave, south of Madras, on the coast of the Indian ocean, to see something of the remarkable organisation which has grown up there under the inspiration of the religious philosophy and writings of Sri Aurobindo. This Indian guru, born in 1877 and educated at Cambridge, made his home in Pondicherry. A revolutionary thinker, he took up the study of yoga and meditation in 1910 and was joined, some years later, by a remarkable French woman, who, under the name of 'The Mother', took charge of the ashram and all of its many activities.

In the main building is Aurobindo's grave, wreathed in flowers and visited by a continuous stream of disciples and admirers. I found the atmosphere somewhat monastic and not a little pretentious. I was fortunate to secure a room in the ashram's international guesthouse, a stone's throw from the main kitchen, and lived there for three days as a member of the community. This is self-supporting, owning as it does several large gardens and farms, one of which I visited. In addition, there is a printing press, a bakery, furniture and light-engineering factories, a paper-making workshop, handloom-weaving sheds, a tapestry-fabricating works, an art gallery and a library. Some four miles from Pondicherry lies Auroville, 'City of Dawn', which (when I was there) was being built on a ten thousand acre site. It is intended as a city of universal peace and harmony, where people from all countries will be able to settle in community "above all creeds, politics, and national ties". Of course, 'The Mother' was the leading spirit in the creation of this city. A huge concrete dome, the Matremandir, is its focal centre, and this will be surrounded by water and twelve gardens radiating therefrom. The educational and social philosophy of the founders must be unique, for the aim is to make education unnecessary, at least in the Western sense of the term. Hence the nomenclature: 'The Last School', and 'The First and Second After-schools'. Teachers work for love, not pay, and indeed all work in the city will eventually be voluntary. The idealism of the inhabitants is tested by a 'Free-sell shop', where one gives and takes. It is hoped that the site will eventually house about 50,000 people, all of whom will work together to seek "a higher consciousness". I noticed a number of Europeans were already in residence – at hamlets rejoicing in the names of 'Promesse' and 'Aspiration'. Since I visited the place,. I have not heard what further progress has been made, but I think such a Utopian experiment could only have taken root in India, where, alongside popular mythologies and almost materialistic religious attitudes, there exist devoted and highly philosophic idealisms. I wonder whether Auroville will succeed in overcoming the innate tendency of the human ego to divide rather than unite, to seek selfish advantage rather than community welfare...?

From Pondicherry I returned via Madras and Bangalore to Delhi.

At Bangalore, however, I broke my journey to spend a few days with John Monach, who was then teaching at a school for blind children, 'The Divine Light School' at Whitefield, which I have already mentioned. It was an education to belong, even briefly, to a different kind of community from that which I had been observing in Pondicherry. This was a group of over one hundred blind children. We shared their life, their simple and – to Western feelings – harsh regimen, their serious moments and their fun. I listened to them singing the school song, not without a distinct lump in my throat: "Lead, kindly light, amid the encircling gloom". The teaching staff were a very dedicated body, some of them blind themselves. I found the food hard to swallow, sometimes even nauseating....

Bangalore, nearly three thousand feet up on the Deccan plateau, is a fine city with notable buildings and beautiful parks. The year I was there, English cricket suffered its sole defeat that season, in the new cricket stadium which is now reckoned to be second only to Melbourne's.

Less than a week later I left for Udaipur in Rajasthan for a meeting with Dr Yohann Paul. Travelling overnight from Delhi on the so-called 'Chetak Express', we passed another prestige train, the 'Pink City Express' from Jaipur, swinging on its way. And here I must pay a tribute to the Indian railways, a good legacy of the Raj, on which I have always travelled comfortably and on the one occasion when I ordered an evening dinner was served with the best meal I have ever had on a train, and it was brought to the compartment in which I was sitting! *En route* for Udaipur, I had rather a cold journey with little sleep, but a young Indian, travelling in the same compartment most thoughtfully spread a rug over me and in the morning awakened me with tea and toast. I mention this to illustrate the sort of kindness which one often experiences in India and which one should never forget. At the station in Udaipur, Ajai Paul, the doctor's son, was waiting for me with a bicycle on which to carry my luggage.

Dr Paul was anxious to discuss his Literacy Campaign, which he had developed since our first meeting six years earlier. He was now proposing to operate in the tribal area of the Bhils, a depressed and poverty-stricken peasantry neglected by Government. There are about four million of these small farmers in a region of which the main centre is the town of Dungarpur. We took the train there and stayed overnight in a municipal guesthouse. Yohann had made an appointment with the chairman of the Village Industries Board for Rajasthan, Sri Bhogi lai Pandya, a fine old gentleman who had been working amongst the Bhils ever since 1919. Meeting us with a jeep, he took us round several primitive and poverty-stricken small-holdings, scattered about the countryside, so that I should see conditions for myself. At this time, I was serving as Hon. Secretary of the Unitarian Peace Fellowship which was considering committing itself to raising funds for World Development and in particular to assist Dr Paul with his Literacy project. Hence I attached great importance to familiarising myself with the plight of Third World people 'on the ground'. The Bhil people are hospitable and charming folk, but manifestly labouring under severe handicaps. They are, for example, an easy prey to rapacious money-lenders, who lend them money on the security of their precious land, which becomes forfeit when they cannot easily repay.... They are, of course, illiterate and innumerate. Sri Bhogi had given his unreserved approval to Dr Paul's project. His plan was this: to set up training-schemes in several key villages where a trained Indian couple would reside and instruct their peers in literacy and numeracy, health and hygiene. He would concentrate on single families specially chosen from a number of villages, bringing them into an educational centre, training them (with emphasis upon the women), and then send them back to their own villages with knowledge and skills which they could then make available to others. Dr Paul reckoned that in the course of ten years the entire population of the Dungarpur district (about half a million) would benefit from this project. Government departments involved in Welfare had assured him of their full co-operation, and in fact he was taking up the work on their behalf. "No project in India hitherto", he wrote, "has had any impact upon the rural *women*, not even in the field of literacy. Our aim is to cater for the needs of women, so that the process of development from a primitive society may be accelerated. It is a truism that if you educate a woman you educate a family".

I was so much attracted to this lively and dedicated educationist's scheme that I was anxious for him to come to Britain to make a direct appeal to Unitarians. The Peace Fellowship made his project the focus of their Lent Appeal in 1978, and in that year I managed to persuade Dr Paul to visit Britain as our guest. He spoke to meetings in both North and South and accepted invitations to address Dutch and German Liberal Christians as well. Unfortunately, the April of 1978 was bitterly cold and our friend came unprepared to face the cold winds of a late winter.

It is to be feared that he caught a chill in England before he returned home, for in June he became seriously ill and died at his home shortly afterwards. The loss of this good and far-seeing man at this particular juncture was a serious setback to a World-Development scheme that promised well for some of the most under-privileged poor in North-West India.

My second visit to India was fraught with difficulties in travel, some anxiety, and considerable fatigue. I missed a good deal of sleep on journeys, several of which had to start at unearthly hours, even before 4 a.m., and often finished around midnight. I covered thousands of miles from the foothills of the Himalayas to the southern shores of the Indian Ocean, and again across to the arid lands of North West Rajasthan. Always, however, I found myself fascinated, marvelling, amused, as well as repelled, disgusted, and almost despairing. The kindness of neighbours to each other was most touching, especially the absolute confirmation of the saying that 'It is the poor who help the poor'. As I journeyed, the concern and sympathy shown me was unforgettable. Unlike the ordinary tourist, I often moved amongst old friends, but I also made new.

In Calcutta, for example, I made the acquaintance of a young man recently returned from British Guiana. He was unemployed, bare-footed, and under-nourished, but seeking work and speaking English well. He helped me when I was trying to obtain permits to enter Meghalaya and Darjeeling, guiding me through the streets to the various offices I needed to visit. Eventually, *at my request*, he took me back to the village (Akra Phatak) where his wife and small daughter were living in a 'lean-to' on the banks of the River Hoogly. I sent to the local shop for some bread and tea, and we ate sitting on the ground near his refuge – it could scarcely be called a home! Basil Carrectus and his wife, Pauli, possessed only a thin rug, a little straw mat and a bit of sacking to cover the stone bunk on which they slept. They had a small stove for cooking but no utensils: they borrowed these from neighbours. Their four-year-old daughter, Mary, slept in a neighbour's house. I was reminded of Ireland, where peasant families treat relatives and poor friends with kindness and compassion. I took Basil back with me to the five-star hotel, in which British Airways had booked me, but he would not even cross the street, whilst I collected some dressings and ointment for his badly-festered hand, cut on some tin.

The contrast between the palm court and swimming pool of the hotel and the squalor of Akra Phatak haunted me then, and still troubles me today....

Shah Jahan's poet-laureate, Abu Talib Kalim, a Persian, wrote of the India he knew in the seventeenth century: "One can say of it that it is a second Paradise in this respect That whoever leaves this garden is filled with regret". There speaks the voice of privilege, always articulate; but there is another side to this coin, what the poet Wordsworth called "the still sad music of humanity", which is seldom heard or noticed by those upon whom the sun of good fortune smiles. In the large cities, like Calcutta, poverty and misery are so patent that I was completely inhibited from using a camera in the streets, because the human condition was often so vile. The hovels and open drains of the bustees, the beggars and the deformed, the blind and the blasted for whom 'home' is the street, must appal any Westerner who passes by. A Calcutta social worker once calculated that in the bustees area there were about eight latrines and two water taps to every four hundred inhabitants. Not surprisingly, infant mortality was 673 per thousand births. Constant immigration from poverty-stricken provinces like Bihar and refugees from other regions, where political and tribal pressures are extreme, pose serious problems for the authorities.

Nehru once said that India's five great problems were 'land, water, cows, capital, and babies'. Cultivable land; clean water, cows that produce milk and other useful dairy products, instead of wandering about and squatting in busy thoroughfares; capital properly distributed and utilised; and last, but not least, birth control: all are highly desirable. Nehru omitted to mention Literacy, but a modicum of education is urgently needed to raise living standards as well.

Yet the world's greatest democracy could enjoy a steadily improving quality of life if social custom could be modified and religious fanaticism expelled. There is no denying that the Indian races are capable of hard work and self-sacrifice. I was constantly startled by the native capacity and willingness to sustain hard labour, in both town and country. Handsome men and beautiful women abound, as do lovely children (even if too many of them!) early accustomed to assist their families by carrying water and fuel and, not seldom, their younger sisters and brothers on their backs. And by far the chief wealth of any nation is its people.

The Delectable Mountains

"Those blue remembered hills"
(A.E. Housman)

My parents spent their Easter holidays, most years, at a farmhouse above Llanfairfechan in North Wales, five hundred feet up the side of Penmaenmawr Mountain. I used to join them there on my way back from school. I can still recall the tremendous thrill it gave me to walk with my father from the railway station through the lamb-skipping meadows up to Tan y Geulan. The local hills rose in procession before us.

But my first intense sighting of mountains was during a cycle tour in Cumberland in the early twenties when, riding from St Bees, we gazed in silence upon Crummock Water and Buttermere, Ennerdale and Wast-water and their surrounding satellites. My walking legs, however, were first exercised in Wales.

In 1928, on holiday with friends at Llanfairfechan, we climbed the Carnedds, and near the misty summit of Llewellyn met a member of the Swiss Alpine Club. Before long, he was asking us if we would care to accompany him on a short rock climb in the Nant Francon valley. Intrigued, several of us met our new friend next day below the Milestone Buttress. It began to rain, and instead of climbing there, we pressed on to the Devil's Kitchen above Llyn Idwal, hoping the weather would im-prove. Ascending to the Waterfall pitch, we were all suitably baptized. Soaked to the skin, I took off my dripping shirt and put on a thin mack-intosh to cover my nakedness. Then the party decided to proceed to the top of Glyder Fawr! The temperature plummeted and it began to hail. By this time I was miserably cold. Walking by compass, we reached the top of the Gribin ridge and came slithering down to the road. (I was wearing crêpe rubber shoes!) I learnt an unforgettable lesson: Never go mountain walking in unsuitable footwear or inadequate clothing! Hot tea and a warm leather motor-jacket alone revived me....

Later that summer, five of us walked over from Llanfairfechan to

Party of Old Willastonians with A.D. Tobler (middle of back row) at Silvretta Hut, Switzerland, 1931

Capel Curig and back, a distance of about 35 miles. Again, I was not properly equipped and was 'rewarded' with badly blistered feet. This completed my initiation: the age of innocence and folly was over!

Lakeland was the scene of my introduction to rock-climbing. A friend led me up D Buttress on Dow Crag wearing heavily-nailed boots. It was my twenty-first birthday and the first of many climbs and walks at home and abroad with Priestley Phillips. In 1930, I joined a party led by W.T. Elmslie, a member of the Alpine Club. We walked the Black Forest from north to south, a distance of about 300 miles, staying at the recently-opened Jugendherbergen. This was the year in which the YHA in Britain was founded. I became a life member. The following year, A.D. Tobler, my old Swiss language-master took a party of Old Willastonians to Seebenalp near Flims and then on to Klosters and the Silvretta Hut, where, despite poor weather, we climbed the Silvrettahorn and the Piz Buin. About this time, the Manchester University Mountaineering Club became very active and I went on meets with them in Derbyshire, Yorkshire, and North Wales. Serious climbing followed with Phillips and

Author leading on Central Buttress, Trifaen, in the 'thirties

Arthur Chisman, both members of the Rucksack Club. Whilst a student in Germany in 1933, I travelled to Czechoslovakia to inspect the High Tatra, and the next year returned with Priestley Phillips to make a number of ascents, with and without guides. We wrote an account of this expedition for the Club Journal of 1935. After this I spent regular holidays at Tal y Braich or at huts in Lakeland rock climbing and mountain walking, up to 1952 when we removed to Northern Ireland. Before that, in Oxford, I used to meet Phillips, then living in Evesham, at Moreton-in-the-Marsh and go for long walks in the Cotswolds and the Malverns. From Oxford, too, my son, Peter, and I made expeditions to the Black Mountains, the Brecon Beacons and the Carmarthen Vans.

To celebrate the 21st anniversary of my first rock climb, I led D Buttress and Woodhouse's Climb on Dow, and a day or two later on Pavey Arc sustained the only accident I ever had, in Rake End Chimney, where a climber dislodged a rock that fell on my head, causing a scalp wound, the mark of which I carry to this day. This was before the general adoption of protective helmets.

During the summer of 1944, before leaving the North for Oxford, I decided to visit parts of the Yorkshire moors which I had not hitherto explored. So, on 1st August, I set out from Dent at 7.15 a.m. and walked over the Three Peaks, Whernside, Ingleborough, and Pennyghent, swimming in the Ribble *en route* and arriving in Litton at 6.40 p.m. Thirty years later, on 6th December, 1981, I walked the Three Peaks again, starting this time at 8 a.m. from Horton-in-Ribblesdale, going over Pennyghent, Whernside and Ingleborough, and reaching Horton in the dark about 6 p.m. A very different trip from the earlier one, since the tracks are now seriously eroded. Another solo walk, which I greatly enjoyed, was that from Bowes over the moors to Grains-of-the-Beck bridge, then up Mickle Fell, down to Maize Beck, and on to Dufton via High Cup Nick, finishing in Appleby at 10.45 p.m. Very rough, but fascinating in variety, thoroughly satisfying, and not far short of 30 miles.

Subsequently, when our family moved to Ireland, I suddenly became aware of the fact that 'The Snowdon Horseshoe' and other similar delights were not the only excitement on offer by the Welsh highlands. There were, for example, Cader Idris and the Rhinogs in West Central Wales, whose reputedly rough terrain I had never sampled. So I arranged to come over from Belfast in August 1955, visiting my father, then living retired in Liverpool, and travelled by train to Dolgelley. I carried a tent and other kit up the Cader road to within a short distance of Gwernon Lake and camped near Rhyd Wen. Next day, I ascended Cader from the West, working round into the head of Cwm Aron, climbing the rocky ridge nearby, and eventually walking along to Pen y Gader and down the Fox's path to camp. On the way down I overtook a family who kindly gave me and my clobber a lift in their Landrover to Tal y Bont, when I walked up to Pont Fadog and pitched camp just above the bridge near Lletty Lloegr. This is the point where the shepherds used to gather their flocks before driving them over the hills to England.

From here I was able to explore the quiet and lonely hinterland near Llyn Dulyn and Y Lethr. Next day, I walked into Cwm Nantol, where there are marvellous views of the Rhinogs, and went on to Maes y Garnedd, the home of Colonel John Jones, regicide and brother-in-law of Oliver Cromwell. From here the way up the Cwm to Drws Ardudwy through a gloriously-tinted countryside beneath and between the two

Author on winter traverse of Crib Goch, Snowdon

Rhinogs was magnificent. Climbing Rhinog Fawr, I came down to the 'Roman Steps' and Cwm Bychan, and from here hitched a lift to Llanbedr and made it home to Tal y Bont. In my log I wrote, "surely one of the finest walks in all Wales.... I must go back". But, like so many hopeful resolutions, I have never returned. So much depends upon opportunity, or lack of it! Moreover, West Wales is not the most accessible part of the beautiful principality. Lakeland, on the other hand I have visited again and again in all seasons of the year, climbing and walking, and never tired of its beauty, variety, and amazing surprises.

I confess I discovered the delights of walking and climbing in Scotland late in life, after my retirement. I had, however, visited Galloway from Ireland in July 1962, when it was still possible to take the train from Stranraer to Newton Stewart. From there I ascended the Merrick and traversed the Rhinns of Kells from north to south, finishing up in New Galloway, painfully sunburnt! True, I also spent two holidays in Arran, walking all its splendid ridges. Yet, not until I was free to attend the Rucksack Club 'Easter Meets' did I become at all familiar with Scottish mountains. The hills of Argyll, Inverness, Wester Ross, and Sutherland remained for me a 'closed book' until 1976. In that year I celebrated retirement by walking 'The West Highland Way' with my son-in-law, James, and his father. As yet, the trail had not been blazed and we met no other pilgrims on the Way, which at times was difficult to follow. We ended with an ascent of Ben Nevis on a memorable and bitterly cold day.

From 1978 onwards, I have been fortunate not to miss a single Easter Meet. Here is the list of the centres and the main summits ascended, usually in good snow conditions:

1978 Crianlarich – Ben More and Stobinian

1979 Alltbeith, Glen Affric – Ben Attow, Mam Soul

1980 Killiecrankie – Schiehallion, Beinn a 'Ghlo (all the tops), Ben Vrackie

1981 Cluanie Lodge – Carn Ghluasaid, Sgurr nan Conbhairran, S. Cluannie Ridge, Forcan Ridge and The Saddle, the Five Sisters of Kintail

1982 Achnashellach – Fuar Tholl, Sgurr a 'Chaorachain, Moruisg, Sgurr na Feartaig

1983 Kincraig – Low level walks (new snow, cold); thro' Rothiemurchus to Lairig Ghru as far as Sinclair hut; two walks in the Monadhliaths

1984 Dundonell – Beinn Dearg (5 Munroes), An Tealach (the whole ridge), Cul Mor, Quinag, Fannichs (3 tops)

1985 Roy Bridge – Creagh Meagaidh

1986 Onich – Bidean nam Bian (in arctic weather)

1987 Kinlochewe – Liathach, climbed on Slioch and Ben Eighe, weather poor

1988 Onich – Garbh Bheinn

1989 Braemar – Morrone, Lochnagar

An unsolicited note appeared in the R.C. Journal for 1984, listing the seven days' climbing in detail and concluding "Totals: 26 tops, 16 over 3,000, 22,250 feet climbed, 78 miles, 64 hours walking".

Other enjoyable walks have been the central (limestone) section of the Pennine Way, the whole of the Cleveland Way, Hadrian's Wall, the New Dales Traverse, and many in the Derbyshire and Yorkshire Dales.

Soon after our arrival in Ulster (in 1952), I joined the Belfast section of the Irish Mountaineering Club and went climbing in the Mournes. A frequent rendezvous for our members was a small cottage on the southern slopes of Slieve Binnian, affectionately known as 'the Bloathouse'. It looked out towards the Irish Sea, a pleasant enough situation, but its interior was less inviting. I stayed in its quaint squalor a number of times, even taking the family there for a week one summer! Unfortunately, not all who frequented it remembered to tidy up before they left.... In practice, mountaineering-club wardens have to exercise a severe discipline in this respect or the huts tend to become uninhabitable. For more than fifteen years, the Mourne Mountains, a compact group of hard granite hills and rocks in the south of County Down afforded some of my most enjoyable outings in both winter and summer.

I managed to fit in two or three days, most years, just before Christmas, often staying at a small hotel in Rostrevor and calling to see one or two of my country members at the same time. After this quiet break amid the Mournes, I was always ready for the busy, eventful days that followed. Winter walking can be a real pick-me-up, for one comes across animals, plants, and scenes not found at other, perhaps more clement, seasons of the year. You have the hills more or less to yourself and the fox, the hare and the buzzard are abroad; you can see farther, the field of view being more extensive than in the thicker atmosphere of summer. The hills are often clearly etched against the sky and there can be that hint of mystery in morning glow and evening shadow which lends depth to living and zest to breathing and movement. Slieve Donard, the highest of the Mournes, no heaven-challenging peak, 'tis true, I have climbed more times than I can remember, in summer heat and winter snow, but never 'came empty away'. On occasion, I have walked straight out of Belfast over Divis or Cave Hill, sometimes seeking permission to trespass on private land, and sometimes not. It always seemed a pity that the city fathers did not encourage their fellow-citizens to 'go walking', when the hills were so conveniently close, by securing 'walk ways' for the people, to take them out of the city and give them new horizons.

It was not long before we ventured, as a family, to take holidays in the Republic of Ireland. Its west coast became a favourite haunt. We started in the north-west by visiting Donegal, north and south, then followed Mayo, Connemara, Achill Island, Clare, Kerry and West Cork. What fascinating country these counties contain. At Easter, the two boys and I would pack our little car with camping equipment and food, and drive west and south, ostensibly to discover a good place for our next summer holiday, but also to get a taste of the hills and mountains of a hardly trodden land. It was rewarding. Ireland came alive for us. As yet, the tourist hordes had not descended and the hotels had not ascended, and you had the feeling that it was all new, unspoilt, and native. In Donegal you could go down to the strand and find not a single other person about: you could bathe 'starkers' and fear no peeping Toms. But to return to walking.

A memorable trip was that across the Wicklows from Blessington to Glendalough, and then on to the two Sugar Loafs and Bray Head, staying a night at the youth hostel in Glendalough. Another satisfying excursion was the horse-shoe ridge-walk on the Twelve Pins of Connemara. My two sons and I were nine hours on the ridge, dropping down to our camp site at Ballynahinch in the failing light, to eat a gargantuan meal cooked by torch-light! Another well remembered hike was in the McGillicuddy's Reeks: up the Hag's Glen, the Devil's Ladder (Oh! those Irish descriptive names!) and up to the summit of Carantuohill (3,414′). As we were nearing the top of the Ladder, Richard called out to me to look at the rainbow on the mist below. I then saw the 'Brocken Spectre' or 'Brocken effect' – my shadow on the mist below, surrounded by a rainbow-coloured halo of light. It was the sight of a lifetime.

Perhaps the ascent I recall most vividly is that of Brandon (3,206′) in County Kerry. I have climbed the mountain many times, and usually by a roundabout route. I used to get someone to drop me at the summit of the Connor Pass, north of Dingle, where I turned west and crossed the moors, taking in Beenabrack, Ballysittera, and Brandon Peak (2,764′). From here I would reach the precipitous edge of the Brandon massif, which R.L. Praeger, in his book, 'The Way I Went', calls "the finest mountain in Ireland". The views are magnificent and I would linger, drinking it all in, before coming down along what is now the mountainous sea coast to find a car waiting for me on a turf road near Ballinahow. Another walk in the Dingle peninsula starts from the top of the Connor Pass but proceeds in the opposite direction through a kind of 'wilderness' where the compass, even in fine weather, must be trusted. Eventually, one comes upon a Hidden Valley with a chain of small lakes and a steep descent and walk-out of the hills into rough farming country, miles from the main road. There one must have 'planted' another car to bring you home. Kerry and West Cork were our family happy 'hunting grounds' in the fifties and sixties, and I can think of no more attractive country for the average walker in the British Isles, unless it were Donegal with its Errigal, Muckish and Slieve League.

Once, when I returned to Ardara in Donegal, after an absence of a year or two, the local grocer, welcoming me back, asked how Kerry compared with Donegal. It was an awkward question to answer, but I had not been living in Ireland for nothing. So I replied, "How can one compare two stars in glory"? It was enough to please my grocer and leave both heavenly counties with honours squared....

One excursion I must not fail to mention, though it was not a mountaineering expedition. This is the sea-crossing from Dunquin to the Great Blasket Island. When staying at Ballyferriter, I often wished to visit this 'seat of learning' – learning, that is to say, about life. Amazingly, this small island has inspired and given to the world three native works of literature; 'Twenty Years A-Growing' by Maurice O'Sullivan, 'An Old Woman's Reflections' by Peig Sayers, and 'The Islandman' by Tomás O Crohan, all unique documents of folk-culture, fascinating reading, and descriptive of a life-style that has entirely vanished. All are redolent of the simple, rough existence made at once possible and unavoidable by the harsh physical environment which imposed itself upon a peasantry living close to nature and often near to starvation.

Not until the year before that in which we returned from Belfast to England did I actually make the crossing. It was accomplished in what the Kerryman calls 'a canoe' and others 'a curragh'*. This is a wooden-framed, shallow-draft boat of tarred canvas stretched round the frame and rowed with long poles, so as not to upset the balance. I was able to join a family party of visitors who spent several hours on the island. I understand the crossing is now commercialised. We visited the deserted village with its schoolroom and desks still *in situ*, climbed the hill and gazed over the 'Dangerous Cliffs', and stripped and swam from its attractive strand, An Tráigh Bhán (The White Strand), which must take its name from the silver sand. I can still 'feel' the wonderful buoyancy of the Atlantic waves and remember the clear water through which you could see the sandy bottom, a dozen or more feet below you. It was an experience not to be forgotten.

We were rowed out by three Dunquin boatmen and landed in the tiny, rocky 'harbour' that served the original islandmen ("All, all are gone", resettled by the government on the mainland years ago). It took about fifty minutes. But on the return journey we needed longer, for the tide had changed and the wind risen, so we were compelled to hug the

*Footnote: (The Gaelic name is *naomhog*, the direct descendant of the craft in which Saint Brendan is said to have crossed the Atlantic

low-lying island of Beg-inish for shelter and then make a dash across the Sound to the safety of Dunquin harbour. I took photographs of the remarkable swell on which the canoe floated up and down, as light as a feather. It startled me at first, as I thought the advancing waves would tumble aboard. But they passed under the craft, which was lifted up by their passage, a peculiar sensation, unlike that of any other boat I ever sailed in.

Perhaps I should now add a few observations about our family holidays. We tended to take these in the summer in the west of Ireland, fishing, swimming, walking, doing our own cooking, usually in modest rented accommodation. It was idyllic. We got to know the Irish and to appreciate 'the charms of Ireland'. As my two sons and daughter have played an important part in my life, I must briefly record their progress here. Peter, born in Sheffield in 1935 and educated at Magdalen College School and Queen's College, Oxford, has had a varied and colourful career, recorded in 'Who's Who?' Richard, two years younger, was educated at the Royal Belfast Academical Institution and Trinity College, Dublin and worked for a time in Enfield in Local Government, then became a teacher in Derby, but found the going hard and unrewarding. Music has been his salvation: he is a member of two choirs. Jane, educated at Richmond Lodge School, Belfast, TCD and LSE travelled widely, worked in Canada and in London as a social worker, and then came with her husband to Sheffield, where she and he are both lecturing in Social Studies. All three are married and gave us seven fine grandchildren. A feature of our family life has been the adventurous holidays we have had together in England, Ireland and abroad marked by much walking and climbing. I fear I have infected all three with a constitutional leaning towards outdoor life and sport.

Postscript

In July 1956, the distinguished vice-president of the Irish Mountaineering Club, Lord Justice Porter, died suddenly. This excellent Northern Ireland lawyer, born in Portrush and educated at Methodist College and Queen's University, was called to the Bar in 1903. He did his mountaineering in the carefree days before the queues formed beneath almost every rock-climb in Lakeland and North Wales and before it became almost conventional to go trekking in the Himalayas. I first made his acquaintance in November 1953, when he started coming to a series of Sunday evening addresses I was giving on 'The New Testament in the Light of Modern Knowledge'. He was very taken with these, and invited me up to his house, where I met Lady Porter and enjoyed their kind hospitality. He paid me the compliment of saying that he had been following the course by reading the appropriate articles in his 'Encyclopaedia Britannica'! A splendid conversationalist, young at heart and most approachable, I cannot think why I never broached the topic of mountains to him. Actually, I think I did not realise, at this date, his interest in this field.

What he did tell me, knowing that he was talking to a kindred spirit, was quite fascinating. He let me into the secret of his appointment. When the Irish law-vacancy arose, the Labour Home Secretary at the time was Mr Chuter Ede, and he had his eye on Porter for the position of Lord Justice in Northern Ireland. But the then N.I. Prime Minister, Lord Brookeborough, a staunch Unionist and a pillar of the Establishment, claimed that the prerogative of appointment was his, and he proposed to put in a Tory barrister. "Oh no, you don't!" replied Shuter Ede, "This is a Crown appointment", and suiting the action to the word, the Home Secretary chose Porter, a sound judge, Crown Prosecutor for Belfast since 1945, and a good Labour man – doubtless to the dismay of the Northern Ireland Tory Establishment. I enjoyed that story, especially as Chuter Ede was a Unitarian and a former president of our General Assembly.

Index